Successful Quality Management

by Frank H. Squires
President, Squires Associates

The best of "On the Quality Scene," a monthly column that has appeared in
Quality magazine for the past 15 years. A condensation of thoughts and ideas,
on a variety of subject areas, that make up the spectrum called Quality.

---

compiled and edited by
Robert T. Linke
Director, Hitchcock Executive Book Service

Publisher:
Hitchcock Executive Book Service
Hitchcock Publishing Company
Hitchcock Building
Wheaton, IL 60187

1st Printing, May 1980

Publisher: Hitchcock Publishing Company
        Hitchcock Building
        Wheaton, IL 60187

The Author

Frank Squires has directed Squires Associates for over 20 years. He has developed quality assurance programs and instituted cost reductions for producers of electronics, plastics, computers, medical devices and nuclear power plants. Frank has been particularly active in product liability prevention.

His education in Electrical Engineering led to his membership on the faculty of Applied Science and Engineering, Toronto University. Wide industrial experience including quality management positions with Thomas A. Edison Industries, Hughes Aircraft and Lear, Inc. make Frank an articulate and knowledgeable spokesman for his industry.

Frank is a registered Professional Engineer, a Certified Quality Engineer, a Fellow of the ASQC and a member of IEEE. An accomplished and sought-after public speaker, he also is an expert witness for the Trial Lawyers Association of America and the Defense Research Institute.

He has published more than 100 articles here and abroad and is the author of "On the Quality Scene" appearing monthly in Quality magazine.

But read on in this book and you will soon get a feeling for how knowledgeable, personable, down-to-earth and on-track the man really is.

Contents

CHAPTER/SUBJECT

CHAPTER/SUBJECT

CHAPTER/SUBJECT

CHAPTER/SUBJECT

CHAPTER/SUBJECT

Preface

This book is meant for managers and practitioners who wish to explore the basic concepts and techniques of quality assurance ... and learn how to "sell" it up the ladder.

The management of overall product quality in mass production operations is a demanding, and often unrewarding task. Quality is *the critical function* in our automated, industrialized society if we, as a nation, are to survive in the marketplace.

But society (and production management as well) does not call for quality ... instead, we hear constant cries for more—more—more (quantity).

These quantitative demands must be balanced by effective quality control if we ever are to improve productivity, regain industrial leadership, and support and fulfill our affluent society.

Successful Quality Management also implies a reduction in the instances leading to product liability suits, recalls, and personal injuries caused by defective mass-produced products.

Don't let it happen to you!

☐ Joe Random was comfortably seated in his office, savoring the day's first cup of coffee, idly leafing through *Time* magazine. Well, not idly . . . he was, after all, reading the Business Section . . . but you know what I mean . . . he was cool. It was early in the day, it was quiet, there was Peace on Earth.

The phone shattered the moment of peace. Joe, alert, watched his secretary. She picked up the phone . . . listened . . . stiffened . . . patted her hair straight. Joe knew!

"G'morning J.B."

"Joe? Is that you? Listen Joe . . . what are you doing to us!" Silence. Joe's mind is racing over the possibilities. What is it? What's bugging J.B.?

"Joe? Are you still there?"

"Yeah."

Then it dawned on J.B. "Joe. Don't tell me you don't know! Those Indians of yours are tearing the place apart . . . and you don't know about it!"

It's too late to hide his ignorance and Joe has to suffer the chagrin of being told by J.B. himself. He promises to look into it.

Another hassle in receiving inspection

It's another hassle in receiving inspection! A shipment of parts just in from Newark has been rejected. It's one of those minor parts, essential to the completion of a major assembly which somehow seem to get overlooked in planning . . . they have to be ordered late from the only supplier willing to take the order on short notice. By the time the parts arrive, production is at a standstill and marketing is in hysterics. To cap it all, the inspectors reject them!!!

The inspection supervisor has already started a couple of inspectors screening. He tells Joe it looks as though there would be enough good pieces to keep the line going. Joe calls J.B. and reports. J.B. says "O.K." none too graciously.

Joe's problem was not that the inspectors had rejected some urgently needed parts . . . Joe's problem was that he hadn't known about it.

How did the word get through to J.B.? The expeditor dashed off faster than Paul Revere to tell production, who told marketing, who had promised to deliver the finished items to Boeing yesterday! Marketing told J.B. But nobody told Joe! ►

Be informed

What Joe should do is to instruct his section supervisors to let him know immediately when there is a catastrophic rejection. A catastrophic rejection is any rejection that wrecks, or threatens to wreck, the schedule, especially when the schedule is already dragging; or any rejection of such large quantity that rework or replacement costs are likely to shatter the cost structure. No "paper," no terrifying rejection notice is to be put into circulation before Joe has been informed.

Joe may then choose to alert the "victim" himself, commiserating with him, assuring him that the lot is being screened and enough parts to carry on with may be saved; or offering to have inspectors stand by while rework is rushed through.

It's ironic that Joe's "Indians" should be accused of "tearing the place apart," when all they did was to discover defects! Why couldn't the chief executive have congratulated Joe! But that's not the way things are done. It's difficult to be grateful when the schedule has been wrecked, no matter who did it, or how, or why. This being the case, quality assurance must be constantly "sold" and resold; the quality manager must be alert to the frequently illogical reactions of his management colleagues. In the case of bad news he must be first with the news and, hopefully, with some word about plans to mitigate the situation. Elegant administrative procedures are as essential to the success of a quality assurance program as technical competence in statistics and metrology. Joe hadn't given enough thought to the effects of a catastrophic rejection . . . to the phenomenal speed of bad news . . . he was caught off guard and it will take him some time to recover J.B.'s confidence. Don't let it happen to you! ☐

How to manage good
... like a manager should

☐ What is it that quality assurance managers manage? Is it the quality of the product? Well . . . no . . . although a quality product is the objective. Is it a system of controls? No, although the objective will not be achieved unless competent procedures are developed.

To manage is to organize and direct the work of others. In the quality assurance context, this is to organize and direct the work of inspectors. The inspectors must be provided with technical assistance, effective supervision, and moral support. Procedures must be addressed directly to the inspector; they must be permeated with a knowledge of the environment in which the inspector works and of the problems created by the environment.

Technical assistance

Let it be assumed:

- That your inspectors are technically competent — because this was the condition of their employment — and furthermore, you wisely provide them with periodic refresher training.
- That you have taken steps to see that the inspectors get the right blueprint at the right time.
- That you have provided instructions detailing the methods of inspection.
- That you have provided all necessary gages and instruments.
- That you have simplified the documentation.

You still haven't resolved the inspector's most difficult technical task: What is he to do about the borderline case?

It's no problem to accept the indisputably good or to reject the grossly defective, but what should the inspector do when the plug gage will go in with a bit of a push, or when the micrometer or height gage reads right on the line, or when the pressure gage, ammeter or voltmeter is dithering on the upper or lower limits?

There are no stock answers. You could say to the inspectors, "When in doubt, reject." But then you'd run the risk of rejecting good material because "doubtful" means possibly good or possibly bad. You could say to the inspectors, "When in doubt, accept if the quality characteristic is minor or superficial; reject if major or critical." But then you've got to make sure that every inspector knows the classification, on every characteristic; and that's quite a problem. ►

Effective supervision

By supervision we mean direct supervision of the inspectors. By managing we mean the development of a policy and the making of plans which are then executed by supervisors and inspectors. The plans must indicate to the supervisor what obstacles to the fulfillment of the plan he may encounter and what to do about them.

The big problem for the inspector is time. There's never enough of it! Material required on the assembly line yesterday or last week arrives in receiving inspection. A change has to be incorporated in finished assemblies and the schedule is knocked for a loop. Scheduling clerks groan with agony at the delay; they breathe down every inspector's neck. In the tense atmosphere, almost anything is likely to happen except good inspection.

Why is there so little time? Perhaps because we are an optimistic people and easily convince ourselves when scheduling that last month's causes for delay won't happen this month. Perhaps because the delivery date is a powerful competitive factor. Whatever the cause, the situation exists and the good manager will do something about it.

He must plan to keep material moving at the same pace as production. He must look out for bottlenecks at inspection points. It's no good complaining that inspection is the inevitable "victim" of cumulative time delays (it's bad enough having to wait while parts are machined or assembled when the schedule's ten days behind, but it's murder waiting for inspection!).

The alert manager will accept the situation and do something. A general policy on overtime, for example, instead of making every request the subject of a major diplomatic negotiation. He might put several inspectors on staggered periods since there's always something to be inspected at the last moment. He might instruct supervisors to appeal promptly to one another for assistance when things are piling up. Whatever is appropriate, but something!

The problem is that the inspector does not reject impersonal material, but the effort of the individual who made it. There is always the probability of a sharp emotional reaction and it will be important to know what effect such emotional storms—or the probability of them—has on the inspector's tendency to reject, or not to reject. It may be appropriate to quote Hamlet, for "to reject" might be to launch oneself upon "a sea of troubles."

The good manager will admit the existence of the problem and will do something about it. Not belligerence and not sweetness and light, but somewhere in between—and appropriate to the situation.   □

The quality manager's dilemma

☐ The quality manager's dilemma is implicit in the objective task he has been assigned, and the subjective environment in which he must operate. His inspectors must appraise the quality of the product, handing out rejection slips when necessary. His engineers must appraise the capability of production processes, and of the manufacturing system as a whole, making recommendations which are, in effect, critical reports on existing practice.

The measure of quality is the blueprint, coldly objective; but for the producer the measure of quality is frequently thought of as the extent and sincerity of his effort. The task of approving or rejecting requires an undiluted objectivity. But what is rejected, or accepted, is not inanimate hardware, but the efforts of production operators, the plans of manufacturing managers and the hopes of salesmen. The quality manager is not alone in the necessity to strive toward an objective goal through a tangle of subjective underbrush. It is the heart of the management problem; it has motivated the construction of various theories of management.

The carrot or the whip

What theories of management are available to provide a strategy for the quality manager? There is the tough approach sometimes identified as Theory X; characterized as "objective" by its practitioners. There is what has been called the human relations approach, identified as Theory Y. Not that X practitioners would count themselves inhuman; it's a shift in emphasis. X managers assert that operators must be directed; Y managers believe the operators should be shown the way. X managers might say that the end justifies the means, the end being the goal, and the directed operators being the means; whereas, the Y manager might say that the end is the product of the means. The two styles of management have been characterized as autocratic and democratic; as authoritarian and permissive; and, popularly, as thing-oriented and people-oriented.

Should the quality manager opt for X or Y? His task demands the objectivity of a ruthless X, but the predictable human reaction requires that he steer with a Y rudder. It's a problem! ►

The problem is further complicated by the cultural conditioning which·predisposes the individual to see himself as conforming to the preferred cultural model. Thus, he may be autocratic and authoritarian by temperament, while protesting that he is democratic and permissive. He may sit through a two hour lecture on human relations, nodding his head benignantly at the proper moments; then go right out and act like Ghengis Khan. Thus, the manager must select a theory of management and make sure he is the man to play the role, or be willing to adapt his behavior to the part.

No theories on the battle line

The manager cannot think about theories of management in the heat of the battle. When the inspectors have created chaos in the machine shop or have shattered the assembly lines (or when it is so alleged) is not the time to debate Theory X or Theory Y.

The quality manager, as an accepted member of the strategy-planning management team, owes it to his colleagues to familiarize himself with contemporary management theory. He may attend one of the various courses being given across the country. My own contribution has been to organize seminars in operational management under the title, "Operation Quality," which provide an opportunity to review current theories of management, and to test their applicability to everyday problems.

What happens if the manager doesn't know whether he inclines to X or Y and will not consider the matter? "Vacillate" is used here, not in the sense of hesitation, but to indicate rapid changes of direction. Because ours is a purposeful culture, we tend to do everything with a fine show of purpose and a manager may vacillate with vigor for a considerable time before his colleagues realize that what they are fascinated by is motion without movement. And so, manager, get thee to a seminar and choose a theory.

I'm participative!
You're authoritative!

□ "I'm participative! You're authoritative!"

Thus spoke a representative sample of industrial supervisors when called upon to characterize the management style of those above them, and of their own style in relation to those below. It might be called the "view from the middle."

The supervisors are from a variety of corporations, utilities and state and federal agencies in the Los Angeles area. They attend a course I conduct in "problems in industrial supervision." All are first or second line supervisors or better.

The subject of one of the sessions had been Rensis Likert* and his division of styles of management into four main systems:

        1. Exploitive-authoritative
        2. Benevolent-authoritative
        3. Consultative
        4. Participative

After some discussion, I asked the men and women in the course to ballot secretly on the style of their superiors. The score was:

1. Exploitive-authoritative	6
2. Benevolent-authoritative	6
3. Consultative	5
4. Participative	3

"You're authoritative!" accused the supervisors looking up.

Later I asked them to ballot on their personal styles in relation to their subordinates. The score was:

1. Exploitive-authoritative	0
2. Benevolent-authoritative	5
3. Consultative	12
4. Participative	8

"I'm participative!" They judged their superiors to be 60 percent authoritative and themselves 80 percent participative! (Consultative is generally included in the participative classification.) ►

What would happen if individuals at higher levels in the organization were invited to look up and down and rate what they saw? It's probable that they would score about the same as our sample.

Why? Why should organizations, public and private, be characterized as authoritative when viewed from below, and as participative when viewed from above? Because the style or system of management in the industrialized world *is* authoritative ... with occasional exceptions such as the Israeli kibbutzim, Yugo-Slav factories and various experiments in the U.S., Canada, Britain and Europe (see "Job Power" by David Jenkins).

The acceptable management creed

Why should supervisors at all levels characterize themselves as participative, although they are generally seen by their subordinates as authoritative? Because participation is currently the most acceptable management creed; it has been explained and advocated by many academic sociologists. There must be very few supervisors in the U.S. who have not taken at least one course in participative management. Thus, supervisors and managers characterize themselves as participative because they know themselves to be trying to the extent that the built-in constraints of the organization allow. But, when they look up it is not difficult to recognize that the ultimate principle of management is authoritative. They may be consulted, but they know who will have the last word.

The crux of the matter is that the pyramidal organization is an authoritative institutional form. It was meant to be that way. It functions the way it was designed to function despite strenuous efforts to graft on portions of participation.

To fulfill the potential increase in productivity claimed for participation, we shall have to design a new and appropriate organizational form. In the meantime, we are stuck with the hierarchical pyramid, which we have had since the Babylonians and Egyptians; it is highly resistant to change.

What has this to do with quality? Everything to do with organization and people has to do with quality. The particular point is that the pyramidal organization protects the chief executive from outside influences and from information in the minds of his subordinates (as it was meant to protect pharoahs, popes and kings.)

As a consequence, chief executives had to be bludgeoned by million dollar product liability awards before they would listen to the warnings and advice of their departmental managers including most importantly, the quality manager. ☐

*Rensis Likert, "The Human Organization," McGraw-Hill

The administrative assumption and operational reality

☐ The manager is constantly confronted and confused by the way things ought to be, and by the way they are. The most precise plans are drawn up and it seems inconceivable that they should not be clearly understood and acted upon exactly as written.

The manager may draw some comfort from the knowledge that this is nothing new; the pages of history make it clear that kings and popes and generals and presidents and many former managers have pondered over the same problem.

Let us distinguish between the administrative assumption and operational reality. Administration prepares a formal plan based upon the assumption that the tasks assigned to various individuals are appropriate to their skills as defined in job descriptions, and to the positions they occupy in the formal organization. Administration assumes, therefore, that the plan can be executed as written. The plan is launched, and founded on operational reality.

What was overlooked? The operational environment, and operational behaviour induced by it, or adopted in reaction to it. Let us take an example. The administrative assumption is that inspectors, guided by administrative instructions, will search diligently for and will cite all defects. Yet defects get by, defects which should have been visible to the inspector since they were subsequently found during a quality audit or by the customer. What happened?

The operational reality is that the inspector works in an environment composed of the attitudes and expectations of those around him, which militates against his willingness to reject any but the most obvious, gross defects.

- He is exposed to the constant prodding of the production expeditors. Expeditors can be very persistent; indeed, they have been known to make derisive comments, characterizing the meticulous inspector as a nitpicker! It isn't permitted to exterminate expeditors, and so the inspector, motivated to minimize the constant aggravation, acquires a tolerance for minor defects.
- He is exposed to the production supervisors who, in the line of duty, challenge rejections. Woe betide the inspector if the defect is marginal; if there is any room for debate! ▶

- The inspector is exposed to the machinists and assemblers with whom he socializes. He tends to award them E for effort and, again, his tolerance for minor defects is reinforced.

It is not suggested that these steps are taken by the inspector consciously and deliberately; they are a series of insensible adjustments to an overwhelming environment.

Another example: the administrative assumption is that "decisions are made" as a consequence of the analysis of relevant data, the ordering of the options, and the making of a rational selection between them.

But the operational reality is that decisions are rarely "made"; they just happen. Or, rather, they develop; they take shape amidst the turmoil of many contending voices and events. Operationally, what emerges is an attitude adopted by a sufficient number of individuals strong enough to push events in a new direction. Administration catches on, the new direction is enshrined in an S.O.P., and it is recorded that a decision was made.

Obviously, it will affect the manager's style and degree of success whether he thinks administrative assumptions and operational reality are identical, or whether he is prepared for divergence. If the latter, then it would follow that he would spend much time in the operational environment observing operational behaviour and sensing the prevailing attitudes. Some managers do, but not enough.

It is interesting to speculate on why there is such a continued strong reliance on the administrative assumption. Why are so many reluctant to learn from experience? Why can so many look directly at operational behaviour, yet not "see" it?

It may be that the indoctrination, the inculturation we receive as children is responsible. We are programmed as children, and when young, with the preferred behaviour for the many situations it is anticipated we shall encounter. A culture is a set of preferred ways of doing things, and the objective of early inculturation is to assure that the individual will follow the pattern and will not deviate. Thus, the individual finds himself imprisoned, as it were, by his early inculturation; he approaches every situation with a preconceived idea of what it ought to be like, and of what he should do about it.

Now, the manager cannot repeat to himself all day long, "I have been programmed by early inculturation to favor the written word and the preconceived idea, and it is likely, therefore, that my problems are caused by the conflict between plans and operational reality, and by my reluctance to test the validity of administrative assumptions." But he can do it occasionally and act accordingly, and he will be that much nearer to success. □

Be prepared!

☐ Are you prepared to answer the following questions:
"What will it do to the schedule?"
"What will it cost?"

These are typical questions which might be put to you by the chief executive, or by one of your colleagues at a staff meeting. "It," of course, is something you want to do about the quality. It might be a new procedure you're proposing, an additional inspection point, an automated testing device for a critical characteristic . . . whatever. The automatic response will still be "what will it do to the schedule" or "what will it cost" . . . or both. Are you prepared to answer these and other likely questions?

The point is that the ability to respond promptly and articulately to questions from your management colleagues may do as much for your career as a well-managed department! Indeed, it may do more, because your competence is taken for granted . . . that's what they hired you for. Furthermore, it's one of the paradoxes of industrial life that the better you manage your department, the less attention is likely to be paid to it . . . and you.

A tight ship equals no pink slip

Which isn't to say that you should start running it badly to attract attention . . . because the only attention that will get you will be a pink slip.

The thing to do is to manage well . . . and to excel at staff conferences by being prompt and articulate in your responses to superiors and colleagues. Your professional stature will increase in their eyes . . . *and the quality of the product you're all making will grow with their opinion of you.*

It is true of any function that it cannot be separated from the individual, but this is particularly true of quality assurance. Management has an ardent affection for production (as indeed they should) and if Capt. Bligh were a production manager he would still be popular . . . or at least acceptable. ▶

Management is reconciled to engineering ... there's no way to get a product designed without engineers. So the chief engineer may be a mumbling recluse and he will still be tolerated.

Polish up your star

But management, especially in commercial production, has long had doubts about the value of quality assurance. It's true that they've been shook up by the glut of product liability suits and the Consumers Product Safety Commission, but it's still the fact that so far as quality assurance is concerned, management is waiting to be convinced. And what will help to convince them will be quality managers who excel in conference by virtue of being well-informed and articulate.

Incidentally, I recall an article several years ago in *Harvard Business Review* on the Young Presidents Organization. You know, guys who made president by the time they were forty. Many comments were made on their abilities and idiosyncracies which were extraordinarily varied, but the one thing they all agreed on was the necessity to be well-informed and articulate. Practically all were still getting education in one subject or another, but the subject that took priority over all the others was public speaking!

So be prepared! You might try making a list of likely questions; ask yourself what you would ask the quality manager if you were the chief executive. It's a marvelous device for getting outside of yourself and seeing yourself in the eyes of your colleagues. □

How many? How much? How good?

☐ These three questions are what industry is all about. Quantity, cost and quality . . . in that order! They are the guts of industry. In more polite language they might be called the "visceral trinity."

If you're a manager, and if you keep these three questions in mind, and if you manage so that you have the right answers, you will succeed.

Have them printed in a fancy script, have them framed, and put them in a prominent position on your desk alongside the photograph of your loving dependents.

It is this irrefragable interrelatedness which drags the quality manager into every problem, either directly or indirectly. The production manager may be asked, "Are you on schedule?" To which he might reply that he would be if he could "just get some material through receiving inspection."

Don't take the rap

This may be a true statement. It may be true because the suppliers have shipped in an excessive amount of junk, but the implication is that the inspectors are sitting on their posteriors. If the output has indeed been jeopardized by the receipt of excessive amounts of unacceptable material, the quality manager should have been the first to recognize it. It is he who should have brought it to the attention of his colleagues and particularly the chief executive. The burden of explaining the deficiency would then have rested with procurement where it belongs.

But, let us say that the production manager is in the fortunate position of being able to say that he's on schedule. This automatically triggers the next question, "What about the cost?" Incidentally, when production managers moan and complain, as they sometimes do, and tell you that they "can't win" you can afford to be sympathetic because it's true enough. ►

However, you still have your job to do. So how might the production manager reply about the cost? Well, he might say, "Quality control's been putting on a quality improvement drive, so costs are up." This too might be a true statement. Quality control might have put pressure on the machine shop to make more parts like the print, but what it sounds like is that quality control is trying to gild the lily!

Once again, the quality manager's colleagues and the chief executive should have been forewarned about what was going to happen and what might be the consequences.

The fustest with the mostest

There was a general who said that the way to win battles was to be there the fustest with the mostest! Who was it? It wasn't Henry V at Agincourt was it? No, it couldn't have been. It was a Civil War General . . . Jackson wasn't it?

Anyway, it's a marvelous policy for a quality manager. Be there the fustest with the mostest information. Frame it, too, and put it on your desk on the other side of the family portrait.

Remember that quantity, cost and quality are irrefragably interrelated, and that quantity and cost are the quality manager's job, too. Keep in mind that every act committed on behalf of quality may affect the quantity or the cost or both. The short run effects of quality programs may be adverse to quantity and/or cost, although not necessarily. It's the long run effects that are beneficial to quantity and cost and which assure the corporation's future.

It's a peculiar world in which you're more likely to be clobbered for what you didn't do than for what you did do, and especially for not doing the things you thought were not your job. The quality manager should have the quantity and cost schedules for the month pinned up on the wall of his office for instant reference. He should know at all times the current status of both. He might assign to assistants the most important tasks of "schedule watching" and "cost watching." Let him always be the fustest with the mostest. □

What to tell top management

☐ If you had the opportunity, what would you tell top management about quality control? Bear in mind that one rarely gets the opportunity to tell top management anything. Top management usually does the telling.

I was presented recently with an ideal opportunity. I was invited to participate in a seminar attended by executives from one of the multi-national corporations and to speak at the banquet.

What I wanted to do was to develop a logical argument for the absolute essentiality of quality control; a demonstration that it is as essential as, say, design engineering. The executives don't know what the engineers know, but they know they have to have them. There is no way to run a production organization without engineers. Management may try to shave the budget, but they do not dispute that there has to be an engineering budget. Likewise with procurement, marketing, personnel and other "accepted" functions; but quality control is not accepted or, at least, only infrequently.

Where have all the craftsmen gone?

I started by drawing a distinction between craftsmanship and mass production. Crafted articles are few in number. They are conceived and molded into shape by skilled individuals, each of whom is responsible for the quality of his own handiwork.

Mass produced articles are not made by individuals; they are produced by the system. Few members of the large work force handling the product at various stages of completion "know" the product in its technical uniqueness like the craftsman knows his product.

While the craftsman is concerned with quality and, moreover, will generally not be pushed for time, the managers, machinists and assemblers in mass production are concerned with quantity and are under constant pressure to meet the schedule—to move it!

Quantity conscious

Consequently, it is a waste of time to demand of managers and operators in mass production that they pay constant attention to quality.

▶

Not that they ignore it, but their primary purpose is to beat the schedule. That is what they are measured by. That is what they are rewarded for. They are QUANTITY-CONSCIOUS. If it were otherwise, there would be no mass production and no affluence for the many.

Individual craftsmen may be spoken to about the quality. But the mass production system (managers, operators, equipment, instructions, etc.) cannot be spoken to. Not that it hasn't been tried. Systems are earnestly exhorted to be "quality-conscious" as though the system were an autonomous individual capable of responding to such appeals by an act of will.

Since systems of mass production are devoted to quantity, and since individuals within the system must, by definition, be quantity-conscious, it follows that an agency must be created to take care of the quality. That agency, an arm of management, is quality control.

Quality is the regulator

Quality control regulates the system pretty much the way a governor regulates a steam engine. Which brings us to a viable definition of quality-consciousness for individuals in mass production: not that they shall be thinking quality every second of the day, but that they shall be as responsive to quality control recommendations for corrective action as the steam engine is to the governor. Well—not quite that automatic, but something like it.

Only when the quantity-oriented nature of mass production is recognized (and that this motivates the behaviour of operators within the system) can management support quality control from a conviction of necessity.

We have spent too much time trying to manage mass production as though it were Medieval craftsmanship on a gigantic scale. It's time to manage it like the complex system it is. □

How to prepare the quality budget

☐ In preparing your annual q.a. budget request, don't lump everything together. Don't submit one round sum of money for approval. Itemize each line and staff activity. For example, using hypothetical costs, see Figure 1.

Even the example is fairly broad, but in this form you can defend your estimates. I say "defend," because what exists between the manager and the budget director, is what lawyers call an "adversary situation." We don't usually phrase it that way, but that's the way it is.

It would be an unusual budget director who did not assume that there's a bit of empire building in every budget proposal. And so he's going to push and question and criticize, and rightly so. The manager who presents his budget in a number of manageable items will be able to offer rational explanations for each separate activity.

Backing up the itemized budget should be a work sheet. The number one item on the work sheet should be the estimated average monthly sales for the budget period. Next come estimates of average monthly purchases of raw material, components and subcontracted work, and of anticipated average costs of production direct labor in the machine shop and the assembly area.

Figure 1
METALUNAR CORPORATION
Estimated cost of Quality Assurance Program for the year

Costs are estimated averages per month for the 12 months.

1. Inspecting purchased material	$2400
2. Machine shop inspection	5000
3. Assembly inspection	4000
4. Functional test	2000
5. Cost of supplier control	600
6. Cost of direct supervision	1340
7. Cost of administration and quality engineering	2080

▶

Matching these will be average inspection costs computed by the quality manager from past records. For example: average inspection cost in dollars per $1000 worth of purchased materials; average inspection cost per $1000 of machine shop direct labor; the same for $1000 of assembly direct labor; and average test cost per $1000 worth of shipped products. From these the manager computes inspection and test costs in specified areas.

Backing these up, he should have the average rates he must pay inspectors in the different areas, together with the number of inspectors he's going to require. For example, if he has to pay an average of $2.60 an hour for receiving inspectors and if he assumes a month of 173 hours, each inspector is going to cost him $450 per month and he may require five inspectors for purchased materials. And so on.

Next he assigns direct supervisors and their anticipated cost. Then the cost of quality engineering and administration, which he should certainly distribute among the operating areas.

Armed with such detail the quality manager can enter into budget negotiations with confidence. By the time he has rounded up and studied the necessary information he will know what he wants and why.

No big lumps

Just a couple of comments on the big lump: Big lumps (or money) and big numbers (of men) invite chipping. In our example, the anticipated total for the average month amounts to $17,420. If the budget was presented in this manner, in one big lump, it's almost certain the budget director would suggest rounding out to $17,000.

Indeed, large sums of money are often subject to "percentage surgery."

"Don't you think you could lop off five percent? It would only amount to $850 (of the already truncated $17,000!)."

While you are chasing frantically through your mind, trying to figure out what such a cut will do to the many things you have to do, it's done!

Again, one big lump of proposed quality assurance budget prompts the budget director to think of other gross sums such as billing, or total manufacturing costs, and to arrive at a ratio of q.a. costs to billing or manufacturing costs. This will start the "ratio game" and while the quality manager is quoting larger ratios, the budget director will be quoting smaller ones and it's your ratio against his. You know where that's likely to end.

The budget director has his job to do, and you've got yours. Both of you are handicapped by one big lump which he cannot digest, and you cannot explain. So break it up.   □

Adversarial occasions

☐ There are many adversarial occasions: some in which the conflict is admitted as, for example, between plaintiff and defendant in a product liability suit; and some in which the conflict is cloaked beneath a presumption of organizational cooperation.

The latter are the ones to watch out for. Every quality manager can recall such adversarial occasions ... the most adversarial being the annual budget conference.

The superior to whom the quality assurance manager must submit the budget may be an occasional luncheon companion; but, on this occasion he comes as a gladiator, armed with the conviction that there is "fat" in the proposed budget—which he intends to cut out. If he had a coat of arms, the motto would surely be "Cut the Fat Out."

Therefore, quality assurance manager, if you were ever a Boy Scout, remember the motto "Be Prepared." Your preparations will determine the future quality of the products.

Keep in mind that while you are interested in a host of administrative, clerical and technical tasks, he is interested only in the overall cost. Nothing will be gained by delivering a learned dissertation on the many diverse and difficult tasks which must be performed to assure the quality. He doesn't doubt your competence; he just thinks you spend too much!

Defend yourself

What should the quality manager use for a shield when the budget director makes his first pass with the modest proposal that the budget be cut by ten percent.

Let me suggest a budget broken down to the utmost detail. It's possible to defend detailed sections of the work; it's difficult to defend one big lump sum. While you're racking your brains trying to think of what a ten percent cut would do to the department, he may take your silence for consent! ▶

But the quality manager with the detailed budget is ready. He spreads it out across the desk and studies it with great concentration. "I'd be glad to, but what shall I cut out? What can we do without?"

"Don't ask me about the details. You're the expert."

"Well . . . yes," the quality manager replies, "but if we are going to cut out essential services, we should agree on which should go." Emphasize that "we"; involve him in the welfare of the corporation you both love and serve.

"Oh, nothing essential, of course."

"But everything's essential," says the quality manager, with an elegant riposte which diverts the discussion from cost to essentiality. From then on, it's up to the quality manager; he may still lose a slice, but it won't be ten percent.

Making-up your budget

The make-up of the budget will vary from manager to manager, but some suggestions may be made. The details which might run down the left hand edge of the sheet should enumerate functions, not individuals. A relatively small department may have more functions than individuals. The quality manager may be doing his own quality engineering, in which case he will divide his monthly salary into appropriate fractions.

Advancing to the right from the long list of functions, the budget will show the following for each section:

- the number of inspectors engaged in the function with the average monthly wage of each in parentheses
- the monthly salaries required along with their costs
- clerical services required along with their costs
- quality engineering costs
- secretarial and administrative functions with fractional salaries as appropriate
- a distribution of the manager's salary.

To the extreme right show the total sum for an average month. Monthly totals are manageable; one can think in terms of a month's activities. The budget director will be quick to multiply by 12 when the final dispositions have been made.

It's a salutary discipline to prepare a budget in this detailed manner even when budget discussions are not pending. It's good training for the manager, sort of like managerial jogging. □

Can you prove you did any good?

☐ Prime mission of a Quality Control Department is quality. Its mission is to assure, by such actions as are necessary, that the product conforms to specified quality requirements. In fulfillment of this task it may, and frequently does, effect very considerable economies. But can you prove it?

Let us imagine that the quality control department of which you're the manager is part of an organization shipping $100,000 monthly. You launch a vigorous quality improvement campaign: Quality analysts identify the operations producing the most defects and indicate the probable causes; quality and manufacturing engineers advance against the sources of poor quality; they are successful in substantially reducing the problem areas. And now it's a year later and guess where you are?

You're on the carpet trying to explain why the ratio of quality control to manufacturing costs has increased! Yes, that's right. As a result of your efforts:

- scrap has been reduced . . . saving material and production labor
- rework has been reduced . . . saving production labor
- schedule emergencies have been minimized . . . reducing production overtime.

Manufacturing costs have been reduced considerably—but your costs are where they were at the beginning of the drive! You look worse, costwise, than when you started!

Records are essential

It's important to remember that money not spent is not recorded. So when you set out to improve quality and, incidentally, to reduce manufacturing costs, make sure you keep a record.

Let us say that 35% of the sales dollar is material and 15% is production labor. Thus, $35,000 should go into material and $15,000 into labor. Both figures are being exceeded because of excessive scrap and rework.

In preparation for the quality improvement drive, you must establish the scrap and rework rates. You must know the average monthly dollar loss in scrap and rework, both as absolute figures and as percentages of total material and manufacturing costs. If you don't know these figures, you don't know where you started from and you'll have no measure of success. ▶

Setting up a hypothetical case

Make sure that manufacturing engineering knows the average cost of rework and the average cost of replacing a scrap part (material and labor). Let us say that the average cost of rework is $5 and the average cost of replacing a scrapped piece is $15. Let the starting average monthly rework loss be 10% (of $15,000); that is $1,500 representing 300 reworks at $5 each. Let the starting scrap rate be 5% (of $50,000, the sum of material and labor), that is $2,500 representing 166 scrap actions at $15 each.

The quality improvement program is launched. You keep score, each rejection being considered as necessitating a rework or replacement. The accumulating record will look something like Figures 1 and 2. The "start" figures are the averages for, say, the previous 6 months.

Observe that the saving for each month is computed as the difference between the cost for the month and the cost for the starting month. Only by keeping such records can you counteract the paradox that the better you operate quality-wise, the worse you may appear to be costwise. □

Figure 1
REWORK

Month	No. of Rejections necessitating Rework	Cost at $5 each $	Saved Month $	Saved Period $
Start	300	$1,500	—	—
January	270	1,350	$150	$ 150
February	240	1,200	300	450
March	220	1,100	400	850
April	200	1,000	500	1,350
May	180	900	600	1,950
June	150	750	750	2,700

Figure 2
SCRAP

Month	No. of Rejections necessitating replacement	Cost at $15 each $	Saved Month $	Saved Period $
Start	166	$2,490	$ —	$ —
January	136	2,040	450	450
February	106	1,590	900	1,350
March	86	1,290	1,200	2,550
April	66	990	1,500	4,050
May	56	840	1,650	5,700
June	46	690	1,800	7,500

The lost computer

☐ Once upon a time there was a computer named Norbert Ampere, who lived in the center of a shining, automated complex. Life was good to Norbert. He was surrounded by adoring programmers; waited upon by monitoring systems which kept his health under surveillance 24 hours a day; he sifted data and rapped out judgments that caused the mighty to tremble; his lights flashing and his reels jerking spasmodically, he looked more alive than the subdued humans who tiptoed deferentially in his vicinity; he was highly productive, yet never overworked; he clamored neither for coffee breaks, nor for vacations. Norbert had it made, or so it seemed.

One day Norbert vanished! There was consternation at the center, there was paralysis at the perimeter. Where had Norbert gone? The mighty and the deferential gathered together in conference; the programmers wept unashamedly. What had they done to Norbert that he should vanish?

Just around the corner

We haven't got as much time as James Bond to find out, nor as many nubile, nude and pliable women to enliven the search, so I'll have to tell you. Norbert had gone off in search of a better computer than himself. That's right! His attendants had unwittingly programmed into Norbert their own cultural attitudes. They had been taught that there is always something better around the corner. The belief had been implanted in them to guard against complacency; to assure that they would never rest content with what they had, but would ever strive for something different and, hopefully, better.

Now this is all very well for humans who are sometimes saved from the worst effects of their best intentions by an inability, or reluctance, to follow through to the logical conclusion. But not Norbert. Once Norbert had an idea he was so constituted as to follow through inexorably to the logical end. ►

The best is yet to be

Furthermore, since Norbert was an Occidental computer, he had been indoctrinated with bipolar or contrapositional reasoning. Things were always black or white for Norbert, right or wrong, wholly acceptable or utterly rejectable. There was no shading in Norbert's reasoning; something could not be capable of improvement, yet be still quite good and beneficial. If the best was around the corner, argued Norbert, then what was here, here and now, must be no good at all! Norbert was never found, and we can surmise that he will continue to search in distant corners of the earth, blind to what he is while looking for the self he might be.

In time we all shall have computers and we will hope to minimize the irrational traits with which we indoctrinate them; in the meantime we are surrounded by a multitude of lost computers. A computer is not necessarily a mechanical or electronic device; it can be any individual who can add and subtract, multiply, and divide. Wherever there is a stack of data, and an individual who could be reducing it manually, but isn't, there is a lost computer.

There must be many plants where managers are waiting until they can afford a computer. In this state of mind there is a reluctance to embark upon a program of manual reduction and all that might be learned from the mass of data goes to waste. (It is to these that the moral of Norbert's story is applicable.)　　　□

Is it too bad to ship?

□ You all know the circumstances. It must have happened to all of you. It's getting towards the end of the month and the bulk of the month's schedule is beginning to move into final inspection. The plant superintendent is picketing final inspection. The sales manager is in orbit. Organizational cool trembles on the brink.

And then it happens! Word flashes through the organization that fourteen units have been rejected! Already the general manager is on the phone. How does it come about that all responsible members of the organization get the message simultaneously? Is it telepathy or what!

Anyway, that's irrelevant for the moment. You tell the general manager you'll look into it and call him back. You dash off to final inspection where you're just in time to save the inspector. A couple of expeditors are beating on him with clip boards.

The units are defective

Your supervisor, who had tried to get through to you the moment the catastrophe occurred but your line was busy, shows you the rejection report. You, he and the battered inspector look at the rejected units. It's right what the report says; the units are defective as charged. You report to management and back comes the challenge, "Alright, but are they too bad to ship?"

Now, what you do about it will depend upon the nature and severity of the defect. If it's a deviation from specified performance, or if it's something that will surely affect performance, then you're going to have to stand by the report. But if it's superficial, if it's something that won't affect performance, then there's room for re-evaluation. ▶

Whichever way you settle it, obviously you'll learn from the experience. You and your staff will investigate to find out why the defect got so far through the system before being detected. Or it may turn out that the defect could not manifest itself until this final stage of inspection. Either way you'll do something to prevent it from repeating. But if this defect doesn't occur again, another may, and you'll be confronted by the same challenge: "Is it too bad to ship?"

Handling the challenge

Why is the challenge made? Why is it reasonable that it should be made? Because, of course, everybody knows that defects are occasionally "bought" in review. If a rejection notice was challenged successfully on Tuesday, then this one can be challenged today. There are many precedents.

But everybody knows that a "defect" bought in review is no longer a defect. Part of the review is an engineering judgment as to whether the defect will or will not adversely affect performance. When the judgment is that it will not, then the defect is no longer a defect, and the engineering requirement from which the part of assembly deviates stands condemned, by implication, as being too stringent. If one engineering requirement is admitted by the fact of acceptance to be too stringent, then other requirements may also be too stringent. Quality managers should, therefore, expect that challenges will be made.

So don't react with self-righteous indignation when confronted by the question, "Is it too bad to ship?" Recognize that many precedents have established the "right" to put the question. Get the material into review to test the validity of the engineering judgment; indeed, you may do this before the question hit you, but you'll have to move fast. Stay cool. And above all, work to bring about that bright day when all engineering tolerances will be the maximum allowable, and the question will at last be out of order. □

What do quality reports measure?

☐ When you analyze the inspection reports from receiving inspection for last month and find that, say, 12% of inspected lots were defective, are you reporting on hardware quality—or what?

The answer depends on what is meant by hardware. If you're using "hardware" to mean the product ultimately shipped out the door and, therefore, the parts and components which go into it, then you're not reporting on hardware. Because of course, the detected defects will not be included in the product but will be returned to suppliers for replacement.

True meaning of the report

What, then, does the 12% represent? It is a measure of the quality of the effort made by your suppliers. Ultimately, it's a measure of the ability of purchasing to find good suppliers.

Similarly, when the rejection notices prepared during the same period in the machine shop or assembly department are analyzed and summarized, you're not reporting on the quality of the company's product since, again, the detected defects will be corrected. You're reporting on the quality of effort made by machinists and assemblers.

Realization that this is the true nature of the report will dictate the best statistic for the purpose. It might be, for example, the average number of defects per machinist or assembler. (I'm using "defects" to represent both defects as they occur in assemblies and "defective" pieces that may be found in the machine shop.)

Let's label them properly

Such reports, then, are measures of quality of performance . . . and they should be labeled accordingly. The "receiving inspection" report might be called "Quality Report on Suppliers" or "Quality Report on Purchasing." Likewise, machine shop and assembly room reports are reports on the quality of production's performance.

The advantage of labeling quality reports in this manner is that it puts the emphasis where it belongs, enabling buyers, machinists, assemblers and managers to take effective correction action. "Effective" is a terribly over-used word but is used here to mean that corrective action has a better chance of being effective when it is aimed at the right target. ▶

Simple gross statistics are needed

In trying to arrive at measures of performance quality, some simple gross statistics are suggested. In the case of purchasing, it could be the percentage of lots in which all or some of the pieces were defective. This lumps together large and small lots, simple and complex parts. Simple parts are just as essential to the end product as complex parts . . . they have to be there.

The discovery that an eagerly awaited small lot is defective and must be rejected can wreak havoc in production. However, if it is felt that you must subdivide purchased suppliers into several classifications and report separately on each, don't create too many classes. As the subdivisions and reports increase in number, the overall significance is (or may be) lost.

What statistics do for you

The point is to develop a statistic which tells at a glance whether you're in serious trouble, or merely suffering from minor perturbations. Take the hypothetical 12% for example: If it happens to you, you and your company are in trouble! The production schedule is in jeopardy, the costs will certainly go up. Your quality analyst breaks down the gross statistic—part numbers, causes for rejection, and suppliers. You, purchasing and production control move into action. But before all concerned explode into activity, you ought to know that you should—which, again, is the point of the gross statistic.

Had the figure been one or two percent, you're suffering from minor perturbations and don't have to get hysterical. This does not mean that it's time to slow down, but it does give you time to congratulate purchasing.

The same argument applies to reports on production. Whatever the quality-of-performance statistic, and whether it's large or small, it will of course be broken down in a search for specific defects and causes. But the urgency with which this is done, and the weight attached to the findings, will depend upon the magnitude of the gross statistic.

One final word of caution: When putting out easy-to-read, correctly labeled and pointed reports of this nature, discuss them with purchasing and production managers before publication. Then it will be easier to pursue plans for joint action to correct a bad situation. Don't let the published reports be the means by which the parties involved first hear about them . . . because that's no way to build rapport. □

Say it! Don't write it.

☐ Say it! Don't write it.

But that's ridiculous! Especially in view of the fact that we all use memo pads boldly imprinted with the slogan "Write it. Don't say it."

However, it's not so ridiculous when you look into it; it's just that the idea is shocking at first glance. What I have in mind is that operating people don't read. I don't mean that they can't . . . but reading is not what production is about.

Production, mass production, is about producing more, in less time, at lower cost. This leaves little time for reading. Indeed, not only is the atmosphere of a busy production area not conducive to reading, but it may be said to be inimical.

Who wants to be seen studying a written procedure, or poring over a blueprint in the midst of a shop full of machinists or assemblers busily charging ahead, cutting metal or screwing parts together . . . getting on with the job . . . not mooning over writing . . . no matter what's written. In fact, if you pay too much attention to written procedures you're liable to be called "professor" . . . and then you've had it!

No time to read

This reluctance to take time out to read applies to supervisors and managers too. There is an urgency in the air of a thriving mass production outfit which cannot be disregarded. It affects production operators and managers alike. One wants to be in motion, to be up and about . . . not "lolling" behind a desk. Yet there are memos, procedures, edicts from management which must be attended to.

Far too many managers resolve the problem by staying after "working" hours to study the accumulated mass of written material piled up on their desks . . . or taking it home. But this isn't the way to do it. Indeed, this method of dealing with the problem almost relegates it to the status of a supernumerary operation . . . something not a part of, or only indirectly a part of the real business. ▶

However industrious and conscientious it may be to stay late or take work home, it doesn't achieve the intention of those who wrote the memos and promulgated the procedures.

Procedures require that many individuals work together cooperatively to attain a prescribed goal. Memos are frequently comments on the cooperative effort . . . or lack of it. What they have to say cannot be appreciated to the full extent when studied in isolation.

Call a meeting

What to do? Write only about what matters . . . then get the individuals together who have to do what has to be done, and discuss it with them. You may have a secretary read associated groups of paragraphs . . . then you know everybody has at least heard the words. There can be no appeal to ignorance.

But much more than that will happen. These are the men and women who have to work together to fulfill the procedure . . . it may turn out that it's not a workable plan . . . you may be shocked and enlightened when you hear what they have to say about it!

So between you, you massage it into a workable plan . . . and you know that everyone who should know, does know. Or you may find that the plan gets general approval . . . and still you know that everyone knows.

There's no substitute for face to face communication between individuals who are expected to work together . . . which is not to say that procedures and memos shouldn't be written.

Procedures are, or should be, operational instructions or guidelines implementing a given organizational policy. They must be written down to fix the policy, to give it permanence. But it still remains to assure that operations people have read them . . . and having read them are in agreement . . . or not. In fact, what has to be done to assure communication, comprehension, and acceptance may be expressed by the slogan, "Write it. Then say it!" □

The stone of Sisyphus

☐ Sisyphus was a demigod in the crowded Heaven of the Greeks. During his time on earth he "ravished" Anticlea (I'm quoting from a "Dictionary of Classical Mythology" compiled by J.E. Zimmerman and published by Bantam), and "violated" Tyro. You might think these were pretty severe delinquencies; but these were not what got Sisyphus into real trouble. Zeus, who also could be turned on by a mini-skirted miss (the chiton worn by Greek women was something like the modern miniskirt), abducted Aegina, the daughter of Asopus—and Sisyphus told Asopus!

So when Sisyphus died and went to Hades, a kind of half way stopping place on the way to Heaven, Zeus socked it to him. Sisyphus was condemned to roll a large stone to the top of a hill, but the moment he got the stone to the top of the hill, it rolled down again; so Sisyphus trundled downhill after it—and shoved it up again—and down it rolled again—and again, he pushed it up—and on and on it goes.

Obviously, at this rate, poor Sisyphus was never going to get out of Hades. Even as you read, Sisyphus is down there laboriously shouldering the stone up the hill or dispiritedly shambling downhill after it.

What's the significance?

Simple, quite a number of contemporary managers feel like Sisyphus. It doesn't matter how carefully they plan nor how hard they work, they never seem to succeed.

They can't succeed because the goals they are striving for are practically unattainable. Consider the production manager responsible for fulfilling the schedule. How often does he meet the monthly schedule? Rarely, or never! How often does he score 100% or better on labor efficiency? Rarely, or never!

Likewise on the assembly lines where, no matter how vigorous the effort, the result will be, at the most, to minimize the days behind schedule—not to achieve a victory.

Confusion in final test where the sales manager is pleading with the supervisor to rush things along so that he can keep his promise to Metalunar Corporation; a promise of delivery which is already the third postponement he's had to make. ►

Why? Because of what could be called SISYFUSTIAN SCHEDULING. That is, scheduling which sets the goal just beyond the reach of the manager's best effort.

Sisyfustian scheduling is common throughout industry. The rationale for its use is the belief that the individual does his best only when compelled to strive for the unattainable.

This belief is held by those who set the schedules, and also by many who must strive to fulfill them. This is not a case of good guys and bad guys, of bad goal setters and good strivers. There seems to be a fairly common belief that if one is not striving grimly for the impossible, one will lapse into perpetual idleness! An ironic comment on this attitude can be seen in cards tacked up over supervisors' desks, "The difficult we do immediately. The impossible takes a little time."

The die is cast

Consequences of Sisyfustian scheduling confront industry every day. Chaos in receiving inspection when material, already ten days overdue on arrival, is rejected. The expeditors, forever chasing that Sisyfustian goal, resent the time that must be allowed for inspection—but to have it rejected; that's a catastrophe!

There is near chaos in the machine shop where the expeditors constantly harass supervisors for parts scheduled for completion yesterday, or last week, or whenever—but the job is only just being set up!

The wounds are deep

And, finally, the monthly post-mortem where the purchasing manager attempts to explain why so many urgently required items arrived late; the production manager offers explanations for a labor efficiency of 82%; the sales manager tells his fellow managers what he told Metalunar and hopes he may yet get a repeat order. But nobody gets a compliment!

That's a by-product of Sisyfustian scheduling which must have a disastrous effect on the motivation of managers. Think what it means— never to be complimented!

The effect of Sisyfustian scheduling on over-all efficiency and on the quality of the product is difficult to estimate but we need have no doubt that it is there, and that it is negative.

The probability is that many companies will continue to believe that the endless labor of Sisyphus is a proper model for operating managers; but some will leave the impossible to Sisyphus and will set rational schedules for their operating managers. They surely will prosper. ☐

Is everybody average?

☐ Quickly! On a scale of 1 to 10 how would you rate your boss? Or a subordinate up for review? Or a fellow manager?

Right down the middle! No, not you, because I'm sure that you would have the courage of your opinion and would score 1 or 10 as you saw fit. But all those other folks rate right down the middle, veering only slightly to left or right to indicate tentative approval or cautious condemnation . . . but not enough to drive it home. Why do they do it? Why can't they recognize outstanding ability and say so with a 10 . . . or blast that persistent pain in the rear with a 1?

It was an article in the December '78 issue of *Psychology Today* that started me off on this matter of appraisals and evaluations. The article was about assessment centers, those remarkable trials at which candidates for management submit themselves to a battery of tests alleged to simulate events in the life of a manager, for example: how to deal with an overflowing "in" basket; how to fire an employee, etc.

The procedure requires that each candidate be assigned an observer at least one level of management above the candidate. The trials usually last three days. On each trial the observer has to rate the candidate's performance on each of 26 "behavioural dimensions" on a scale of 1 to 5.

Right down the middle

How do you think the observers score? Let us quote the author, Berkeley Rice: "There were few 1's or 5's. Only the best candidates averaged about 3.5 . . . the assessors engaged in lengthy disputes over the ratings or the meanings of particular dimensions and behaviour." Incidentally, the author reports that industrial and business users and non-users are divided as to the efficacy of the assessment method.

"Proponents of the assessment method claim it can accurately predict a person's performance in a new job. Critics say it's a pseudo-scientific fad whose predictive ability has never been proven. They argue that it merely puts a certified blessing on 'fast track' prospects already tagged for promotion." ►

What is the generally prevailing attitude toward individuals who offer themselves as candidates for promotion, whether to higher levels of management, or to public office? It's one of caution, of tentative doubt . . . it's strictly from Missouri!

Before I went into the consulting business and was managing quality assurance, I had to review the reviews my assistants had made on their subordinates. I did this routinely enough, until one day it hit me like a sledge hammer that practically all of the scores were down the middle. I called a staff meeting and asked, "Isn't anybody excellent? And isn't anyone just plain inadequate?" They were equally amazed when I produced reams of reviews . . . they hadn't been aware of the constant centralizing tendency.

No tails

We plotted a histogram from the data . . . and produced a distribution with a towering column in the middle and no tails! It got a bit better after that and we arrived at a better estimation of who had it . . . and who didn't.

Why this middling tendency? It's so common that it must be a cultural attribute. We don't learn it; it's just there and we do what everyone else does. If challenged, we would say that we aren't given to flattery. We never tire of asserting with pompous modesty that "flattery will get you nowhere." How do we know? There's so little of it. It might be as welcome as water in the desert!

Anyway, flattery is not what we're considering, but the widespread reluctance to put anyone at the top of any given scoring system. It's as though the scorer thought that by scoring 10 or excellent, he or she was admitting that someone was better than him or her. This, of course, would imply that the scorer thought of himself as average, or a little better perhaps, which might be true, too. I mean the tendency to such self-evaluation, not the accuracy of such a self-applied score in any given case.

I think it would be a good idea to give it some thought, and to check the practice of scoring in our areas of influence. In the meantime, managers can make a start tomorrow by congratulating a subordinate for a job well done. When the subordinate recovers from the shock, the word will go through the department like wildfire . . . HE NOTICED! It will do wonders for the quantity and quality of work. Don't do it too often . . . but do it. □

B.F. Skinner and the quality manager

☐ B.F. Skinner and the quality manager have a common problem. Both advocate new ways of thinking while most people prefer the old ways.

B.F. Skinner is that famous Harvard psychologist so many love to hate. His "thing" is the behavior of people; his cure for it is Behaviorism. This implies that the behavior of people needs to be cured, an assumption I think we can accept, except, of course, for you and me.

The quality manager's "thing" is the quality of manufactured products, the functional behavior of which, he thinks, should be improved. The implied assumption is confirmed by the mutterings of the consumers and the mounting flood of recalls.

B.F. Skinner's thoughts about how and why human behavior can and should be improved are best summed up in "About Behaviorism."* Professor Skinner had published six or seven books on the subject beginning in 1938. Apparently, he began to suspect that he wasn't getting through. So in 1974, 36 years after his first attempt to tell the world, he published "About Behaviorism." You can get it now in paperback for $2.45.

The why, not the how

You are familiar with the increasing library of books on quality control, many of which are concerned with the "how" of quality control instead of with the "why." One can understand why it should be so: the "how" is so precise, whereas the "why" of anything is difficult, especially when the explanation challenges old familiar ideas. I made a small attempt at explication by putting together a piece called "About Quality Control" (with apologies to B.F. Skinner) when I had the opportunity to address a captive audience of corporation executives as the banquet speaker. It was subsequently published by the System Safety Society in their journal, *Hazard Prevention* (Nov—Dec 1976).

What do B.F. Skinner and quality managers find so difficult to explain? B.F. Skinner says we have spent 2,400 years (since Socrates) looking inside ourselves for guides on how to behave. And look where it's gotten us. The biggest wars ever, street crime on the increase, politicians with ►

Korean connections, etc. It's time we realize that behavior is largely conditioned by the environment. We should consider what can be done to the environment to condition us to behave better.

The quality manager's voice from the past is the craftsman. The idea of the craftsman, highly skilled, resourceful, capable of making furniture from hedgerow sticks, of making a silk purse from a sow's ear, warms the heart. How nice, how traditional if we could all claim such ancestors.

But craftsmanship is not mass production. It's mass production that leads to affluence, which leads to consumerism. It's fashionable to deride consumerism nowaways, but before you join the chorus try to imagine what it would be like to be without all those consumer items . . . and then, try to imagine what it would be like if they were all as good as they could be.

System variability and quality

They won't be that good until the managers of the mass production industries accept that mass production is not craftsmanship. I don't mean the machine tools, the molds and dies, which are the work of craftsmen, but the products made by them. The quality of the products is conditioned by the environment; the environment is the plant, the equipment, the managers, engineers and manual operators. All constitute one system. Every action of every individual must contribute to the needs of the system. How good the product of a given system can be in terms of the percent yield of acceptable products is a function of the variability of the system as a whole. System variability, or capability, has to be measured; it cannot be surmised or dictated by fiat.

Quality control was invented to measure system variability and to control it at the optimal level by continuous statistical monitoring. Mass production without such controls is like a steam engine without a governor. It can only behave out of control and unpredictably, which is how B.F. Skinner says many individuals behave for lack of the proper controls in the environment. The majority of the populace still prefer Socrates to Skinner and old time craftsmen to statistical quality control . . . we just have to keep working at it. □

*"About Behaviorism," B.F. Skinner, Alfred A. Knopf, 1974.

The dire consequences of unilateral cost reduction

☐ Cost reduction is, by its nature and by the interconnectedness of the operating departments, a cooperative enterprise; but, all too frequently, a department will act unilaterally with good intentions and dire consequences.

Such was the sad fate of the Janus Corporation. The vice president called a meeting of his operating managers: the chief engineer, the managers of Production and Quality Control, and the chief purchasing agent.

"Times are bad," he intoned, "we have to reduce costs." The managers listened attentively. The vice president continued, "During the next three months, I want each of you to reduce costs by five percent per month without, of course, reducing the output."

"J.B.! That's going to be tough."

"It's a challenge," shot back the V.P., who knew that the tougher the task, the harder the effort. "You can do it."

So the managers departed and arranged to get together to make plans. The chief engineer thought he might release a couple of people from the print room. However, the production manager objected that it already took forever to get anything out of the print room. The production manager's supervisors assured him they were already understaffed. The quality control manager reviewed what every individual in the department did and could see no way to reduce except by a purely arbitrary cut. A typical start, a kind of ritualistic protest before getting down to business. The purchasing agent didn't say much; when they pressed him he said he was looking around.

He looked around, all right

The consequences of his "looking around" weren't felt until well into the third week of the first month. The quality control manager was checking the results to date when a bewildered receiving inspection supervisor staggered into the office and barely made it to a chair.

"For heaven's sake, what's wrong?" ►

The supervisor thrust out an arm; the manager extracted from his clutching fingers a handful of rejection notices. As he glanced over them, his eyes narrowed in disbelief; the materials and components cited for numerous defects were those most essential to the end product.

The stunned QC manager demanded, "What happened?"

"Look at the vendors' names."

The QC manager read off the names, "No!"

"Yes," the supervisor replied. The names the manager read off were some of the best schlock houses in the business.

The purchasing agent had done what every procurement manager can do when pushed. He had given the suppliers of good material the opportunity to continue supplying at reduced prices. A few wanted the business badly enough to cut deeply into the profit margin, but most said "No dice." So he sent the purchase orders to the vendors who would.

Chaos broke out

Chaos broke out. Squads of inspectors worked into the night screening the junk in a search for sufficient quantities to keep the desperate production manager in business. The purchasing agent was saved from lynching by taking sanctuary in the V.P.'s office.

There was an emergency meeting; the V.P. said that this was not what he meant; the purchasing agent was instructed to get back with Quality Street vendors; it was agreed to work out a joint program.

It took up to four months to get back to quality normal. The problem is that, even when a joint program is agreed upon, it is difficult to eliminate the tendency to act unilaterally. The departmental managers cannot be holding hands all the time. Most of the time the managers must run their departments more or less autonomously.

It's in the nature of operations. Since everyone cannot do everything, the main functions must be performed by particular individuals, who may inadvertently interfere with other functions while driving hard to complete their own tasks.

The solution lies in the sometimes despised art of coordination. The problem is to find coordinators knowledgeable enough not to attract the scorn of the professionally knowledgeable managers; persuasive enough to extract the needed information without offending the managers; and possessed of the patience of Job. They're hard to find. □

The Henry Higgins' syndrome

☐ There is a complaint that Rex Harrison sings in "My Fair Lady" as he despairs of ever teaching Audrey Hepburn how to speak the Queen's English.

What's it to us, in quality and industrial management, that Henry Higgins (Rex Harrison) cannot accept the difference between man and woman, especially when the woman is Audrey Hepburn?

Well, we hear something like it at staff meetings when chief executives complain about the lack of cooperation. "Why can't we have more cooperation? Don't we all belong to the same team?"

Well . . . yes. But the team is one thing, and the members of the team are something else again. The "team" is an abstract concept; whereas the members of the team are competitive individuals. Each one has made it competitively to his position at the 2nd, 3rd, 4th or nth level of the management pyramid. Each is biding his time until he can make the attempt to the next level above.

Building a team attitude

To be surprised at the lack of cooperation among the members of such a team is to fall into the Henry Higgins' syndrome. It is to ask "Why can't competitors be like cooperators?" The Henry Higgins' syndrome is to assume that the individual will conform to the situation; whereas the situation is much more frequently shaped by individuals.

To recognize this is not to come to the conclusion that cooperation between competitive individuals at different management levels and in different departments is not possible. What it forces upon us is a recognition that the main task of the chief executive is to coordinate the activities of his competitive subordinates. That way he will minimize the potential for conflict, diverting competitive energy to fulfillment of the organization's plans. ▶

The wise chief executive will know that it's equally important for him to be aware of the character traits and idiosyncracies of his managers, as of their technical qualifications. He will expect conflict and seek to anticipate it. He will avoid the Henry Higgins' syndrome and be prepared to make changes to accommodate quirky but competent individuals . . . so long as the vector sum of all changes is in the direction and magnitude of the over-all plan.

Coordination is all important

What is true for the chief executive is true for each department manager. He also must recognize the necessity to coordinate the activities of competitive subordinates.

Now, not only is this true for the quality manager, but he has the additional task of coordinating the quality assurance program up and down the hierarchy, and across all departments.

He, least of all, can afford to be blinded by the Henry Higgins' syndrome. When purchasing men are shocked by the rejection of long-awaited supplies, and production supervisors cry out against the rejection of fabricated parts, it's not the time for the quality manager to ask, "Why can't victims be like beneficiaries?" Because of course, "victims" are what they feel like. The organization benefits from the detection and rejection of defective parts . . . but don't expect the men who made them or bought them to jump for joy.

Chief executives, department heads and quality managers all have to operate in an environment where cooperation is essential for success, but which is peopled by members of that competitive species, *homo sapiens*. Successful groups are stuck together by that much maligned function, coordination. ☐

Organization and Entropy

☐ Every thoughtful manager has observed the tendency of schemes and programs, no matter how enthusiastically launched, to lose steam. It seems to be only a matter of time. It manifests itself by falling short of a goal that was thought attainable at the start of the year. Everyone is working as hard now as in the first months of the program, but the goal stays just out of reach.

What has happened? We might find an analogy in the concept of entropy. "A Compact Science Dictionary," (edited by G.E. Speck and published by Fawcett Premier) says of entropy that "it can be said to represent the amount of disorder or dissipation." This is appropriate, but I came across a far more applicable description in an unexpected source.

I had picked up "The World of Black Humor" (edited by Douglas M. Davis and published by E.P. Dutton). It is a collection of examples of black humor taken from contemporary literature, and critical comments by various writers. One of the latter is Wylie Sypher whose "Existentialism and Entropy" is quoted at length. In it he says, "Jacob Bronowski compares the future to a stream of gas shot from a nozzle: the farther the gas is expelled from the nozzle, the more random the motion of the molecules. The gas diffuses; it loses direction. Thus, during the course of time, entropy increases."

It starts with a bang . . .

That seems to be a fair comparison with what happens to the best laid plans of men and organizations as they advance in time from the moment of promulgation. At the start, the program is clearly understood and agreed upon by the managers. There have been meetings at which diverse points of view and alternate goals have been exchanged and discussed. Agreement has been reached, ways and means have been outlined and the goal — perhaps 12 months away — is clearly visible. Enthusiasm is high. The starting gun is fired. Let us assume that there is no objective reason why the goal should not be attained. ▶

There is rapid progress in the early months. But by the 8th or 9th month, the achievement curve begins to level off. The goal is in serious jeopardy.

What has happened is that the once compactly designed program has diffused into a thousand implemental tasks, many so diversified as to appear to have little connection with the grand design. Not only has it become difficult to find the once sharply defined goal in the mass of discrete actions, but the cohesion of the managers has been dissipated in the pursuit of many divergent tasks. We might give this organizational phenomenon a name and call it IMPLEMENTAL DIFFUSION.

Step aside to look ahead!

What to do about it? In the first case, we should not expect energetic line managers to stop suddenly in their tracks and exclaim, "My God, we're going in the wrong direction!" Such detachment is not to be expected.

The solution is for managers to gather together in an environment in which, temporarily detached from the daily hurly-burly at the plant, they can reassemble the program in its original form and reaffirm their faith in the organization's ability to attain it. A kind of retreat . . .

For this purpose, the best occasion is the staff seminar held in pleasant surroundings away from the plant. A number of large corporations already hold such seminars once a year and it can be expected that the practice will increase. But to make them effective it must be believed that they are necessary to the health of the organization and not merely a pleasant dalliance in the country. The foundation for such belief is recognition of the tendency to entropy, tendency to implemental diffusion and need to cure such an ill.   □

The McNamara Effect

☐ Robert McNamara has gone from the Department of Defense but the "McNamara Effect" remains. The McNamara Effect may be thought of as a tendency to emphasize cost during contract negotiations. It manifests itself at public gatherings of managers and engineers when, if the after-luncheon speaker is a prominent military personage, the speech is likely to be peppered with references to cost.

If a visitor from another planet sat in on many of these meetings he would get the impression that there wasn't much more than a dime left in the treasury. This would be equally true whether the speakers were military, or company executives, or engineers.

And so the visitor would dash back to Venus to take up a collection—only to be confronted by a well-informed economist, a kind of Venusian Galbraith, who would ask, "Who's the collection for?"

"America."

"You mean the United States of America?"

"Yes."

"You must be kidding! You can't have heard correctly. Why, they're the richest nation on Earth! They're so rich the imagination boggles at the thought of it."

"What's 'boggles'?"

"Oh, never mind. What made you think you should take up a collection for the United States?"

"Every time an important man makes a speech he complains about high costs. He says they have to have more for the dollar. I couldn't bear it. Several times I was reduced to tears."

"Oh, that! Why that's the McNamara Effect."

"What's the McNamara Effect?"

"McNamara was this remarkable Secretary of Defense who promulgated the idea of system effectiveness. System effectiveness is availability plus reliability, plus the cost of maintenance, plus everything that is relevant when you consider acquisition and use. Since the cost is an

►

element in every one of the conditions which must be studied, spokesmen for system effectiveness appear to spend most of their time talking about cost reduction. What McNamara had in mind was that everybody should strive for the optimum."

"What's 'optimum'?"

"Oh, go back to Earth."

So, back on earth

One of the by-products of the McNamara Effect is tendency to think of quality assurance as cost reduction.

The objective of a quality assurance program is not cost reduction. The objective is to assure that what is shipped, or provided as in a service contract, has the specified quality.

It happens that quality assurance has developed into a rational philosophy of management which creates a high probability of cost reduction if its recommendations are adopted and conscientiously conformed to. But cost reduction is not its prime objective.

When a quality assurance program is "sold" to staff and operators as a cost reduction program, it's handicapped from the beginning. It's a matter of attitude. When you're striving to achieve something positive like quality, you're strongly motivated. And when your efforts are guided by a rational quality assurance program, you're likely to perform at lowest cost.

The quality assurance manager ... like design engineers, production managers and purchasing agents ... must strive to operate within the prescribed cost constraints. But neither he nor they must ever forget the specific task for which each will be held accountable; that task, for the quality assurance manager, is to assure the quality of the product or service. □

The organizational imperative

☐ The organizational imperative is the one thing a manager must succeed at to be successful in the eyes of the organization. It's what the organization expects of him; it's what he will be measured by; it's the best measure of his own performance, once he's identified it. Furthermore, when he's identified it and when he is sure that he and the organization see eye to eye on what he has to do, the manager is provided with a focal point for all of his planning.

What's the organizational imperative for the quality manager? *It's preventing customer complaints!*

The quality manager must also work with purchasing to assure that raw material, components and other supplies are at a satisfactory quality level. But if the quality of supplies isn't so satisfactory, he will be involved but not finally judged.

The quality manager must work with production to keep down rework and scrap, but if rework and scrap rise to uneconomic levels the quality manager will, again, be involved but not finally judged.

It's only when customer complaints rise to an anguished shriek, when the volume of complaints drowns out the warbling of musak back at the plant, that the quality manager stands alone. *This is the final judgment.*

Sad but true

It's ironic, because, of course, everyone is involved in the quality of the product that finally gets into the hands of the customers. It may even be true that the quality manager met some resistance in his efforts to up the quality; he may have suffered from budget trimming, it is not unknown; but none of these will be rated acceptable alibis when the customers complain. ▶

It's on such occasions that one realizes the great significance of one's title. When customers complain about the quality, the general manager naturally turns to the "quality" manager for an explanation.

It should be pointed out that while no alibis are acceptable from the quality manager when customer complaints are excessive, or from the sales manager when the backlog drops too low, or from the chief engineer if the design is poor, or from the production manager if he misses the schedule, it is also the case that much is forgiven when the manager succeeds. At least, the manager's explanations will be listened to tolerantly.

It may be alleged that quality control costs are high, or that selling expenses are excessive, or that the design staff is too large, or that there are too many production expeditors, but the managers will be listened to and their explanations accepted (at least in part), if they have succeeded.

Nothing succeeds like success

It's nothing new, it's simply that old axiom that nothing succeeds like success, but you must know what to succeed at. So, know your organizational imperative and bend every effort to its fulfillment.

One final word to quality managers: Your organizational imperative requires that you know what the customers are saying. This means, obviously, that you must have access to field reports. These, typically, are addressed to service or sales and it might be some time before copies trickle through to you. Try to arrange that you get copies on the day of receipt. Treasure them, collect them, analyze them, measure past plans against them, make future plans from them. *They are your most important reading!* □

The qualities of a quality manager

☐ What kind of individual operates best as a quality manager? What are the desirable traits and characteristics?

As the manager of the inspection function he should have an aptitude for management: a predisposition to take command and a willingness to accept responsibility for the actions of his supervisors and inspectors. He should have a sufficient knowledge of the technicalities of inspection and test: sufficient to appreciate a good inspector when he sees one at work and sufficient to support the efforts of his metrologist as the latter strives to advance the state of the art.

As the manager of the quality engineering function he must, again, be a good manager. Technically, he must have a competent knowledge of the statistical techniques of process analysis and control which constitute quality control's unique contribution to manufacturing technology.

As the quality manager he will be a part of the company's facade. He is likely to receive the largest fraction of the company's visitors, excepting only salesmen calling on Purchasing. The quality manager must know how to conduct himself amicably and forcefully in such contacts. He must know that his every word will contribute to, or detract from, a favorable company image.

An aptitude for managing

Thus, the quality manager should have what all managers must have: an aptitude, indeed an appetite, for managing. He should be qualified in metrology and statistical technology. He should recognize the part he plays in establishing the company's image and should accept the role of an occasional public relations man.

But these qualifications are shared by many; all managers should have an aptitude for directing the work of others; metrology and statistical manufacturing technology are the specific concern of quality control, but all can learn them who will; many individuals function as spokesmen for the company and must be adept as part-time PR men.

What, if anything makes quality assurance unique? What would demand a special qualification? ▶

It is the nature of the task itself. Quality assurance is, or is thought of, as the company critic. Critics have never been popular, nor will they ever be. The human being is so constituted that a word of censure breathed against him, or against anything he has made or planned, is received, not as an objective appraisal, but as a personal condemnation. Thus, the receiving inspector does not reject defective material, but the effort of the supplier and, indirectly, of the purchasing agent who selected the supplier. Inspectors do not reject defective parts, but the efforts of the machinists; testers who reject the finished product are seen as driving a dagger into the heart of the sales manager.

You must sell quality control

The quality manager must have sufficient detachment to recognize that this is how he is seen by his colleagues, no matter how saintly he and his inspectors feel as they dot the i's and cross the t's on the rejection notices. The quality manager's prime requirement is the ability to create in the company as a whole an attitude favorable to, or at least tolerant of, the activities of the inspectors. To do so he must recognize and accept the necessity. Only when the necessity has been recognized, only when he has rejected the idea that quality control is self-evidently good and need not be "sold," will the quality manager approach the task of selecting an appropriate strategy in the proper frame of mind.

The problem exists to some degree when attempts are made to apply statistical controls to manufacturing processes. The manager may take the position that statistical controls are essential to the rational utilization of the company's production facilities; and indeed they are. But, again, manufacturing engineers don't always see it that way. To put forward a new technique of process control is, by implication, to condemn the old and to risk offending the vested emotional interest in the *status quo*. The quality manager must again give thought to a strategy which recognizes the need to "sell" statistical process control and to keep them sold.

The quality manager must recognize that the beneficiaries of quality assurance activities will more frequently feel like victims. He must plan accordingly and do so without resentment; he must be quick to perceive the hidden resentment beneath the perfunctory acquiescence. He must fulfill a major part of his assignment by persuasion of powerful individuals and groups over whom he has no line authority. He must then, above all, be a capable negotiator and coordinator.

To summarize, the qualities of a quality manager are an aptitude and an appetite for directing the work of others; competence in metrology and statistical technology; some ability in PR; perception; and a high degree of skill as negotiator and coordinator. □

What does the
Quality Manager manage?

☐ What does the quality manager manage? The quality of the product. To comprehend the situation which created the necessity for quality management, which literally created the quality manager, it is essential to distinguish between two aspects of the quality of industrial products:

- Design Quality
- Conformance Quality

Although the two aspects of quality are completely interdependent, they are handled separately as a matter of design and manufacturing procedure. The design, as developed by the engineers, is an abstraction—just so many drawings and specifications. It will not become a reality until converted into hardware.

Thus, the engineers design a product; purchasing buys raw material, parts and components; production puts them all together into the end product.

What do you do?

What, then, does the quality manager do? How does he manage the quality? In the first case, *he promotes and participates in design reviews.* The intent of design reviewing is that the participants (executive management, production, purchasing, quality control and engineers other than those responsible for the design of the product under review) shall be thoroughly briefed as to the over-all logic and details of the design. The briefing enables them to ask questions, to make suggestions and, in general, to "massage" the design until all are satisfied it will accomplish its purpose, and can be manufactured within the proposed cost constraints.

All sign an approval document committing the design to production, a valuable document which becomes a most important part of the quality history of the product. So far the quality manager has participated in design review; in many organizations he promotes and coordinates them too. What next?

The quality manager turns his attention to "conformance quality." He must inspect the product to make sure it "conforms" to the engineering drawings and specifications which means, as we all know, that all quality

▶

characteristics of purchased materials and of the manufactured product itself shall measure within the specified tolerance limits. Quality characteristics being linear dimensions, chemical compositions, performance characteristics, etc.

Thus the two aspects of quality are brought together in hardware in conformance with the design; hardware which must then possess the quality inherent in the design.

We said that the design is an abstraction until converted into conforming hardware; hardware that doesn't conform cannot possess the quality inherent in the design. *It can be seen therefore that the quality manager "manages" the quality (of the hardware) by detecting defects (deviations beyond tolerance), and by causing them to be corrected by repair or replacement.*

What do they think you do?

This is what the majority of employers and consumers think of as quality control, quality assurance, or quality management; the detection and exclusion from the hardware of defects.

But quality management does much more than this. Inspection reports are collated and analyzed in a search for the causes of defects. *Recommendations* for correction action are made to purchasing and production to prevent the further purchase and production of defects.

The quality manager cooperates with purchasing in the evaluation and selection of capable suppliers. He works with production by making statistical process capability studies. These make it possible for production to assign jobs to processes with the assurance of a high yield of good (defect free) parts.

These quality engineering activities are aimed at preventing defects. They constitute the difference between the "popular" idea of quality management as inspection; and the more comprehensive knowledge of quality management as inspection; analysis of inspection reports, recommendations for corrective action to operating departments, supplier surveys and evaluation; the application of various statistical techniques and the specific management function of integrating these quality-related activities with over-all operations.

To condense: *The quality manager manages the quality by the detection and prevention of defects.* It is this stark definition of quality management that I find most comprehensible to my clients and to audiences. The "detection of defects" encompasses measurement from the most simple to the most complex applications of metrology; the "prevention of defects" leads into the many ramifications of statistics. □

Quality Manager to General Manager?

□ Might quality management become one of the roads to general management? The signs seem to be pointing that way.

Let us consider the quality manager's assignment: It is the development of a quality program capable of achieving an optimum combination of quality and cost within the constraints of specification, price, and schedule. Since the quality manager neither designs the product, nor produces it, nor prices it, he can only fulfill his assignment by influencing the efforts of those who do.

To do so, the quality manager must have a particular set of qualifications. He must have a sufficient technical knowledge of the product; he must be familiar with the statistical techniques of quality control and know when to apply them; he must be up-to-date on metrology and other inspection techniques; he must be an able supervisor, capable of formulating policy and giving firm operational guidance to his staff; and above all, he must be a capable coordinator. He must be able to persuade the highly differentiated individuals who are his fellow managers to agree on the quality program and the best way to implement it.

Coordination is the essential mode

There is a sense, of course, in which every manager must be a coordinator. But coordination is not the essential operating mode of any manager's job except the quality manager's . . . and the general manager's.

Sales managers search for new contracts. In that search they tend to operate alone, which is not to say that they do not make themselves familiar with the company's design and production capabilities; but once that knowledge is acquired they are to a considerable degree self-sufficient and operate as such.

The chief engineer must direct the design of the product. He cannot disregard his colleagues, but since the design will be dictated by the required performance, and by his technical knowledge of materials (an objective body of knowledge not dependent on the opinions of his fellow managers), he also tends to be operationally self-sufficient.

Production managers and purchasing agents have specific tasks to perform, subject only to their understanding of blueprints and schedules. They are considerably involved with their colleagues, and yet so long as a set of blueprints (which may come from outside the company) and a schedule are provided, they can plunge straight ahead in fulfillment of clearly defined tasks. ►

Tying it all together

But not the quality manager. His quality program is a tying together of the activities of sales, design, purchasing, and production as they affect quality. His program, the company's quality program, can only be implemented by them.

The quality program requires that the company watch quality control commitments when negotiating a contract, because the company's program is keyed to certain procedures and not indiscriminately to anything and everything a potential customer may demand. The quality manager must persuade the sales manager to be watchful.

The quality program surely requires that maximum tolerance limits be allowed on all dimensions consistent with the designed performance. Such a policy minimizes production costs, minimizes debates in material review, and tends to induce a disciplined regard for the validity of engineering tolerance limits in the shop. The quality manager must persuade the chief engineer to give some consideration to this controversial issue.

The quality assurance program aims at preventing the production of defects. It is the quality manager's task to make production personnel familiar with the concept of statistically measurable variation, to provide control techniques, and to assist in their installation.

The company's quality program leans heavily upon the quality of purchased materials; which requires a selection of suppliers based upon a knowledge of their willingness to maintain disciplined inspection. The quality manager has the task of persuading the purchasing manager to cooperate in a plan for the control of suppliers.

Thus, the implementation of the quality program depends mainly upon the efforts of sales, design, purchasing, and production. Therefore, the quality manager must be an individual of considerable diplomatic ability. He must have an understanding of the subjective nature of knowledge so that he will be prepared for the differing interpretations his colleagues may arrive at from the same set of facts. He must not be too surprised when equally conscientious colleagues set off in opposite directions for the same goal. He has to know how to use the powerful tool of inspection without alienating his fellow managers.

Increasingly, companies are asking for men with coordinating ability to fill the onerous positions of quality managers. The demand may foreshadow a recognition of quality managers as candidates for general management — the ultimate goal. ☐

The last word!

☐ Who has the last word on quality? Who, that is, makes the final decision on the disposition of urgently needed nonconforming material?

Suppose that a frantic marketing manager has appealed to the chief executive against a legitimate rejection. If the disputed material is for the military, the government's Q.A.R. will have the last word.

But what happens in the case of a commercial product? There may be a formal or informal review board, consisting of representatives of quality assurance and engineering. Let's say that there is such a board, and that the engineer supports the quality assurance rejection. The heart-rending cries of the marketing manager are heard in the remotest corners of the plant!

Suppose also that the marketing manager's frenzy is justified, that there's a probability of losing a part of the market if this shipment is not made. Let it further be the case that the chief executive is just as anxious as the marketing manager to see the shipment made and that he has convinced himself that the defect is not critical. Quality assurance and engineering are of the contrary opinion.

May the chief executive override the quality manager? The organization chart says . . . Yes!

What about the wife and kiddies?

If he does; what can the quality manager do? Well, he can quit. But what if he has 3 or 4 children and a heavy mortgage? Assume he doesn't quit but having made a vigorous attempt to persuade his superior to let the rejection stand, and having failed, invites him to accept responsibility by signing the rejection notice release. The chief executive does so.

Are the quality manager and the chief executive in order? If the organization chart is to have any validity, they both are. It is unlikely that the quality manager would be overridden in the case of a critical defect.

►

However, that is not the issue. The question is whether the organizational superior may override the organizational subordinate ... and the organization chart replies in the affirmative regardless of whether the defect is great or small. This is what the hierarchical organization is about.

Such actions as we have described, until recently, were confined within a given organization. It wasn't a matter of public concern.

However, the times are changing and now that plaintiffs' attorneys threaten to penetrate the organization in a search for individual officers and employees to be named in a product liability suit along with the company, it's something we have to think about.

I checked the Code of Ethics for members of ASQC. It states under "Relations with Employers and Clients" that:

ASQC Code of Ethics

"Each Society Member will act in professional matters as a faithful agent or trustee for each employer or client ... He will indicate to his employer or client the adverse consequences to be expected if his professional judgement is overruled."

This would appear to sanction the behaviour of the quality manager in our hypothetical case who, having failed to convince on this occasion, may succeed in the future. □

EGQ-1 — The Executive's Guide to Quality

☐ Do executives need a guide to quality? I think so . . .! To function successfully, quality needs the strong support of the top executive. And strong support can only be motivated by a clear understanding of what quality is and what it does for the organization. Perhaps comprehension would be a better word than "understanding."

For example, the executive may not understand the principles of mathematics and physics the engineers apply to the design of the organization's products, but he comprehends the necessity for a design group capable of keeping the organization's products abreast of the state-of-the-art. He comprehends this as an over-arching necessity of the total socio-industrial environment of which he, and the design group, and the organization, and its products, and the desire to make a profit are all mutually supportive parts. The executive comprehends that the organization has no future without a competent design group. But, there may be executives who do not comprehend that quality is equally vital for the organization's future.

Is quality a burden?

What do executives, or at least some, think of quality? In the first case, and never to be forgotten, all executives are adversely influenced by the fact that Quality is designated "burden." A polite euphemism for parasite, and who wants it? It is true that Design and Sales are labelled "overhead" or "burden," but the curse has been taken off them somewhat. It might be said that comprehension of the necessary and essential nature of Design and Sales has neutralized the adverse effect of the pejorative designation. Not that the curse has been lifted entirely. Only the other day I saw a headline: ". . . lays off engineers to reduce overhead!"

There are executives who resent quality as something imposed on industry by the government. Even those engaged largely in production for the commercial market tend to feel that the quality departments, which

▶

have somehow sprouted within their organizations, are a pernicious spill-over from military contracting. There's no point in denying that the military has had a considerable influence on quality procedures and attitudes, and on what could be called the popular myth of quality. We shall have to examine the procedures, both for the benefit of those executives contracting for the military, and to extract from them what may be beneficial for commercial production — but later.

Quality is the critical function

What I want to do now is to identify what, if anything, makes quality uniquely necessary and essential. Quality is the Critical Function. It is that delegated part of the top executive which must address itself to assuring that what was planned was carried out successfully — or not so successfully. The quality assurance manager is, in a sense, the top executive's *alter ego*.

It is because quality is the critical function that it must be independent of those organizational groups whose work it is called upon to criticize. But, it might be asked, can't these groups, production and purchasing for example, be trusted to criticize their own work? It isn't that they can't be trusted; it is that they, like all of us, suffer from a common human trait. No man is an objective critic of his own work, or of work done by others for which he is responsible. Indeed, it may be that the inability to see the defects in oneself, or in the products of one's hands and mind, is a necessary condition for psychic survival. Robbie Burns said: "O would that God the giftie gi'e us; To see ourselves as ithers see us."

If God should ever grant that gift, I suspect that many would cry out for the merciful blindness of vanity. However, nothing in history indicates that it's likely to happen, no matter how many ardent poets call upon the deity, so we must accept the fact that the critical function is necessary and it must be independent. This is what the general manager should comprehend. With such *comprehension* it would not matter that he did not *understand* all of the intricacies of statistical evaluation or the complexities of measurement.

It is not merely that such comprehension on the part of the general manager is necessary to secure his consent to necessary staffing and funding, but it is equally important that quality shall have his moral support. This is the essential requirement. Essential for the successful functioning of quality and for the survival of the organization. □

EGQ* 2.   A clamor of consumers and a delusion

☐ Dear Executive: I hope you aren't ignoring the vociferous clamor of the consumers and their advocates. And, most importantly, the response of the courts and what seems to be the developing attitude of judges and juries.

Not, God knows, that the consumers don't have something to complain about, but the disturbing element in the situation is the apparent assumption on the part of consumers, plaintiff's attorneys, judges and juries that products are, or should be, perfect.

Anyway, consumers' hardware isn't perfect, and what's more, it can't be. Even on Apollo, the reliability engineers could only predict a probability of success of something like 99.943%. I don't know the actual figure; if it's been published I haven't seen it. The point is that, whatever it was, it was not 100%.

Now, if this is true for Apollo, on which vast sums of money were spent, it's surely true for mass-produced commercial products. It's an ironic joke, therefore, that the belief seems to be gaining ground that competitively-priced consumer items are, or should be perfect.

But they aren't—and they cannot be, not even if the consumer were prepared to pay what the nation paid for Apollo. By the way, you don't share the popular belief yourself, do you? After all, you, too, are a consumer when you're not being a chief executive.

A common delusion about sampling

I'm assuming that you're in mass production, that you're not hand crafting a few special items, in which case what I have to say would not apply. If, then, you're in mass production, you're using mass production methods and your product is being inspected by sampling. Which brings me to the heart of the matter, which is to make sure you don't share a far too common delusion about sampling. ►

What delusion is that? The belief that finding no defectives in the sample assures you there are no defectives in the balance of the lot. At first glance, it seems to be a logical conclusion. But it's a delusion nevertheless. To take a typical case: the lot size might be 10,000 and the sample size 200. Let's say that no defectives are found in the sample. Does this mean there are none in the remaining 9,800? WlI, it may be true—but the inspector doesn't know, you don't know, and the deluded don't know. There is no sampling plan (short of 100% inspection, which is no longer sampling), which can provide the assurance that the lot is defect free. No one in the manufacturing business should ever forget this dominant fact about sampling.

The probability of defectives

Why is this delusion so widespread? Perhaps because people want to believe it. It would be so marvelous if it were true! It's pretty disheartening to discover a fantastic cost reducer like sampling, and then to discover that the cost reduction has to be paid for—by accepting the probability of some defectives.

Now, inspecting only 200 instead of 10,000 allows a tremendous reduction in the cost of inspection, a reduction which contributes heavily to the competitive price. But the cost of the cost reduction is the probability of some defectives.

The thing for every manufacturing executive to do is to get together with his quality manager and find out what sampling is being done and what is the estimated probability of defectives in the competitively-priced products he's shipping to the consumers' market. That's the first step; then a way must be found to correct advertising so that it doesn't give the consumer the impression that he or she is going to find joy everlasting in articles bought at the local hardware store.   □

*Executives Guide to Quality

EGQ* 3.   The difference between quality assurance and quality control

☐ Dear Executive: Whenever I speak at a management conference, there's always someone who puts the question, "What's the difference between Quality Assurance and Quality Control?" It occurred to me that the same question may have occurred to you, so I thought I would attempt to differentiate them.

There is Quality Assurance, Quality Control, and Inspection. Let's start with Inspection.

INSPECTION is the examination of raw material or manufactured parts to assure conformance to specification. The specification may be an engineering specification, blueprint, catalog description or advertisement. Inspection may be dimensional, or tests of chemical or physical properties, or functional tests of mechanical, electrical or hydraulic characteristics. Whatever and however an act of inspection is performed, the objective is to find an answer to the simple question: Is this material, part, or product like the spec—or is it not? Thus, the many acts of inspection taking place at various locations throughout the plant result in the acceptance or rejection of raw material, component parts or end product. And that is where INSPECTION ends and QUALITY CONTROL takes over.

Why are there any bad apples?

I wouldn't be surprised if you were to explode at this moment and exclaim, "Oh, does it! Before anyone else gets into the act, I want to know why anything at all had to be rejected. I don't pay anyone to buy defective material, and I surely don't pay anyone to manufacture defective parts!"

You would be right! You don't pay for the purchase and manufacture of defects, but you get them! There are various causes which account for this unprofitable practice of getting what you don't want and didn't order. Some causes are fairly obvious but the worst offenders are deeply embedded. Quality Control is concerned with the detection and correction of the causes for the incidence of defects.

The quality control engineers, or "quality engineers" in contemporary usage, perform this highly profitable task by collecting, sorting and arranging inspection reports and subjecting them to statistical analytical techniques of great diagnostic power. They condense their findings into corrective action recommendations which are fed back to Purchasing and Production. When Purchasing and Production act upon them, improvement in quality is reflected in subsequent inspection reports. Thus, quality engineering is a closed system which penetrates to the

▶

causes for the incidence of defects, recommends action for their correction, and automatically records the improvement.

Such diagnostic analysis and corrective action are, in the sequence I have shown, after the fact. But the same statistical analytical techniques may be applied to mass production processes before the process (machine tool, plating vat, heat treating oven) has been committed to a large production run.

The natural or normal spread

These techniques measure the so-called "natural" or "normal" spread of the process. Armed with such information, and with a knowledge of the specified tolerance, and assuming jobs are matched to processes in such manner that the tolerance exceeds the process spread, Production can roll into production with the certainty of a high yield of good parts. Quality Control, or Quality Engineering, performs many more tasks including assistance to Purchasing in the selection of suppliers, planning inspection and test, selecting sampling plans, collecting and analyzing field performance data, etc. But it will sharpen the distinction between quality Control and Inspection on the one hand, and between Quality Control and Quality Assurance on the other, to think of Quality Control as being mainly concerned with the prevention of the production of defects.

What about Quality Assurance? QUALITY ASSURANCE is the management of Inspection and Quality Control, plus a whole raft of coordinating activities on the part of the quality manager, whereby he strives to keep you and his fellow managers informed on the quality situation and, hopefully, involved. Typically, the quality manager will circulate a Monthly Quality Summary which indicates the percentage of purchased material found defective during the month, and whether this was better or worse than last month; and the percentage of scrap and rework in the production areas and whether this was better or worse than last month; and a summary of field complaints and what is being done to eliminate them; and various other items.

When I said that you should be involved, this was done advisedly because if you aren't involved, or if it is believed by the work force that you aren't involved, the quality manager, the quality engineers and the inspectors might as well go home. I don't mean that you have to be involved in every single action, but you should see that Monthly QUALITY SUMMARY. Then you'll know what percentage of purchased material was defective and what percentage of parts had to be reworked or scrapped in the machine shop, and, if there's good cause to speak to the Managers of Purchasing or Production, you'll have the facts.   □

*Executives Guide to Quality

EGQ* 4.   The quality balance sheet

☐ Dear Executive: The other day I received in the mail an invitation to send for a brochure, "How to read a (financial) balance sheet." You know, the kind of bait stockbrokers cast upon the waters.

It occurred to me that you also might receive such an invitation since you, like the rest of us, are on everybody's mailing list. This possibility amused me, because your daily activities are the material from which balance sheets are made and reading a balance sheet is surely one thing you can do backwards and forwards.

But then a kind of associated thought came into my mind: can you read a QUALITY BALANCE SHEET?

A quality balance sheet should show how much quality has been produced in return for a given expenditure. But there's a problem right at the start. "Quality" is a vague term; so too, for that matter is "profit." However, the moment you think "profit," you think "dollars," and dollars are a nice hard quantitative entity. They're a bit inflated at the moment, but you can allow for that. You still have a firm number and I hope it's a good one.

But what do you think when you think "quality"? I mean, how do you quantify it? The thing to do is to count defects. Ridiculous isn't it, to count quality by counting defects, but that's the way it's done.

For example

Let me give you an example. Let's assume you mass produce a moderately complex device and machine many of the component parts yourself. The machine shop consists of 100 men plus supervision which represents a fairly substantial investment. You know what the shop costs are and you want to find out how much quality you're getting for the money. So you phone the shop superintendent.

"How's the quality, John?"

"Fine, J.B., just fine."

That doesn't tell you much although it's a typical reply. How should you frame the question to get something specific?

Try this: "What percentage of parts were defective last week, John?"

Assuming that John doesn't collapse from shock, and that he has the info, he may reply, "Three percent," or "Six percent," or whatever.

►

Your next question might be "And how does this compare with last week?" Depending on the reply, you congratulate him, or listen to his explanation of why it's worse. In any case, you're both talking numbers; you both know the quality situation in terms of the proportion of defective pieces.

Now, if the shop supervisor has the info, the probability is that he's quoting from an inspection summary prepared by the Quality Manager. This is a report which might contain the following:

QUALITY SUMMARY
Machine Shop
Period: (Week) (Month) of

1. Total number of parts inspected . . . . _____
2. Number of parts found defective . . . . _____
3. Defective parts as a percentage of total . . . . _____ %
4. Percentage of parts defective for the previous period . . . . _____ %

Comments: An explanation of why the percentage of defective parts had increased, or decreased or remained the same.

This is the absolutely basic pared-down information; but even so, when you know this much, you know a lot. The summary may go into more detail, listing the specific defects in rank order from the most frequently occurring to the least. As a consequence, the machine shop's corrective effort can be directed at the worst offenders.

It's for you to decide whether you want to receive a copy of the periodic Quality Summary. But keep in mind that, if it's known that you're receiving a copy, and if it's further known that you read it, your operating managers will read it too. Then you'll see some vigorous corrective action and those defect percentages will come tumbling down!

I'm not suggesting that your operating managers won't study such reports unless it's known you do, but hell, they're so busy that if they never looked at a report they would still have many tasks to perform.

It's shocking isn't it, how many things are up to you, but that's what it is to be the chief executive. You don't have to run the Sales Department, or Engineering, Purchasing, Production or Quality Control, but you must direct them, coordinate them and, above all, develop quantitative measures of performance. In regard to quality, if you don't know the defect rate, you're flying blind. □

EGQ* 5.   Think defects!

□ Dear Executive: Did you happen to see my piece on "Science Fiction" (see page 213)? In it, I pointed to the shockingly high proportion of books on management that make no reference to inspection, to quality control, or to defects. I asked the question, "Don't they (the authors) know about the high incidence of defects?"

Don't they know that defects in purchased materials may wreck the schedule and send costs rocketing sky high? Yet most books on management elaborate on the making of schedules. They get lyrical on the matter of cost reduction. They devise beautiful channels of communication. But *what information travels along those beautiful channels?* Is it ever a count of defects? Rarely.

I can think of several books in which it is said that cost overruns and delayed schedules are evidence of deviations from planned procedure. And so they are. Simulated case histories are presented and it usually turns out that some individual departed from the plan, or there was a technical difficulty, or something. But rarely does the investigation lead to a stack of defective material.

Welcome to the real world

Yet the incidence of defects may be the most frequent cause of high costs and shattered schedules. It's weird how defects hide so effectively from the light of day in these remarkable texts. It's as though the reader were not expected ever to come into contact with hardware! But hardware, good enough to survive inspection and test—and to survive in the market—is what industrial production is all about!

These are the books your management colleagues are likely to be reading. If you give them time out to attend a training course, they're likely to spend five days or whatever and never hear a whisper about defective material!   ▶

Why? It may be that there's no reference to defects because the authors assume (correctly) that managers don't plan to make defects and that, therefore, there's no point in discussing them. But I doubt it. I think it may be that authors and managers think "quality." Quality is such a positive, heart-warming word; it invokes such a gratifying sense of accomplishment that one simply cannot think of defects in the same breath.

The absence of defects

And so it seems to me that you and your colleagues ought to start thinking "defects." Only then will you think of quality as *the absence of defects*. Only then will you ask the right questions about quality. Not "How's the quality?" But, "What's the defect percentage today, or this week, or whenever?" Only then will you know when the quality is improving (by a reduction in the incidence of defects). Only then will you have a reliable, quantitative measure of the performance of your operating managers in the matter of product quality.

It is probable that we in quality control haven't gotten through to you, or at least, not through enough. Our titles, "quality manager" and "quality engineer," suggest that all is well. Perhaps if you thought of us as defect detectives, and as investigators of defects and their causes for the purpose of preventing their further production, you would get a better idea of what your quality control specialists are trying to do for you.

Anyway, let me recommend that you try thinking "defects"; let nobody talk to you about quality except in terms of the presence or absence of defects. You may be shocked, if you haven't heard them before, when those defect percentages are first quoted to you. But you will be deeply gratified by the reduction in those percentages, and by the consequent reduction in cost overruns and schedule delays. Just ask the right questions. □

*Executives Guide to Quality

EGQ* 6.   Don't shoot the quality manager!

☐ Don't say you haven't wanted to. It's a natural impulse.

At any moment during a busy day your phone may ring—and who·is it? It's the procurement manager reporting that "they" have just rejected that consignment of parts production needed to complete the assemblies that the sales manager has been anxiously awaiting to complete the overdue shipment Metalunar is screaming for!

You don't have to ask who "they" are. "They" are the quality manager and his subordinates.

You inquire, "What happens now?"

"Well, they (the parts) are going into review."

"Any chance they may be accepted?"

"I don't know. I'll let you know when the review's over."

"O.K. Let Don (the sales manager) know and please keep me informed."

You shouldn't worry. You'll be informed all right: The phone will blast again and it will be the production manager who excitedly explains, "the sales manager wants to know what he should tell Metalunar?" This rejection has thrown the organization into chaos.

"Shoot the bastard!"

Now wouldn't it be marvelous if, in response to your question, the procurement manager replied, "Well, we just shot the quality manager and now we're trying to find his assistant to sign the release." Indeed, there is precedent for such behaviour. Our ancestors killed the bearers of bad tidings; and who are we to be better than our ancestors!

However, you could handle it another way. You could ask the procurement manager:

"Why were the parts rejected?"

"Quality control says they're defective."

"Well, are they?"

To which the procurement manager, greatly embarrassed by such an unexpected question, might reply:

"Hell, J.B., I suppose there's some little thing wrong with them. You know what a gang of nitpickers they have in quality control."

"No, I don't," you might say, "I only know you say so. Would you mind bringing me the rejection notice?" This will shatter the poor man. He wonders what pill you're on, but he procures the notice anyway.

The rejection notice informs you that the urgently awaited consignment ▶

of 540 widgets deviates from the blueprint on three characteristics; and one of these three is the prime critical dimension! If, at this moment, you were to roar, "Why the hell d'you buy such junk?", the quality of your purchased material would change overnight! Believe me!

Temporary solutions

You can expect that your managers will solve the problem one way or another. If the deviations from blueprint are on the plus side, your production manager may rework enough pieces to get a token shipment to Metalunar. If the deviations are undersize, you're sunk. There's no option except to harass the life out of the supplier until he gets with it and makes some good pieces.

But transcending this particular catastrophe are the following questions that should be asked:

(1) Why did it happen?

(2) What must be done to prevent it from happening again?

(3) Why did the procurement manager refer so casually to the detection of such serious defects as "nitpicking?"

The last question is by no means the least. It may be the key to the whole train of events. Unfortunately, and this is where it may hurt, it may come back to you!

The procurement manager's casual comment is a manifestation of an attitude toward rejection reports and, by extension, to the activities of quality control in general.

Attitudes are powerful motivators of action. The attitudes of individuals in a hierarchical organization are commonly acquired by emulation of organizational superiors.

The procurement manager's supervisor is you. His attitude is, most likely, a reflection of yours, although he may not be overly conscious of it. If your response to complaints about rejections has been to express impatience with quality control, instead of anger with the manager who bought or made the defective pieces, then you may have laid the ground work for the loss of the Metalunar account.

"My God!," you might exclaim, "Do I have to become a quality control expert? Do I have to watch every word I speak, every gesture I make?"

You don't have to become a quality control expert. If you want quality purchased material and manufactured product (and by "quality" I simply mean defect-free), then you should demand to see every rejection report that any supervisor considers unrealistic. Blast off when the defects are gross and plentiful. Don't shoot the quality manager because his inspectors found deviations. □

*Executives Guide to Quality

EGQ* 7. Quality and quality improvement

☐ Dear Executive: Have you ever overheard your production managers muttering darkly about "never-ending" quality improvement programs? Like "When are we going to stop improving the quality and make some profit?" and "Do they expect us to turn out a Cadillac for the price of a Chevrolet?" And so on.

Even if such complaints have not reached your ears, it's almost a certainty they are being made. We bring it up because the next quality improvement program you authorize may be the straw that breaks the camel's back; you should be prepared.

Enough is never enough

The production managers have a point; they are constantly being urged to "improve" the quality. Even when they're successful, that strident demand never ceases. As the production managers say, it's endless! And so it is, for "improvement" is an open-ended concept. No matter how good a product may be, there's still room for improvement . . . there's never enough improvement.

To develop an approach to the problem, we have to consider two aspects of quality:

(1) *Design quality:* The design developed by the engineers to fulfill the customer's requirement or, in the case of products for mass consumption, to fulfill the promises made in advertisements. The design exists as so many engineering drawings and specs.

(2) *Conformance quality:* The degree to which the product conforms to engineering drawings and specs.

To be in full conformance, each measurable characteristic must measure within the tolerance limits specified by the designers. These might include the composition and physical properties of a material, a linear measurement, a weight, or a mechanical, chemical or electrical property. The end product then will possess the "quality" inherent in the design. If the design is adequate, the product will perform as specified or advertised and all will be well. ➤

Greater conformance

When we speak of quality improvement, what do we have in mind? A better design? Greater conformance? We could mean either or both, but in general it is assumed that the design is adequate, and that what we have in mind is greater conformance.

The assumption that the design is adequate is not left entirely to the engineers' competence, as excellent as that may be. There are design review procedures (which I'll describe in a future article) that seek to assure the adequacy of the design. In any case, let us make this assumption: By the time you go into production you must believe that the design is adequate. This leaves improved conformance as the principal goal of any quality improvement program that may be launched.

But what is "improved conformance"? It is fewer defects. Since defects are characteristics of materials, parts and components which do not measure within specified tolerance limits—i.e., which do not "conform"—it can be seen that what we need is not "improved" conformance, but only "conformance." In other words, we want only that which is specified.

"Quality attainment" is more accurate and less aggravating than "quality improvement." Conformance to specs and advertised capabilities is an attainable goal; quality improvement is an ever receding unattainable goal.

We must say, however, that conformance or quality "attainment" doesn't sound very inspiring. Who's going to exert himself to attain conformance? Especially when conformance is almost always coupled with "mere" conformance. But "quality improvement" has a fine onward and upward thrust to it.

Consequently, we think it might be better to stay with "quality improvement" . . . but be prepared for those sometimes bitter complaints. Be ready to keep peace in the family by pointing out that nobody wants the quality improved beyond conformance to design specs—not you, not the designers, and not quality assurance.   □

*Executives Guide to Quality

EGQ* 8.   Who sets quality standards?

☐ Dear Executive: Who sets the quality standards?

Not Quality Assurance!

This may surprise you because it seems natural that "quality" standards should be set by "Quality" Assurance. But it depends on your definition of "quality standards."

There is a definition of Quality Assurance which reads: "A management function to assure that products conform to quality standards." The quality standards are "set" by the designers in the engineering specification (in which term I include all blueprints). The specification breaks down into descriptions and drawings of many parts and their quality characteristics. The designers specify the allowable tolerance on each characteristic.

For example, a characteristic of titanium is that it shall not contain more than a specified percentage of hydrogen (which has an embrittling effect). The designers specify the maximum permissible percentage of hydrogen. It is the job of Quality Assurance, by making appropriate tests, to assure that incoming lots of titanium do not contain more than the permissible percentage of hydrogen. If the permissible percentage is not exceeded, the titanium is said "to meet the quality standards," or "to conform." If it doesn't, the material is rejected because it's "out of spec" or "nonconforming." Quality Assurance has the unenviable task of recording and publicizing (by way of a rejection notice) the failure to meet the quality standard . . . but it did not set the standard!

Check to spec

The quality standard set by the specification on a given dimension may be that it shall measure 0.500 in. ± 0.002 in. Thus, the dimension may vary from 0.498 to 0.502 in. Every piece which Quality Assurance finds between 0.498 and 0.502 in. will be accepted. Pieces measuring above or below will be rejected. It may happen that some pieces measure 0.4975 in. If there is an urgent need for the parts, it's likely to be asserted that these are "close enough." But, however close, they're out of specification; they don't meet the quality standard.   ▶

The procedure in such cases is to submit the "nonstandard" parts to the Material Review Board, known as MRB. The Board consists of responsible individuals from Engineering and Quality Assurance. If you're contracting for the Department of Defense, the third member of the Board will be the government QAR (Quality Assurance Representative). If you're supplying masses of anonymous consumers, the Board is generally confined to Engineering and Quality Assurance with someone from Production to advise on manufacturing problems.

The essential function of the Board is performed by the engineer. He, in effect, is invited to rethink the design and to decide whether the performance of the end product will or will not be adversely affected by the use of these nonconforming parts. If he decides that the performance will not be affected, the parts are "bought" and all members of the Board sign an appropriate document.

You may wonder why the engineer can modify his own quality standard in this manner. If you should ask your Production Manager, he's likely to tell you that "The engineers always make the tolerances tighter than they need to be." If you spoke to the Chief Engineer he might say, "It's the only way to keep Production in line. No matter how much tolerance we give them, they take more!" I tell you these things because there's a certain amount of turmoil going on out there in the manufacturing areas. Sometimes you're the only one who can moderate it. It's important that you know the attitudes of your managers. Certainly you should be aware of this almost traditional antagonism between Engineering and Production.

Another point: When the engineers "buy" parts in MRB, Quality Assurance should press for a specification change. They should present the logical argument to the engineers: "Your acceptance of these parts is, by implication, a confession of an error in design, insofar as it is an admission you made the tolerance tighter than it need be. Therefore, change the specification so that we don't have to go through this hassle in the future."

You might think that the engineers would automatically change the specification to allow broader tolerances in such situations ... but they don't. At least, not always, and indeed not very frequently. You might talk to your Chief Engineer about it sometime when you've gathered some statistics on the operations of the Material Review Board. Anyway, Quality Assurance should keep trying because, all other things being equal, manufacturing costs go down as tolerances are opened up to match need rather than desires. ☐

*Executives Guide to Quality

EGQ* 9. Pareto, mon amour

☐ Dear Executive: I know it's ridiculous to speak with affection about a technique to analyze production performance (The Pareto Analysis), but I wanted to catch your attention. The Pareto is one of only two analytical techniques that might be described as fabulous (the other being the Frequency Distribution).

Nearly a century ago, Vilfredo Pareto, an Italian economist, discovered that where *many* things or people may deviate from an established norm, *a few* deviate the most, often accounting for a majority of total deviations. It is this tendency toward disproportionate deviation that we seek with The Pareto Analysis.

For example, let us imagine that you have an Assembly Area in which 80 assemblers are putting together a moderately complex device. Week by week, month by month, you hear mutterings from Production about the nitpicking inspectors, and from Quality Assurance about the assemblers whose fingers are all thumbs. There's no focus to all these complaints, but quality is neither improving nor declining, and you don't know what to do.

A Pareto analysis

What you should do is have Quality Assurance make a Pareto Analysis. Here's how you do it. Start with a preliminary one-day seminar at which you and your department managers learn what it's about and get the opportunity to ask questions of an expert. To stimulate participation, it may be better if the expert is from the outside.

Now you've completed the seminar and you all agree to take the first reading at the end of the first week of next month. It's most important that the *status quo* shall not be disturbed. Let things proceed in the usual manner so that when the defect rate is cut way down you will know the point from which the improvement began.

The week passes, rejections are made, and products move to the end of the line and on to shipping. Monday morning, the quality engineers collect all inspection records and make The Pareto Analysis. Briefly, they: (1) count total defects, (2) separate out defects according to type, (3) place groups of defect types in rank order, and (4) compute the size of each group as a percentage of the total number of defects. Tabulate this information and you have The Pareto. ▶

Monday afternoon you get together with your managers. If The Pareto is decently tabulated, it will tell you the story at a glance. It will be obvious that *only a few* of the many types of possible defects *account for the bulk of the total defects.*

Let's say the defects that week totaled about 900, and that 25 different types were recorded. The Pareto might look something like this:

Kind of Defect	Rank	No. of Defects	% of Total	Cumulative %
	1	198	22%	22%
	2	189	21%	43%
	3	171	19%	62%
	4	162	18%	80%
	—	— —	— —	— —
	—	— —	— —	— —
Totals		**900**	**100%**	**100%**

We see by The Pareto that only 4 of the 25 possible defect types accounted for 80% of *all* defects.

Customarily, The Pareto is referred to as "The 10-90 Effect" because approximately 10% of the things that *may* go wrong are likely to account for 90% of what *does* go wrong.

Confronted by The Pareto, almost anything you and your managers might say would be gratuitous. It's obvious what has to be done and, concentrating on those four "worst defects," the corrective action commandos act.

With another reading next week, there's a change for the better . . . not startling, perhaps, but a change. Within a few months, you may reduce the 900 total defects down to, say, 150.

Think about your reduced manufacturing costs, with 750 fewer reworks, 750 inspections you need not pay for, and 750 schedule disruptions that no longer spoil the charts. Where could you get so many profitable benefits for such a small effort?   □

*Executives Guide to Quality

The crucial question

□ If an industrial executive could ask his managers one question only, what should that question be?

It's ridiculous, of course, to imagine an executive tied down to one question only. He's at liberty to ask one or twenty-one. But it's an interesting exercise to select one question only, if one is all that is to be allowed. It's like the game of "What would you wish for if you only had one wish" that we used to agonize over as children.

Let us imagine that our executive is on a business-cum-pleasure trip. He's checked things in Bombay; business was moderate in Singapore; Hong Kong should be good for a few more years; he's now in Tokyo and he's relaxing in a teahouse.

He's had thirty-six cups of tea and he just can't face another. The smiling geisha has picked up the samisen and has begun to pluck gently at its three strings. As one soft pathetic note languidly follows another he begins to suspect he's been misinformed about geisha girls. Feeling restless, he decides to call Pittsburg and find out what's happening back at the plant. Since the executive's ancestors came from Aberdeen, he's determined not to let the call go more than three minutes. So he's going to ask one question only. What shall it be?

The executive could ask "Are you making a profit?" But what could the plant manager reply except "Yes"? And then, who knows how much profit is being made until the accountants pull the figures together?

The executive could ask "Are you on schedule?" If the answer were "Yes," what would that tell him? The plant might be on schedule with a pile of junk, and what good is that to him! He could follow up with, "Are you on schedule with good material?" . . . but he's only got one question.

He could ask "Are you keeping within the budget?" The plant manager might reply "Oh yes!" . . . but what does that tell him? It's possible to be within the budget but behind on schedule, or low on quality, or both.

He could ask "Are you making quality parts?" The answer's certain to be "Yes." The plant's sure to be making some good parts; it's rarely the case that all parts being produced are bad.

So what one question is the executive going to ask? He should ask *"Are you maintaining the predicted percent yield of good parts?"* If the answer is "Yes" he has learned the most that can be learned from one question about a mass production operation. ▶

Evidence of good planning

The fact that he can ask the question is evidence of the excellent planning that was done before plunging into production. We infer from the form of the question that:

- The quality engineers had been required to determine the natural "spread" of each production process by statistical analysis
- That this information had been disseminated through all levels of management
- That the chief executive (now in Tokyo) had promulgated a rational production policy which required that no job be assigned to a production process unless the engineering tolerance limits were equal to, or in excess of, the natural "spread" of the process
- That when circumstances made this impossible, the quality engineers were to be called upon to predict the yield and that the predicted yield is to be noted on the work order as an attainable target
- That each production process is controlled by a control chart prepared by the quality engineer, posted by the operator, frequently checked by the supervisor, and monitored by the inspector
- That production management, quality engineers, production (or industrial) engineers, operators and inspectors cooperate to maintain the yield at the predicted levels
- That indications of abnormal variation appearing on the process control charts trigger prompt corrective action
- That all production control records highlight actual percent yield, comparing with the predicted yield

When there is a recognition by all levels of management that the tendency to variability in each production process is as arbitrary as the engineering tolerances; and when it has been recognized that the profit projection, to be reliable, must be based on a predicted percent yield of good parts; and that this depends on the known degree of compatibility between process capabilities (natural spread) and engineering tolerances; then, and only then, can the production plan be said to be rational.

No other choice

Therefore, the crucial question must be "Are you maintaining the predicted yield?" For if the answer is "yes," it's highly probable that production is on schedule and costs are within budget. An unforeseen event which reduced the yield below the predicted level would disturb schedule and budget.

Anyway, that's the question the executive asked and to which the plant manager said "Yes." And the executive, his mind at ease, returned to the bright eyes of the geisha, the sad notes of the samisen, and his thirty-seventh cup of tea. □

The ultimate criterion

☐ Starting from the premise that the objective of an industrial manufacturing organization is to make a profit on the investment, it is submitted that quality is the ultimate criterion.

To achieve its objective, an organization must confirm that what it is offering for sale is what the public believes it is buying.

However, these two conceptions of the objective product are not necessarily one and the same.

What it means to the company

The objective product is a means to an end for the general manager . . . the end, of course, being the projected profit. The objective product is a means to the fulfillment of the quota for the sales staff; it means fulfillment of a problem in the application of scientific knowledge for the designers.

The end product is a bewildering variety of materials, parts, and components for the purchasing people. It is a problem in the utilization of resources for the manufacturing manager; for him, it may very well become a severe scheduling challenge . . . particularly if there are frequent engineering changes, delays in delivery of parts, and an abnormal number of rejections.

For the quality assurance manager, the objective product is a multitude of multi-various activities which finally culminate in an end product for inspection and quality control.

What it means to the customer

But for the customer, the objective product is none of the foregoing. What he buys is the *quality* of the product! The "quality" of the product is synonymous with what it will do for him . . . or, to be more exact, what he has been led to believe it will do for him. The customer doesn't "buy" all that hardware, the accumulation and assembly of which has "cost" so much sweat and, possibly, so much organizational friction. ▶

It follows that everybody's efforts . . . from top management all the way down the line . . . will be lost if the customer does not find in the product the quality he has been led to expect. For if the quality is not there, the word will soon spread, sales will languish, and management's alimentary tracts will become ulcerated.

What it means to you

The quality of the product as understood by the customer is, therefore, the ultimate criterion. It assures continued sales . . . and, presumably, continued profits. The fate of the organization and of the projected profit hangs upon this quality.

As a result, management must recognize that while the objective product is a "quality" of performance, of appearance, of duration for the customer, it does not carry the same connotation for many members of the organization.

Ultimate quality represents *a great variety of activities of which the product is, as it were, a by-product.* This fact must be kept in mind at all times by all members of the company, if the end product is to contain the quality expected by the customer.

A *total environment* must be created in which the situation is not so much that everyone is deliberately quality-conscious, but one in which it would be impossible, or at least difficult, to function without contributing to the "quality" of the product as understood by the customer.   □

Quality-Mindedness

☐ If there's one subject that can turn a staid meeting into an enthusiastic rally, it's a stirring call for quality-mindedness. But when the meeting's over, you're apt to wonder what the cheering was all about. Who is going to do what?

I decided to discuss the subject with Si Si, a kind of personal yes-man whose criticisms are always constructive.

"Si Si, there's something bugging me. You know this quality-mindedness that everybody talks about?"

"Yeah."

"Good. Then perhaps you can tell me what it is."

"Well, man, it's like when everybody's mind turns toward quality."

"But nobody's mind turns away from quality. It's like Mom and Apple Pie, you daren't be against it."

"Well, man, there you are. What more do you want?"

"I want to know what the Quality Minded do about it. Give me an example."

Si Si thought a moment, and said, "Top Daddies wanna ship product that satisfies the money-payers. Like that's being quality-minded."

"I see. Give me another."

"Production scrooges wanna keep scrap and rework low. Like that's being quality-minded, too."

"Right. But there's still something bugging me."

Si Si shrugged. "You're hard to please, man. Everybody knows what quality is and everybody has a mind. Put 'em together and there it is."

"Ah, that's it. Quality. Does everybody know what it is?"

"Sure, man."

"Well, would you agree that quality is the degree of conformance to specification?"

"Yeah, man."

"And that any attempt to achieve conformance at minimum cost is quality-mindedness in action?"

"Why the 'minimum cost' bit?"

"Well, surely you're not thinking of quality apart from the cost?"

Si Si hesitated. "Yes. No. Check one, man."

"No, of course."

"Right. No."

"Okay. Now where shall we start?"

"Let's begin with the design lines, daddy. Let's see what we have to conform to." ▶

"Right. Would you say that the designers should discontinue the practice of tightening the tolerance limits more than is strictly necessary? Assuming that they do so, as so many production supervisors allege."

"Sure, man."

"Don't be so quick to agree. Perhaps it's a good thing to tighten down the tolerance limits a little. You know what the designers say, 'No matter what you give 'em, they take a bit more!'"

"Well, dad, I've made lots of them design-production battle scenes, but this whole gig has to be solved and the flag has to be run up somewhere. I don't see how anybody can be quality-minded if there's any doubt about what the quality is!"

"Si Si, you're beginning to . . . What's the word I want? Something like 'evacuate,' 'bulldoze,' 'eviscerate'?"

"Dig, man."

"That's right. You're beginning to dig the problem."

"Thanks, dad. What else do you suggest for the quality-minded check list?"

"Would you agree that quality-minded inspectors should work strictly to the drawings? That they shouldn't base judgments on the memory of what went through material review?"

"You said it, man."

"Would you agree that quality-minded production engineers or industrial engineers, or whoever has the responsibility for scheduling jobs onto manufacturing processes, should be concerned about the capability of the processes? That they should request process capability studies from the quality control engineers, and should be guided by that knowledge when assigning jobs?"

"Yeah, man. You got more, I s'pose? . . . "

"Would you agree that quality-minded purchasing agents should be guided by q.c. recommendations when issuing purchase orders?"

"Okay, dad, but you're tirin' me . . . "

"And would you agree that General Managers should demand to know the cost involved in arriving at the optimum combination of quality and cost, and that it would be quality-minded to sanction such expenditures?"

"Gimme a f'rinstance on the 'optimum' bit."

"Well, you know. It's like the most quality for the least cost. Except that 'most quality' doesn't mean absolute perfection, whatever that is. It means quality by definition. And 'least cost' doesn't mean zero. There's some optimum combination inherent in the circumstances prevailing in each plant."

"Right, man."

Si Si declined any further argument and we joined the crowd at the coffee truck. □

The quality explosion

☐ Is there a quality explosion? Is there such an increase in the quantity of quality activities that a behavioral change has been induced? Something happened recently that prompts me to believe there may be. I was making a call on a medium-sized company to consult with the quality manager on a reliability program. As I chatted with the receptionist, a gorgeous creature as beautiful as Venus and as affable as Aunt Vera, I glanced idly at the entries ahead of mine. Something about the page of entries seemed to demand more attention. Looking more closely, I was astounded to find that 6 out of the 7 visitors ahead of me were calling on quality business!

"Is this usual?" I asked, turning the sheet toward the receptionist.

"Oh, yes. We get a lot of quality people." The manager's secretary arrived and escorted me to his office.

"D'you get many visitors?"

"Indeed we do," she replied, "I could make this trip with my eyes closed!"

Swamped with visitors

When the quality manager had outlined what he wanted done, I questioned him about the number of visitors. "I'm swamped," he exclaimed, "I could spend all of my time with them, and it still wouldn't be enough."

"How many do you see in an average month?"

"Plenty! I don't know exactly how many." We decided to check the record. We found that in the previous month there had been 510 visitors of whom 156 had called on q.a. business! We went back four months and found comparable figures: people calling about q.a. varying between 20% and 35% of the total.

Subsequently I checked in other plants and found pretty much the same picture. The proportion on quality assurance business was never less than 10% and occasionally hit 40%.

The rising tide of interest in quality assurance, the increasing proportion of all supplier-customer communications that are concerned with quality makes it reasonable to speak of a quality explosion. ▶

Mr. outside or Mr. inside

To qualify as an "explosion" there must be a qualitative change in the nature of the activity, or a potential for qualitative change. This manifests itself in quality assurance by the disproportionate amount of time the quality manager must spend with visitors; so much so, that quality managers are faced with the problem of deciding whether to function predominantly as "outside" men or as "inside" men.

The quality manager must, as it were, select his major. He may concentrate on the visitors, explaining the quality assurance system, debating the applicability of certain requirements, responding to complaints, constantly projecting the company's quality image. He may then occupy the balance of his time making sure that the manufactured product will support the image. Or, he may go for an "inside" major, concentrating heavily on departmental administration, hoping that the product will project its own image.

It is possible to hope that a good product will sell itself; this is one of those beautiful sentiments we piously intone on suitable occasions, but the volume of advertising does not decrease. The substance and the image are one, or become so in time; neither can be neglected.

Obviously, every quality manager devotes his efforts to both. The point is that the increase in the absolute and relative quantity of q.a. business threatens him with a behavioral change in function. He can get a grip on the problem by checking the statistics on visitors; he can take a position and allocate his time before he is swept by the flood into almost 100% interviewing.

By recognizing the problem and by making plans, he ought to be able to confront the q.a. explosion with more equanimity than, for example, society anticipates the population explosion. □

Quality improvement or quality attainment?

☐ "Quality improvement" is, at first glance, a fine thing. Who would dare to be against it? It would be like rejecting Mom and Apple Pie! But it has some interesting implications.

What is the quality being improved from, to?

The implication is that the product is already at some acceptable "level" of quality and that we are making a determined effort to improve it beyond that level. The implication is that we are already giving the customer the quality he specified; nevertheless, here we are generously striving to give him even more.

But is this the case? We must have a definition of quality to know what we mean when we talk about improving it. Quality is conformance to specification. A quality product is one on which all measureable characteristics (material, dimensions, function) are within the specified tolerance limits. This is "quality" as implied in the contract: complete conformance of all characteristics to blueprints and specifications.

Do we propose to improve upon it and if so, what might we do?

Slice the tolerances?

Well, we might cut some or all of the tolerances in half. Would this improve the quality? Not by our definition. Any and all characteristics are "in conformance" whether they measure smack on the nominal dimension, or measure anywhere between the upper and lower tolerance limits. If quality control arbitrarily cut the tolerances, production, purchasing, and general management would raise the roof, and properly so.

It is true that q.c. will occasionally slice a bit off a tolerance, but this is usually done to guard against the possible rejection of borderline measurements by the customer's receiving inspectors. Such action should be explained by the quality manager to his colleagues for what it is—defensive action, not quality improvement. If Engineering should cut the tolerances, then we would have, by definition, a different product and the price should be renegotiated. ►

What we are engaged upon is an effort to attain the quality, to manufacture and deliver a product in conformance with the specified requirements. Indeed, we ship the product when we believe this to be the case.

Just give me what I specified

Of course, we might suspect that the product is not entirely in conformance; in which case it would be proper to speak of "improving" the quality from some level below complete conformance, to conformance. But if the customer thought this was what we meant by "quality improvement" he would quickly sound off, "Don't give me that stuff about quality improvement! Just give me what I specified."

The word "improvement" applies in full force to quality control's efforts to improve manufacturing processes so that they will produce a high yield of conforming parts and reduce the cost of manufacturing. The goals of a quality program might be stated therefore, as:

- Quality attainment
- Process improvement
- Cost reduction

Such a description of the quality program is accurate and defensible; it avoids the daily and frequently acrimonious debates about "quality improvement." The phrase angers production men who demand to know why "they" (the customers) should get more than they contracted for.

There is, of course, the case where an AQL (1.5% or whatever) is specified in the contract. Quality attainment is still the appropriate phrase, supported by process improvement, to attain the specified level of quality at the lowest cost of manufacturing.

This is much more than a semantic problem. It is a question of establishing an environment favorable to the quality assurance task. We are frequently accused, like Oliver Twist, of asking for more! No matter how hard the producers strive, no matter how much quality they feel they have provided, we constantly demand improvement. We rob them of the satisfaction of success, for whatever level they arrive at, the cry is still, "Improve! Improve!" Our colleagues in production, purchasing, sales and general management are immunized by constant repetition; the cry falls on deaf ears.

"Quality Attainment" makes it clear that the goal of the quality program is not more and more and more; only what was specified, no more, and no less. □

An organizational dilemma: Where to place Reliability?

☐ The participants at the West Coast Reliability Symposium held in Los Angeles in February (1977) voted overwhelmingly in favor of making Reliability organizationally independent of Design Engineering and Quality Assurance.

I was scheduled to speak on the "Reliability—Quality Assurance Interface." When I looked closely at the assignment I realized that the word "interface" implied that Reliability and Quality Assurance were two different departments. In that case the problem was to comment on the overall efficiency of such an arrangement and on the probability of harmony (interdepartmental harmony being as difficult to maintain as international harmony at the U.N.)

Interface or intraface

Perhaps the word should have been "intraface" which would establish that Reliability and Quality Assurance were two sections with one chief. How then should they face up to one another for the good of the product? The latter is likely to suffer when members of the technical staffs feel that they are not properly placed: that they have not been accorded appropriate organizational status.

I decided to put it to a vote. I defined reliability as the specific mathematical function of reliability analysis and prediction. The reliability analysts would accumulate failure rate data from all available sources. They would apply state-of-the-art predictive techniques and would indicate to the engineers which parts, components and subassemblies had failure rates especially detrimental to the whole product.

They would not do the reliability engineering. Both the initial design and changes made in response to the findings of the reliability analysts were defined as tasks of the design engineers. ►

They would not monitor the product for reliability characteristics during procurement and fabrication. This was defined as a task for quality assurance who should have the responsibility for monitoring all quality characteristics in the work areas. Incidentally, the production people, managers and workers are beginning to feel oppressively spied upon as technical staffers crowd the work areas monitoring quality, reliability and safety. Then, too, there are the time and motion study specialists, expeditors et al. This is a problem I'll return to another time.

The results of the vote

With this narrow definition of reliability, I invited the participants to vote on their preference by marking E on an unsigned piece of paper if they felt that Reliability should be subordinate to the Chief Engineer; Q if Reliability should answer to the Quality Assurance Manager; and IND for independence. I emphasized that a vote for IND would mean organizational equality with Engineering and Quality Assurance, the Chief of Reliability having equal rank with the Chief Engineer and Quality Assurance Manager and equal direct access to the Chief Executive. The vote was:

Independent	31
Quality Assurance	17
Engineering	14
Undecided	6
	68

It's a particularly interesting score because most of the participants were members of West Coast ASQC sections. It might have been expected that they would favor the inclusion of Reliability with Quality Assurance. As a representative sample of the quality assurance and reliability community, the vote has significance for all of us. □

Operational inertia

☐ Operational inertia drives corporations along courses which may or may not be the routes set by top management. The probability is that the course is more likely wrong than right, due to the nature of operational inertia and the situation which allows it to take the helm.

There is an ever-constant likelihood of catastrophe, or near catastrophe, in the daily life of every industrial organization. Many daily deviations from the planned schedule cannot be anticipated. For example: late delivery of raw material; too many people out with the flu; unanticipated breakdowns of equipment; abnormally high rejection rates.

When such problems explode into being, the operating managers must do something at once. They can spend little or no time on investigation. If there isn't a ready solution, a chain reaction of disaster can begin. Operating managers act time and again in such situations.

Fight the cause, not the symptom

However, when the symptoms are attacked but the cause is left undisturbed, outbreaks multiply and there is more and more fire fighting to be done by vigorous operational managers. The managers are apt to enjoy it even while protesting. Provided one has enough authority, it can be an exhilarating experience to rush from fire to fire; to be able to sit in the office for no more than a few minutes before being snatched back into the fray by a frantic telephone call. One becomes the star trouble-shooter; it's exciting and gratifying. But situations which provide excitement and gratification tend to perpetuate themselves, and operational inertia takes over.

Emergency solutions tend to fall outside of established procedures. As they multiply, established procedures are forgotten and the organization proceeds vigorously in an unknown direction. Since operating men get things done, there is a reluctance to challenge them, to call upon them to pause and give thought, not only to the problem, but also to the cause of the problem. Indeed, they cannot pause because of the possible consequences of delay; they must provide prompt solutions. With characteristic energy, they drive on at an equally fast pace in the wrong direction as if they were on a true course. ▶

Sit back and think

A solution is to give the operating managers time out to think about the problems they act on so vigorously. At one plant, the v.p. of operations told each of his departmental managers to take 30 minutes out each day. "Shut the door of your office. Don't answer the phone. Just sit and think!" he said.

But the phones wouldn't stop ringing. Such vigorous men could not disregard them. The think interval shrunk to 15 minutes. Next, it was forgotten. The idea was good but the methodology was inappropriate.

Managers may be allowed time for contemplation and evaluation by attending one of the scores of excellent seminars staged in various parts of the country. Another method—which I am hesitant to make reference to, but which simply must be mentioned in this context—is the use of a consultant. The consultant, not burdened with operational responsibility, nor prejudiced in favor of the operational status quo by personal associations, can compare procedures established and the course set, perhaps a year ago, with operations as they are now and the new course. There is then material for a dialogue between the general manager and his operating managers, with the consultant's report and probably the consultant acting as a sounding board.

In quality assurance, the tendency to being nudged off course is inherently high because of environmental pressures. Furthermore, quality assurance practice is constantly changing with the changing technology. Possible deviations from the planned program, and possible methodological and technological obsolescence, should be investigated periodically.

Cycle time for review is probably about two years. Longer than that may make it too late for a mid-course correction. □

QC, systems analysis and cost reduction

☐ Does quality control really reduce costs? The claim is frequently made, but it tends to confuse management because the ostensible activities of quality control appear to increase costs, not to reduce them.

Now, while the prime task of quality control is not to reduce costs, but to assure conformance of product to quality standards, it can be demonstrated that quality control must reduce costs in the long run. It does so because the daily activities of quality control constitute, in the aggregate, a technique of systems analysis. Inspectors probe the system in a search for defects. Quality engineers analyze the inspection reports in a search for the deficiencies in the system which caused the defects. The deficiencies in the system are corrected; the proportion of defects is drastically reduced; production rework and scrap costs are substantially reduced as a consequence.

Defects may be . . . the attempt to catch up with unrealistic delivery dates

What are the components of the system and how may they contribute directly or indirectly to the production of defects? The "system" consists of the direct labor force, supervisors, production staff (scheduling, production engineers), procurement, design, sales and management. Defects may be directly or indirectly caused by the line workers, who may need more skill or motivation, or both; or by the supervisors who may have failed to train and motivate them. Defects may be the consequence of an over-optimistic schedule which encourages everyone to cut corners in the attempt to catch up with unrealistic delivery dates. Defects may be a consequence of inadequate instructions issued by production engineering.

Defects may occur in supplies from vendors whose quality matches their low prices. Or in the product itself because of extreme complexity of design. Pressure from sales to lower the selling price may adversely affect

►

quality of design and supplies. Management's influence on quality and the incidence of defects are both direct and indirect. Directly, it may cut budgets in areas vital to product quality; indirectly, it may motivate the corner cutters by a display of impatience with the inspectors instead of with those who make the defects the inspectors discover.

Quality control's sensor is the presence (or absence) of defects. . . .

The concept of quality control as a technique of systems analysis puts the quality manager in a favored position. It identifies him as an integral part of the productive system. Furthermore, he can keep in mind that the validity of a technique of systems analysis is determined by the nature of the probe, or sensor with which the system is tested. Quality control's sensor is the presence (or absence) of defects, a most realistic measure of system capability.   □

Profit and the quality function

☐ "Does quality control contribute to profit?" This question was part of a questionnaire sent out by Hartford Section, ASQC, to 74 firms in the Hartford area. The section asked that the questionnaire be answered by someone other than the quality manager. Slightly more than half of the firms replied. Top executives made the responses with 53% indicating they believed that quality control did make a contribution to profit; 47% thought "not" or were "uncertain." Only 18% felt they could *measure* quality control's profit contribution. These figures are from the June '70 issue of ASQC's "Quality Progress" where the results of the survey are reported in detail.

The question and the answers raise issues which are fundamental to industrial producers and their quality manager. What is the significance of this score to q.c. managers? To the extent that the sample may be considered representative of industry in general, it indicates that about 50% of q.c. managers may be existing under the suspicion or belief, on the part of general management, that they don't contribute to the very thing for which the organization exists! It would be difficult to imagine a worse handicap!

Passing out the pink slips

Now why would general managers reply "no" or "I'm not sure" to this vital question? Why don't they blast off: "You'd better believe it! If I thought quality control wasn't contributing to profit, they'd be outside as soon as I could get the pink slips made out!"

They don't because they have been conditioned to think of some departments as contributing to profit, and of some as detracting from the profit by activities variously labeled "burden," "overhead" or "indirect." Thus, in this context the question is a valid question.

O.K.—since 47% replied "no" or "not certain," if quality control doesn't contribute to profit—who does?

Does the sales department? But the entire sales department is designated "burden," or in plain English, "parasite." Salesmen have to be paid out of receipts; the more they're paid, the less there's left for profit! But salesmen don't see it that way. "If it weren't for us there would be no orders and nothing from which to make a profit anyway," they say.

▶

What about the engineers? They are typically labeled "indirect" and appear in the accounting records as a frightful sum of money that must be deducted from receipts and, therefore, from the potential profit. It is true that, on occasion, engineers find themselves labeled "direct," but this is an accounting device only applicable in certain contractual situations. Engineers are but temporary residents within the sanctified circle of the "direct."

No profit in pushing pencils

What about the accounting department? You must be kidding! Surely accounting is a star example of a non-contributor to profit. Many of them have only the faintest idea what the product is from which profit is supposed to be made. But accountants will tell you, and you better believe them, that until they sort out and arrange receipts and expenses and taxes and arrive at a rational balance, nobody knows whether there is a profit, or how much.

What about the production department? Do they contribute to profit? Don't be ridiculous! They make all of it! Everyone else detracts from it. But even within the production department, who makes the profit. Certainly not the plant superintendent and certainly not his supervisors; they are "overhead;" they eat up the profit. Then who, for God's sake, makes the profit? Who's working at it? Show me a "contributor to profit!" Well, there's one standing at that machine. There's half a dozen more working at that assembly bench. There they are, the profit-makers by accounting definition; those labeled "direct," "productive," the non-parasitical few!

Finally we come to quality control. Parasites by definition! But as everyone knows or should know, highly productive parasites. At the least, they inspect defects out of the product and what mass producer would survive for long if this essential task were not performed? At their best, quality control departments develop, and persuade their companies to adopt, production policies based on statistical analysis of production processes. They assure compatability between process capabilities and engineering tolerances. For the mass producer there is no single greater contributor to profit.

It would seem logical to take the position that since industrial production organizations exist to make a profit, then everyone on the payroll should contribute to that end. There should be no doubt about it.

But doubts will continue to haunt the minds of general managers as long as we are influenced by the invidious comparisons prompted by a discriminatory accounting terminology. The question should be not "Whether?" but "How much?" □

Who are the parasites?

☐ You, if you're a manager and are designated as "overhead."

You, if you're a brilliant designer and are designated as "indirect."

You, if you're a manufacturing engineer and the best efficiency expert since Frederick Winslow Taylor, but are designated "burden."

You, if you're the best statistical analyst that ever came down the pike, but are labeled "non-productive."

Now—those are accounting terms with which we have long been familiar. They look innocent enough but they are loaded with implication. Let's look at them again.

"Non-productive" in relation to what or to whom? In relation to those who produce!

"Indirect" in relation to whom? To those who act directly to "change" the product, that is, to those who produce!

"Overhead" in relation to whom? Over whose head? Over the heads of those who cut metal, and operate presses and solder and assemble!

A "burden" on the backs of whom? On the backs of those who labor in sweat and discomfort while you loll about in the front office, or at a drafting table, or tinker with a sliderule! Parasites! One and all!

What's in a word?

Now it might be said that the words are to be thought of only as neutral classifications—but the cloud of implication cannot be dispersed in this manner. It isn't enough to say, "It's only a word—that's not what I'm thinking when I use it." One cannot think without words; words shape one's thoughts even while one is attempting to express one's thoughts with the words.

But let us say that the words do indeed mean what they appear to mean, and that those designated as non-productive, indirect, overhead, or burden should be identified as parasites and cast forth. In that case, we would make a Pareto analysis to identify those few who cost the most; the most burdensome, and out they would go! ►

But pause a moment. Let's not be hasty. Before we toss them out, let's read the names on those pink slips. My God, there's the chief engineer! And the entire production control staff! And the budget director! And the quality assurance manager—but that's you! Now—that's taking it too far!

There can be little doubt that cost accounting terminology, as presently employed, adds to the already difficult task of determining the appropriate relative numbers of engineers and machinists and supervisors and clerks; appropriate, that is, for your product and its level of technology sophistication. Furthermore, the use of the terminology tends to perpetuate ratios of direct to indirect which are constantly being outdated by increasing automation. Our Victorian great-grandfathers would be stunned if we could get word to them about currently "acceptable" ratios!

It's time to change the negative designations

What nomenclature shall we use? Well, we could designate engineers as engineers and clerks as clerks, etc. If you think you've got too many clerks, address yourself to the problem in that form. Don't ask yourself if the "burden" is too great because, by virtue of the disparagement implicit in that term, you've already answered the question in the affirmative!

It's time the managerial and engineering fraternity got together with the accountants to devise an approach and terminology appropriate to the new and still rapidly changing technological environment. Parasites of Industry, Unite! You have nothing to lose but your demeaning designations. □

Democracy in quality control

☐ What would democracy do to quality control?

According to your grade school teacher and to Webster, democracy is "government by the people; esp. rule of the majority."

That's the key to democratic procedure: rule of the majority. Let us imagine it is sometime in the future. Industrial companies are managed by worker-management committees. We are in the MRB room reviewing a quantity of rejected parts. The debate is getting hot and furious. The production manager is convinced that QC is conspiring against him! The marketing man is distraught; he dare not tell the Great Kallipygos Corporation that he cannot deliver on time!

They plead with the QC manager. But he will not be moved. "In that case," they say, "we are going to refer it to the worker-management committee."

"No!"

"Why not?"

"Because this is a technical problem. The defect in these parts is one that will have a detrimental effect on the long-run reliability. You can't ask the committee to vote on such a question. I mean, what do they know about reliability?"

The production manager objects, "If you think they don't know about it, you tell them. They can form an opinion and vote on it. In any case, they have the last word."

Tell it to the committee!

"Reliability isn't a matter of opinion! If you're not technically qualified, you can't understand it any more than the color blind can see colors."

"Tell it to the committee."

And so they went before the worker-management committee. Since this is all in the future like science-fiction, we cannot know what decision will be arrived at. But it is interesting to speculate on whether a worker-management committee would have more regard for quality than quantity, when and if they came into conflict, than hierarchical management does now. ▶

These thoughts were provoked by the increasing flood of books and articles on democracy in industry. First among the books is David Jenkins' "Job Power." It's a good introduction to the subject because Jenkins records what has been done in Sweden, France, Britain, Yugoslavia, Israel and the U.S.

Jenkins emphasized in the preface that it is not the message of his book that the goal of democracy in industry is increased productivity, although he quotes instances where that has happened.

Jenkins has published another book, "Sweden, the Price of Progress," which has much to say on the same subject. There's also "Democracy and the Workplace" by H.B. Wilson. This is a moderate statement of the problem from the worker's point of view which is that the workers would be both more content and more productive if included in the management structure by participation.

But what about day-to-day decisions?

What I do not find is any appreciation for the details of daily life in a mass production plant and for the sometimes excruciating decision making problems which arise. Management may, for example, wish to relocate a plant in an area where there is cheaper labor. If the workers are represented on a worker-management committee, they are in a position to raise objections and may, or may not prevail.

When these conflicts are concerned with product quality, as they so often are, how are they settled? By an appeal to the Material Review Board. How has quality made out at the hands of the MRB? Remarkably well, considering that its members were always subject to organizational over-ride by top management.

So we come back to the question I put at the beginning: what would democracy in industry do to quality control and product quality? Will it fare better when the question of whether to use non-conforming material is submitted to the majority vote of a worker-management committee than it does now, when the quality can be "saved" by the veto of any one member of the board? We don't know, but we can be certain that the demand for more and more of everything by the world's increasing population will place a premium on quantity. Suspicious eyes will be turned upon anyone attempting to hold back the flood of quantity for anything but the most obvious defects. If quality decisions are submitted to a majority vote, it would seem logical to expect the majority to vote for much needed quantity. □

Nobody's perfect!

☐ "Nobody's perfect," you must have heard it many times. For example, in Chick Walsh's editorial in the March '72 issue of *Quality Management & Engineering,* he reports a conversation with a quality manager who said " . . . 30% of incoming material is out of engineering specifications."

It's likely that when this was reported to the responsible individual, he shrugged it off with, "Oh well—nobody's perfect." To which one might reply, "Granted. But how imperfect can a body be!"

When it is reported that the defect rate in the machine shop is about 9%, some hard-pressed supervisor may mutter, "nobody's perfect."

That beautiful cliche

When defects on a moderately complex assembly are running at an average of, possibly, 14 defects per unit, that beautiful cliche, "nobody's perfect," will pop up to confound the critical inspector.

Even the engineers, caught with conflicting tolerances, may use it. So will the payroll people when the computer makes a mistake on someone's pay check. Although I suppose the right thing to say then would be "nothing's perfect," since the computer isn't a "body"—or is it? But nobody is *required* to be perfect, and nobody is asked to manufacture perfect products.

A product could be described as "perfect" if every characteristic (linear dimension, chemical composition, electrical current—whatever) measured smack on the specified nominal value. But this is not required. However welcome it would be to Engineering and Quality Assurance, neither insists on it. *To be accepted, it is only required that the various characteristics of a product shall measure between the specified tolerance limits.*

Quality is not their primary goal

"Nobody's perfect" has become a cliche which excuses numerous deviations from specified quality standards, while implying that an heroic effort is being made to achieve perfection. Its frequent use is symptomatic

▶

of an attitude which militates against quality. It is not that operating managers are opposed to quality. On the contrary, they are very much for it—but it is not their first priority.

There are three goals that every operating manager must strive for: to produce on schedule; to keep costs down to budget; to achieve specified quality. Every management text states that these 3 goals are of equal importance—but in daily practice (and to paraphrase George Orwell in "Animal Farm") some are more equal than others. Schedule and costs are "more equal!"

Why should the use of this comforting cliche be challenged at this time? Because the advent of "consumerism" has made it more imperative than ever before that industrial products shall conform to advertised quality standards. The daily use of the cliche "nobody's perfect" serves as a veil shielding the reality of potentially dangerous defects from schedule-driven managers. If you're hauled into court on a product liability charge, it will do no good telling the plaintiff's lawyer that "nobody's perfect." □

What can we learn from the Japanese?

☐ What can we learn from the Japanese? Let's look at what the Japanese do and see whether we can do the same in the U.S.

Lifelong employment

There are many who question whether lifelong employment is a reality or just propaganda. It is attested to by J.M. Juran, who has brought us most of what we know about the Japanese industry.

What does lifelong employment do for the Japanese worker and manager? As Juran writes, it gives them "freedom from fear of layoffs."[1] Workers in quality circles participate enthusiastically in cost reduction as well as in quality improvement, knowing that their jobs will not be the cost reduction. Loyal participation is assured.

Promotion based on seniority

This is a matter for constant debate in U.S. management circles. "Rationalists" are all for younger, cheaper, more "dynamic" replacements for the "deadwood" in the organization. Young and cheap is not necessarily "dynamic"; those over 30, or 40, or whatever the dividing line is at the moment, are not necessarily moribund, but these labels, once applied, are hard to remove. The rationalists frequently succeed in placing an unsenior, whose manic style conceals his ignorance, in the position operated successfully for years by a moderately well-paid senior, whose sober style fails to accent his wisdom. The word "deadwood" would have no meaning for the Japanese. It is a patriarchal society in which age, as such, is honored.

"Participation"

I put participation in quotes because it is a controversial subject in the U.S., and in Europe, too. Does it mean participation in management planning or in the execution of the plans made by management? U.S. management, in general, is opposed to participation in planning; this is a "management privilege." But participation at the hardware level is encouraged, as witness the quality circles organized by some U.S.

▶

corporations. There is a problem here which is a manifestation of Western culture. There is some hesitation on the part of the unions to condone participation. They wish to maintain the "adversary" attitude which is traditional in the relationship between labor and management. The mechanics and assemblers are imbued with this attitude, too. They tend to suspect that they are being "conned" when management talks about "participation" in quality and productivity improvement programs, less so in the case of quality. But we should keep in mind that successful quality improvement programs also reduce costs in the long run ... and sometimes in the short run.

Nevertheless, the reluctance on both sides to participate is to be deplored. As Dr. Juran says, "... the collective worker education, experience and creativity is the major *under-employed* asset in the economy of the U.S."[1 & 2] But, again from Juran, "As a mechanism, the QC circles are merely the visible evidence of invisible prerequisites— mutual respect, industrial democracy, spirit of participation, etc."

Vertical monopoly

As Dr. Juran tells us, manufacturing, marketing and field service in Japan are one. If marketing and field service are not directly a part of the manufacturing organization, they are essentially controlled by the original producer.

So what can we learn from the Japanese? Well ... if we are prepared to engage in lifelong employment with one company, and to adhere to a policy of promotion based on seniority, and if we can learn how to participate without adversarial undertones, and if we are ready to welcome the vertical monopoly, we can learn a lot. But to do this, we would require a new cultural outlook and we would have to change the law of the land on monopolies. Until then, if "then" is even in the future, we can hone the techniques we already employ and strive for more cooperation. It is ironic that the mass production and statistical quality control techniques which the Japanese utilize so effectively were developed largely in the U.S. It appears that certain "mechanistic" techniques may be transferred from one culture to another with, as in the case of Japan, an amplification of performance. It's something to keep in mind when we consider the potential competitors rising up around the world. □

---

1. Juran, "Japanese and Western Quality—a Contrast," *Quality Progress,* December 1978.
2. Juran, ditto, *Quality,* January 1979.

East is east, and west is west:
More on Japan

☐ What makes Japan such a formidable competitor? What do they do that we might profitably emulate? Let us consider further aspects of the industrial scene in Japan.

Following are the words of Hiroshi Takeuchi, general manager of the Economic Research Division of the Longterm Credit Bank of Japan: "The abilities required of a senior manager are not mental; they are an intuitive sense of assessment and a charismatic power of command. Both can be acquired only through experience." He is writing in *Japan Echo* of Tokyo; the excerpt I quote from appeared in the May '79 issue of *Atlas World Press Review.*

This attitude contrasts with our belief in the U.S. that management can be taught in the classroom. Here it is believed that what the mind can certainly learn about administrative procedure can be converted by the heart—the guts—into instant executive action in the confused and controversial atmosphere of the workplace.

"Wage differentials in Japan are smaller than in other countries," Takeuchi continues. "The average Japanese company president earns four to six times the wage of an unskilled worker of the same age, and only 50 percent more than the wage of such skilled workers as welders and steeplejacks. In contrast, American and European company presidents earn more than ten times the wage of the average worker of the same age." It is unlikely that management will press for the reduction of wage and salary differentials, although the unions are working at it.

Teamwork is everything

"At Japanese companies an egalitarian attitude about ability prevails," write Hiroshi Takeuchi. He cites a hypothetical case: "If Taro Sato, who works in a company research laboratory, achieves a revolutionary breakthrough in technology, the workers will give him credit, but they will not value his abilities above those of fellow workers. They regard his feat as the result of a team effort."

By contrast, we operate a star system which gives exclusive recognition to the individual. This is not surprising; we are a part of—and have been conditioned by—a socio-political system based upon the concept of the uniqueness of the individual. ▶

A consequence of the star system is that stars are coveted by other companies. They are lured away by competitors, leaving behind unfinished research programs, unfinished designs, unfinished plans for the manufacture of a new product.

As an example, a company of which I was once the quality manager lost its chief engineer in the final stages of an innovative design; it was this innovation which had secured for us a valuable contract. Most of the profit was eaten up in the effort to get the bugs out of the new design in the absence of the chief designer.

Cover yourself with a part-life contract

There's no strong sentiment in favor of lifelong employment with one company in the U.S., either on the part of management or the unions. But we could do something to keep managers and engineers around long enough to finish the projects they are working on. We could hold them for the length of the project with a *part-life* contract.

Unfortunately there is a snag; I can best illustrate it with a true story about an engineering manager. The manager was doing quite well with one company when another company came fishing for him. You know how it goes . . . the VP invites you out to lunch and after the second martini he puts the question, "Are you happy where you are at?" Soon you're off and running.

Negotiations were going along nicely (a substantial increase in salary, stock options, fringe benefits, etc.) until the manager said that he had one last request.

"What's that?"

"I would like a contract."

"A contract!" The VP was horrified. "I don't have a contract myself. What d'you think would motivate you if you had a contract?"

What was he to do? No contract was offered; but then, there was no contract where he was at. He took the job leaving behind a fair amount of unfinished business.

If we can overcome the cultural conviction that security—even a bit of security—discourages hard work, we can effect a massive and most profitable reduction in the amount of unfinished business. We cannot go all the way with the Orient, but we could take a small step.   □

Kissinger, Crosby and quality control

☐ One of Henry Kissinger's favorite expressions while he was Secretary of State was "conceptual flaw." The term speaks for itself. This reminded me of a reply given by Phil Crosby of ITT to a question from the floor at a management seminar. To the question "Why doesn't management show more interest in quality control techniques," Phil replied, "Management knows concepts, not techniques."

Now, if we combine the thinking of Kissinger and Crosby, we arrive at a useful guide for behaviour in the presence of top management—don't blind them with techniques. Communicate conceptually and make sure there's no flaw in your concept.

The why, not the how

What is conceptual thinking? It is to think about the *why* as distinct from the *how*.

What fundamental belief about the nature of modern mass production is essential to a conceptual grasp of professional quality control? It is that the system as a whole produces the articles the corporation is in business to manufacture, market and make a profit from. Although the articles ultimately arrive as single items in the hands of individual consumers, the system of production does not "see" the articles as single items. It sees them en masse; it sees them in vast quantities.

As a consequence, the central point of interest is the *yield* of acceptable articles as a percentage of total production. It is not the quality of any particular article; it must be known that the manufacturing processes are capable of producing articles which meet the absolute quality requirements. By "absolute" I do not mean that every quality characteristic is within the drawing tolerance limits. The question is: What proportion of the total will be "quality" articles when the system is operating under mass production conditions? ►

The percent yield of acceptable articles

The basic concept in quality control as applied to mass production is that the essential "product" on which the fortunes of the company depend is the percent yield of acceptable articles. This might prompt the alert executive to ask "Why should there be any question? Why isn't the yield 100 percent?" The quality manager must then be prepared to launch into a dissertation on the inherent, ineradicable tendency of all repetitive production operations to vary, and the danger that the variation on one or more operations may exceed the drawing tolerance limits.

The chief executive, being in a humorous mood, may ask, "Why don't you have the engineers open up the limits?" To which you might reply, "Oh, we do. But they tell us the limits are already stretched to the maximum extent."

"Since the engineers won't relent, what do you do?" And then you tell him in as few words as possible. When you consider the millions of words written on the subject, it's difficult to find the appropriate few! You might hand him a copy of Shewhart, or Juran, or "Modern Quality Control" by Glen Hayes and Harry Romig, but that won't do either, because he pays you to know, and to know it well!

Keep the concept in mind

Keep the concept in mind: that the system as a whole produces the product, and that the "product" is the percent yield. Tell him that what quality control does is to measure the variability on each process, and to advise production in the hope that production will match jobs to processes in such a manner that the tolerance limits exceed the process variation. This isn't always possible, but whether it is or isn't, the yield can be estimated and marketing plans can be made.

Try to avoid statistics, but in case he asks, be prepared. You may get him interested in control charts, in which case he might walk into the production area with you and the control charts can do the talking for you. A control chart, zig-zagging nicely around the center line will tell him more about variability than a thousand words. But for heaven's sake, make sure the charts are up to date! ☐

A mathematical model for people

☐ There are psychologists who assert that it should be possible to condition the individual to the point where his or her behavior would be completely predictable. Prediction requires a mathematical model or the gift of prophesy. Since the gift of prophesy does not seem to be widely distributed, we must look for a mathematical model.

It occurred to me that we might try the exponential model which has been fairly successful in predicting the behavior of hardware. Let's try it on a simple assembly of ten components, all of which are in series so that the system reliability, or probability of success, is the product of the individual reliabilities. Let the reliabilities of 8 components be 0.9 and let the reliabilities of the 9th and 10th components be 0.99 and 0.8. The overall reliability equals 0.9^8 x 0.99 x 0.8, which equals 0.34. Observe that the overall reliability is not only worse than the best component (which seems reasonable), but is worse than the worst!!

Fitting a model to a manager

Now let us see if this model will fit an organized group of managers; will it enable us to make a prediction as to the group's probability of success? It's difficult to measure with any exactitude the abilities of individuals and to identify the least able. But let us assume it can be done. Whatever the figures might be and whoever the least able might be (not you or me, but somebody), the exponential model would predict that the probability of success for the group as a whole must be less than the probability that the least able will succeed at his appointed task!

But who would believe it? No one that I've spoken to. It would sound good at a company dinner to have the leader declaim after the third bourbon and branch water: "As a group we are no better than the weakest link in the chain. So let us all strive to be the strongest link!!" Such rhetoric! ►

But if this were true, if group activity fit the exponential model, we would still be in the tree tops, waiting for the least able to learn how to get down.

Let's try again

We have to look for another model; one not dependent so much upon the relative ability of each, as upon the degree to which each individual acts in support of the others, and in the right direction. The problem is not that everyone shall be a Faraday or Edison but that the efforts of the competent individuals who comprise most management groups shall be coordinated and kept moving in the right direction. For a company as a whole the coordinator is and must be the chief executive. Each manager must coordinate the work of his departmental subordinates.

A few years ago there was a tendency to equate "coordinator" with "messenger"; to put down the idea of coordination. Many companies suffered while competent, conscientious managers raced forward on their uncoordinated paths, sometimes 180 degrees out of phase with their fellow managers.

The only model that seems to fit organized group behaviour is one based on the premise that individuals, however competent and conscientious, are motivated to action by a highly subjective perception of what is expected of them, and an equally subjective evaluation of group success. As a consequence their interpretations of the company program may differ considerably; what looks like success to one may look like near disaster to another; and if their efforts aren't coordinated, disaster it will be! Subjectivism is the problem, and coordination is the solution.   □

The intelligent woman's guide to quality control

☐ Dear Virginia: I thought you'd like to know what it is your husband does all day. This "something" that you find so hard to explain to Veronica, and Eva, and Hilda. Like that time you told Veronica he was in quality control and she said,

"Yes, I know. You told us. But what does he *do*?" And Hilda chimed in,

"Yes, tell us Virginia. We know what salesmen do, and what engineers do, and what accountants do, but what do the people in quality control *do*?"

"Well," you replied. "They control the quality."

"Ha!" said Hilda, "Light in our darkness!" Then Eva saved you saying,

"Oh well, whatever he does, he's doing all right. Look at the new Mustang that Virginia's driving. Why don't we all pile in and drive over to the Avantgard to see the latest Fellini." Which you all did.

Now the first thing you have to do, Virginia, is to dig the terminoloьy. When we say we control the quality we mean that we exert a directing and correcting influence on all activities which may affect the quality of the product. You might ask, "Like what?" to which we would reply,

"Like persuading salesmen to make sure they've read the customer's inspection requirements before they grab the contract and sign on the dotted line. Like persuading the designers to allow broad tolerances; at least, as broad as the intended function of the product will allow."

"Why do that?"

"To make it easier for production."

"Why should they make it easier for production?"

"To keep the manufacturing costs down."

"I see. What else?"

"Like persuading purchasing to buy from qualified suppliers. Like persuading production to assign jobs to machines that are capable of making 100% good parts, or nearly."

"Don't production people do that without being told?"

"Well . . . yes and no. Yes, because that's their intention. No, because we have this thing called statistical quality control that really tells you what the machine capability is, and they don't make too much use of it."

"What is it exactly?" ►

"Well . . . there's the peculiar phenomenon called variability. Like you and Hilda, and Eva, and Veronica are all similar but not identical. Yet you were all produced by the same process."

"Please!"

"Sorry, but it was just an illustration. Hasn't it ever struck you as remarkable that there should be so many people, yet no two are ever exactly alike?"

"Yes, I suppose so. But what's this got to do with machines?"

"Machines making parts don't make them identical either. There's this tendency to variation. What we do in statistical quality control is to measure this tendency and 'control' it."

"And also, Virginia, there's the schedule and other legitimate pressures; there has to be somebody whose prime concern is the quality of the product. Which isn't to say that everybody else isn't concerned about the quality. But you know how it is."

"All right, you've told me about persuading, and variability, and statistics. But what do you *do*?"

"Oh, I see what you mean. What *physical* thing do we do? Well, we have these inspectors who measure parts and if they're not right they reject them."

"What d'you mean? Not right. How could they be 'not right' after all the advice you give them?"

"It's a pretty complicated situation, Virginia. We're in the midst of a technological revolution, in case you hadn't noticed it. The engineers may agree to allow maximum permissible tolerances; but even so, they may be so narrow on these new space products that they are still less than the natural spread of the best machine tools. Which means there's bound to be some parts outside the tolerance."

"But if they're the best machines available, the production people can't help it, can they?"

"No, but they can aim at the best use of the machines and this is where we can help them."

"Can you give me a short phrase summing it all up?"

"I suppose you could say that quality control, or quality assurance to use the current term, is the management of inspection, the use of statistical controls wherever applicable, and the development of an informed company-wide attitude favorable to quality."

"Couldn't I just say that quality control rejects the defective products made by Hilda's husband from non-conforming material bought by Eva's husband, in an attempt to meet the too-stringent requirements of the design made by Veronica's husband?"

"Virginia! Please!" □

Jack of all trades

☐ Is it true that "no one field seems to qualify someone to be a QC professional?" This is the conclusion arrived at by Catherine Gaubatz in an article in the September '79 issue of the American Society for Quality Control's *Quality Progress.*

Ms. Gaubatz, senior supervisor, Product Test Laboratory, Information Terminals, Sunnyvale, CA, and a student at De Anza College, Cupertino, has selected for a class paper the subject "Quality Control as a Career." She interviewed individuals of various rank and function at ten companies, from which sampling she arrived at the conclusion that "no one field seems to qualify someone to be a QC professional." In effect, the QC practitioner is seen by others—at least by some others—as a jack of all trades.

It is not true, but Ms. Gaubatz is not alone in her impression. In June, I was in San Francisco, at the invitation of a national association, to speak at a seminar on quality control management. I had asked the association what theme I should attack. "Give them an identity," I was told, "Outline the specific duties of the QC professional."

Identifying the QC professional

Identity and specific duties are what we need. It is the performance of specific duties—and the public recognition that these are the province of a particular group of qualified individuals—that confers identity and professional status.

Everybody knows what doctors, lawyers and engineers do, but who knows what the quality control professional does? I made an attempt to answer this question in the March '79 column of *Quality* magazine "Victims and victors of variability" (see page 339). There I referred to the knowledge of variability and of statistical techniques for its measurement and control as the *professional-specific* activity in quality control. ▶

No plans for the mass production of any product, or for the provision of health care, transportation or other public service should be completed without input as to the probable effects of variability—that is, input from the variability specialist, the QC professional.

But it's not that easy

Unfortunately, there is an obstacle to the widespread demand for specialists in variability. The public, including potential employers and industrial colleagues, are not aware of variability—despite its ceaseless impact on their daily lives. Every individual is made by the same process, but no two are identical! (Incidentally, there are hot debates about the complete identity of identical twins; but, we need not go into that). It is sufficient that we live in a sea of variability. But few arrive at a recognition of variability as a determinant of the quality and quantity of daily life. Fewer still make the transition from biologic variability to its baleful presence in mass production.

Angered by defective products, it is unlikely that a consumer will exclaim, "Why weren't these variations anticipated and corrected? Who is looking after the variability?" Not only would the enraged consumer not respond in this manner, neither would management.

Management could be expected to accuse quality control of malperformance in one or several of the tasks enumerated by Ms. Gaubatz; but, there is a low probability that the failure would be seen as a manifestation of uncontrolled variability and attacked accordingly.

The establishment of the identity and *professional-specific* duties of quality control is a task which demands early attention; we cannot survive as Jacks and Jills of all trades. Meanwhile, you will be glad to know that Ms. Gaubatz is not discouraged and has decided on a career in quality control.   □

The hunter and the Bengal tiger

☐ Once upon a time there was a hunter who felt his life would not be complete until he had shot a Bengal tiger. So he bought a beautiful high-powered rifle and went to India and organized a safari. He wore a pith helmet, and adopted an English accent to impress the beaters, and pushed off into the jungle.

They journeyed for days through the torrid heat.

Suddenly they were rewarded. There was a Bengal tiger staring straight at them! The hunter threw up his beautiful rifle, aimed and fired . . . but nothing!!! No sound! No explosion! No dead tiger!

What in heaven's name? Ah, of course, the safety catch. But the safety catch wouldn't come off! It was defective! The beautiful rifle couldn't be fired!

The Bengal tiger stuck around to see what would happen, but the hunter looked so mad as he tried to wrestle the safety catch off that the tiger got scared and dashed off into the jungle.

In times gone by that would have been the end of the affair. The hunter might have thrashed a couple of the beaters to vent his rage; the manufacturers would have probably replaced the defective safety catch; and the hunter would have swallowed his disappointment.

But not this time

But not now. On this occasion the hunter sued the producer of the rifle. What transpired is reported by Danny R. Jones, Esq., attorney-at-law in Los Angeles, in an article, "The Serviceman's Right to Sue," which appeared in the April-May 1970 issue of the magazine, "Trial." He writes: "The Appellate Court of California upheld his right to seek recovery for the cost of safari and traveling expenses, which amounted to $6,000, plus $10,000 for loss of honor, prestige and victory involved in killing a Bengal tiger." So you see, it wasn't the tiger who got shot by the defective rifle, but the manufacturer! ▶

This ruling was made in 1967 which, at the time of writing (mid '73), is six years ago. But only a few years prior to that, say in the mid fifties, it is most likely that even had the hunter sued, the cost of safari and traveling and "the loss of honor, prestige and victory" would have been dismissed as contingencies. The manufacturer would have disclaimed responsibility, and it is most likely that his disclaimer would have been upheld.

From our present vantage point, it seems incredible that we once accepted the position that, while the producer was responsible for repair or replacement of a defective part, he was not responsible for contingent effects resulting from the defect. But when you come to think of it, what might be called beneficial or positive contingencies are what we buy various products for.

All of life is contingencies

Consider the problem of getting to an appointment on time. Being blasted out of bed at 6:30 A.M. is contingent upon the alarm clock going off. Shaving to achieve that suave, sophisticated look is contingent upon an electric razor performing as advertised. A satisfactory breakfast, to put you into a good state of mind for the interview, is contingent upon mixer and toaster mixing and toasting without failure.

Now you're out of the house, shaved and satiated; now you have to get the car out of the garage, which will be contingent on the engine starting, which is contingent on reliable performance from ignition key, solenoid switch, starting motor, carburetor, igniter (timer) and plugs . . . any more? . . . anyway you get the idea. Assuming that you make it out of the garage, your arrival at the ultimate destination is contingent only upon your car being able to maintain 14 MPH, the average speed on a busy LA freeway!

The moral of the story is to make sure that your company does not get shot down by its own product . . . that it is not impoverished by having to provide compensation for contingent losses caused by a defective product. When you and your management are debating quality and cost, make sure you weigh the present cost advantage against the staggering cost of compensating for contingencies caused by possible future failures. □

Crisis in quality

□ Is there a crisis in quality? Well, there's a crisis *about* quality, which is not quite the same thing. Actually, the quality of common consumer hardware is better than it was years ago.

Dr. Juran makes this statement in his comprehensive review of "Consumerism and Product Quality" in the July '70 issue of ASQC's *Quality Progress*. Furthermore, says Juran, "failure rates have decreased (on automobiles for example), but there are more failures because of the 'product's population explosion.' The situation is that there's much more of less."

Nevertheless, the threat to industrial producers and their technical assistants is not the less severe because the popular view of the situation may be a bit distorted.

"Quality is being attacked on two counts:
- Bitter complaints against shabby, shoddy, glutinously slow after-sales service.
- The rising tide of claims for injuries caused by defective products or, if you like, by alleged defective products."

Time magazine's feature article, "America the Inefficient" (March 23, 1970) was largely a blast at atrocious after-sales service. Betty Furness is quoted as advising housewives who want to keep kitchen appliances in good order to . . . "have a repairman living with you!"

Elizabeth Hanford, former executive director of the President's Committee on Consumer Interests, speaking at ASQC's Annual Technical Conference, quoted from the *Wall Street Journal* the case of a Mr. Comstock who tried for 6 weeks to get a replacement thermostat for an electric oven. In the end, Mr. Comstock had to pull rank to command attention. What kind of rank? He's director of public affairs for the Association of Home Appliance Manufacturers!

It's not this prong of the attack that I want to consider, although it's here that the greatest good could be done the quickest. In the case of product failures that aggravate and inconvenience but don't injure, much would be forgiven by consumers if they got prompt, courteous service.

Prompt, courteous service! It sounds ridiculous doesn't it? It's as though "prompt" and "courteous" were antithetical to the idea of

▶

"service;" as though it were an impropriety to unite them! Anyway, it's a measure of how bad the situation is that so many speak bitterly and/or contemptuously of after-sales service. There can be little doubt that we, the professional quality people, will become involved in the service scene, but that's another problem for another time.

Should you be blamed for a defective product?

For the present, I want to make some comments on "quality" as it appears in product liability injury claims. In many cases the claimant can produce a part which is shown to be defective and to be the cause of the injury; in general, the doctrine of strict liability has applied, and the plaintiff is awarded the judgment.

Now, the question I want to raise is: does the plaintiff have the right to the judgment even if the part is defective as claimed? It's a shocking question, but what I have in mind is a number of factors which bear on the situation and must be given serious thought by industrial producers and their quality advisors:

(1) The defective part is (presumably) mass produced.
(2) The fact that it and (undoubtedly) all other parts in the end product were mass produced had a decisive effect on the price. Indeed, were it not for mass production, the product would not have been on the market at a popular price. An electric washer, for example, made from hand-crafted parts is inconceivable; at least, at a price that anyone would be prepared to pay except a Rockefeller.
(3) The fact that it (and all other parts) were mass produced in large quantities dictated that inspection would be by sampling.
(4) Inspection by sampling is based on a readiness to tolerate some defectives, the probable proportion of defectives being roughly expressed by the AQL.

Thus, assuming that the plaintiff had been injured by a mass produced article bought at a popular price (largely a function of production and inspection methodology), it was an implicit probability that someone might buy a defective product and might, indeed, be injured by it.

But the mass of anonymous consumers who buy mass produced products don't know it! All that the consumers hear about the product is what they're told by Madison Avenue. And what Madison Avenue tells them is that the product is the next best thing to salvation. No—not that, because that admits there's something better than the product. The product must be presented as the supreme example of excellence, Man's ultimate accomplishment! Would anyone on Madison Avenue dare mention the probability of failure? He would be tossed from his 22nd story window! ▶

It is one of Dr. Juran's recommendations that advertising material be reviewed before release, as we now review design. But it isn't only the consumers who don't know about the probability of failure. Many industrial executives don't know either. To this extent they are severely handicapped. They don't know how to respond to the growing flood of complaints. Not having a "position," they tend to be defensive. As many reports indicate, they've made a poor public showing.

Industrial executives have to be informed about the facts of life in mass production. And their quality assurance managers have to see that they know. What executives have to know is the 4 points I made before. They may be summarized as: "Popular consumer items can be sold at popular prices because they are made by mass production and inspected by sampling, but some probability of failure is an inherent feature of the system."

We are all familiar with the usual claims that 100% inspection is only 80% efficient or whatever. It seems to me that we entrap ourselves when we make such statements without qualification. For if we, the quality assurance experts, say that 100% inspection cannot be relied upon, what are we going to do when a characteristic is classified "critical" and zero defectives of 100% inspection is specified?

It's important to get this 100% inspection thing right. If someone is willing to pay for it, we can do it. We could, for example, deduct from each end of the tolerance on each specified characteristic (mechanical, electrical, or chemical) a generous allowance for instrument variability.

And what about inspector fatigue?

This would cut deeply into the tolerance. Consequently, it would be murder on production since many probably good parts would be thrown out. As for inspector fatigue (the usual explanation for the "unreliability" of 100% inspection), don't fatigue the inspectors; change them frequently. Automated inspection devices don't get fatigued but an allowance would have to be taken out of the tolerance for the variability of the measuring device.

We could do more. We could assure that no part would be made on a production process unless the tolerance on the dimension were substantially in excess of the natural spread of the process. *Instead, the situation is more frequently the other way 'round as industry strives to get the most out of the machines.*

Our position should be that 100% inspection is possible and reliable, but at frightful expense. Then we can take the position "We know you're not willing to pay that kind of money, so what percentage of defects are you willing to tolerate?" ►

Quality managers should be ready to give their top executives a dissertation on sampling and AQL's, on screening and replacement and on the estimate of the average outgoing quality (AOQ).

That's the question general managers *should* be asking their quality managers: "What's the AOQ on this or that (mass-produced) item?" The AOQ is essential to the development of an after-sales service program and to the funding of it. It's the prime statistic that every mass production organization should know about its product. All company spokesmen should know about it.

I admit it's not easy to get executives to sit still long enough to really "dig" the company's statistical program and the resulting AOQ. It cannot be explained in 3 minutes at the coffee machine. But executives must listen, or they're going to run into more trouble. They may be stuck with government quality evaluators for commercial products; they may need his stamp before anything can be shipped!

Now, we can make sure that industrial executives know the probable failure rates on products they ship to the market, but who's going to tell the consumers? Who's going to tell them, for example, that there's a 1% probability of failure on a particular product as an inherent concomitant of the mass production and inspection methodology which made the popular price possible?

Run it up the flagpole

Can you imagine Madison Avenue doing it? I can already hear the jingle:

There may be one failure in a hundred.

But it won't be you!

No, it won't be you!

I suppose that what will happen will be that industrial producers will get wise and will overhaul their service programs to assure prompt repair to replacement and courteous treatment. As a consequence, the unfortunates, randomly chosen by fate to suffer from the statistically probable failures, will tend to forget the failures and remember only the prompt and courteous service.

But a lot of blood is likely to flow before that happy time. In the meantime, quality managers, make sure that the sampling plans you selected are being used exactly as you planned them (they aren't always, you know), know your AOQ and make sure your general manager knows it. You will then be better prepared for the claims if and when you're hit with them. Whether you can make it stick in court that an advertised probability of failure is not an offense when and if it occurs, remains to be seen. But, of course, if you didn't advertise it, it's hard to make a case. □

What happened to the quality?

☐ What happened to product quality?

Why do you ask?

Well, look at all those product liability cases. All those claims for compensation for injuries caused by defective products. The number of claims increases every year.

I suppose you feel that the increase in the number of claims is evidence of a decline in product quality?

Isn't it logical?

On the face of it . . . yes. But let's look at the numbers. About a million claims were filed in 1973. In 1965, the number of claims filed was 100,000. Would you say that 1974's quality is 10 times worse than in 1965?

Well . . . no. Not when you put it like that.

It's questionable whether product quality is worse at all. The sheer momentum of ongoing quality control and industrial engineering activities ought to assure that manufacturing processes and the products they produce will improve, perhaps stabilize at a particular level, but not decline.

If quality didn't suddenly take a nose dive, what happened? Many social events, but four in particular:

Four special social situations

1. The legal case of Henningsen versus the Bloomfield Motor Co. and Chrysler. Mrs. Henningsen was driving a new car when it suddenly veered off the highway, plowed into a bank and seriously injured Mrs. H. A suit was filed, charging that the steering mechanism was defective.

The defense counsel contended that the steering system was damaged sufficiently so that it could not be determined if it was defective at the time of sale. Furthermore, said the defense, the car was sold to Mr. H, not to Mrs. H. There is no link, no privity between us and Mrs. H. Not that we are not deeply sorry for what happened to Mrs. H., but the law is the law.

The lower court dismissed the claim. Nevertheless, the Henningsen lawyers appealed and appealed until the case reached the Supreme Court of New Jersey in 1960. The Supreme Court decided for the plaintiff, citing (in this famous landmark case) the legal principle of strict liability. While it could not be proven that the steering was defective, the court ruled that

▶

the behavior of the automobile left little doubt that the steering must have been defective. It was inconceivable that Mrs. H. deliberately drove the car into the bank.

Furthermore, said the court, the defense of privity must be reconsidered. The producer's responsibility for making a safe product does not stop with the purchaser but applies to his wife, children, friends and subsequent owners. So out went privity.

2. In a similar case which reached the California Supreme Court in 1962, Greenman versus Yorba Tool, the court ruled in favor of the plaintiff.

Out went privity in California, as in New Jersey, and out went the defense plea of "no negligence." By the same token, out went the necessity for the plaintiff to allege and prove negligence in manufacture.

3. The third event was the Ralph Nader incident in 1965. You all know what a great deal of publicity the case attracted. The consumers now had a champion. Soon they had others. The President (Lyndon B. Johnson) took note of the situation and appointed special assistants for Consumer Affairs. In time, Richard Nixon followed, and in October, 1972 the law which authorized the present Consumer Product Safety Commission was signed.

4. The fourth event is the growth of a corps of trial lawyers who make a living handling product liability cases on a contingency fee basis.

Watch your step!

For the first time, the quality of mass-produced consumer goods is under penetrating social scrutiny. The scrutineers are the consumers, consumer advocates, lawyers and the courts. It's a powerful combination. It remains to be seen how far it will go. In the meantime, the producers have to cope with the situation. And we in quality control must assist to the best of our ability.

How? Now, as always, we must apply those statistical quality control techniques that help eliminate defects and correct processes which produce defects. Now, as never before in commercial production, we must urge that design review for safety and quality control actions be strictly formalized, and that formal records be filed in such a manner as to permit quick retrieval.

We cannot persuade our colleagues in management to cooperate in a comprehensive program until the program has been "sold" to top management. In the prevailing consumer-oriented social atmosphere, this should be easier than in the past. It will still require considerable diplomatic skill and powers of persuasion on the part of the quality control manager. But go to it. There never was a better time. □

Zero probability of failure

☐ A number of judgments have been made favoring plaintiffs in product liability cases, and substantial compensatory awards have been made, in cases where the elapsed time appears to be excessive between the manufacture of an article and an occurrence eventuating in injury to a consumer. By "excessive" I mean in relation to the stated warranty — and I don't mean a couple of days or weeks over the warranty, but years.

This raises the question of the inherent limit on product capability. By capability I mean designed performance, reliability and safety.

To further define capability: performance is the ability of a product to function as specified or advertised; reliability is the probability that it will perform on demand and that it will continue to perform without failure for a specified period of time; safety is the probability that it will perform for the specified period without injuring the consumer.

Two kinds of safety

In the matter of safety, I think we must distinguish between objective safety and subjective safety. By objective safety, I mean those guards against injury designed into the product. For example, guards on presses and actuating devices which require the use of both hands so that the operator cannot possibly get his hand in the press; or arrangements of the circuitry of electronic devices that prevent the user from removing or opening a door to make an internal adjustment. By subjective safety, I mean those hazards created by the consumer's misuse or neglect of operating instructions. Therefore, safety as a component of product capability should read "objective safety."

Product capability must surely be a function of price — but a product cannot be manufactured with zero probability of failure — not at any price!

It is here that a problem arises for producers and consumers alike. The legal principle of strict liability in tort implies, or appears to imply, that the

▶

liability of the producer is not limited in time. There are judgments, which appear to have been inspired by such an interpretation of strict liability, that I referred to in the first paragraph.

There is no zero probability of failure

We must all bear in mind that no journey of Apollo was entirely free of mishaps. There was one occasion when it had to be decided not to land the astronauts on the Moon—there was some question whether we could get them back to Earth, but the ingenuity of the astronauts and brilliant instructions from Houston succeeded in bringing them back safely.

The point is that if zero probability of failure cannot be assured for Apollo, despite the vast sums of money expended, it surely cannot be expected of mass-produced articles at competitive prices.

There is a fundamental principle at issue in these transactions between producers and consumers: the liability should not exceed the capability. But for this principle to prevail, the capability of consumer products, in regard to performance, reliability, safety and elapsed time, will have to be quantified . . . and consumers will have to be made aware of how much capability they can expect for whatever price they're willing to pay. Which brings us to consumer advertising, and that's something else! ☐

Advertisements and product liability

☐ The other night I was watching a 2-hour "special" on TV. Contrary to my usual habit, I compelled myself to look and listen through the commercials. Have you ever done it? It's quite an experience!

I was overwhelmed by a flood of articles of such excellence, and so seductively presented that I would have dashed out and bought all of them . . . had I believed them! There were automobiles that started up with such promptitude . . . that were so responsive to the steering over the most harrowing surfaces and 'round the sharpest corners . . . that were so spacious and palatial inside . . . that even without the mini-skirted blonde, each was still an irresistible bargain!

There were shaving creams that promised, not merely to soften up a bit of hairy stubble, but to elevate the user to near orgasmic heights of euphoria. There were refrigerators with ice cube trays that never stick. There were perfumes, sprays and cosmetics which promised to make a woman so ravishing as to distract her man from following the Watergate incident! But we don't believe them . . . and there's the rub! We have the right to believe them because they are presented in an effort to persuade us to buy.

Imaginative puffery

Plaintiffs' attorneys take full advantage of the right to believe. The consumer's right to believe the advertisement has been a severe handicap in many product liability cases. The court will not accept a plea from the defendant that "We were only kidding . . . that was just a bit of imaginative puffery . . . everybody knows ads exaggerate."

This raises the interesting question as to what ads would be like if they were strictly factual. For example, "Don't expect too much from this extremely competitively priced article. You're a sensible person. You know you aren't going to get more than you're willing to pay for." Would sales really drop off if such ads appeared? ▶

What happened? How did ads progress to their present state? I mean, they are quite an art! Was it the consumers who refused to buy until they were flooded with hyperbole? Or is it that the imaginative efforts of Madison Avenue have so accustomed us to fantasy that we prefer fantasy to reality? Is it that we demand to luxuriate in the fantasy of the ad as a necessary preliminary to enduring the reality of the product itself? It certainly appeared so thru the Fifties and into the Sixties.

Puncturing the facade

However, about the middle of the Sixties, the advertised fantasy was punctured in one product liability case after another. And not by indignant social reformers, but by attorneys who turned a cold, legal eye on the fantastic ads and asserted that the product should do all that the ad promised, or that compensation should be provided in lieu thereof.

Is Madison Avenue going to come down out of the clouds? There's no sign of it. Will the producers demand realistic advertising . . . after all, they pay for it? That depends upon how they are approached. It seems to me that the quality manager should enlist the aid of design and production in a movement to make the product like the ad, or the ad like the product! You remember all those times we pleaded with our colleagues "to make the product like the print . . . or the print like the product." Well, it's the same thing, except that in 1973, we were confronted by the threat of more than 1,000,000 product liability claims before the year was out. Once the strategy is agreed upon, I think the more effective tactic would be to propose making the product like the advertisement. This would require that the ads be taken apart meticulously to find out exactly what they promise and what they imply. It would almost certainly be a shattering and most salutary experience for management.

And finally: Have you any idea what it will cost to make it like the ad? That's the clincher! Once you begin to put those figures together, you will know where you're at! ☐

Professional or practitioner?

☐ Should employees be referred to as professionals or practitioners? An employee should give it some thought before he claims, as so many of us do, that he's a professional.

If an employee finds himself called as a witness in a product liability case, it's likely to be a matter of some importance whether he's identified as a professional or a practitioner.

Why?

Because the title "professional" implies that the individual is *independent,* not under direction, free to do whatever he or she, as a trained "professional" considers necessary.

But are employees independent? Obviously not. How would the organization survive if this were so? An individual member of an industrial organization, an employee, no matter how exalted the rank may be, and no matter how "professionally" competent, is not a professional in the traditional meaning of the term.

Pulling in the reins

Employees, of whatever rank, and at whatever level of "professional" competence, are hired to apply their competence to a particular segment of the organization's work . . . within such constraints as may be imposed by, or are implicit in, the corporation's manufacturing policy. It may seem, on occasion, that there is no discernible policy! But there must be one somewhere and the employee will run up against it sooner or later. Sooner rather than later, if what he wants to do designwise, productionwise or qualitywise costs too much. "Too much" means more than the cost constraints imposed by the over-all policy.

An employee may be able to persuade his organizational superior to spend a little more on design, on production facilities or on quality, but even so, it is the superior who decides whether the proposal shall be cost-supported. ►

A few years ago it didn't matter much what you were called. You were part of the corporation; you recognized the constraints. If you could satisfy your own personal "professional" technical standards while operating within the constraints ... fine. If you couldn't, you could attempt to persuade your superior. He might be persuaded ... it happened occasionally. But if not ... well, you could quit. And you might find another company with a more tolerable set of constraints. In any case, it was between you and the company. Plaintiffs' attorneys were not then digging down into the organization looking for "professional" engineers and technicians with the idea of naming them in the suit along with the defending company.

Better a practitioner than a defendant

This was done in the case of FDA versus Abbott's I.V. Solutions. Four "officers and employees" were named, of whom three had quality control titles. The case never came to trial. Abbott charged the FDA with prejudicial pretrial publicity; the judge agreed and dismissed the case. Consequently this "test case" was never tested. If there's a probability that this may happen to you, check that you are covered by the company's product liability insurance.

Don't be reluctant to call yourself a practitioner. It doesn't mean you're less technically qualified than a professional. The ultimate definition of a professional is not technical competence, but independence. A lawyer may be incompetent (I suppose there are some) but he's still an independent professional. Likewise with medical doctors, some of whom may be way behind the times in medical science, but they are still independent professionals; whereas an employee may be as brilliant as Einstein, but as an employee he is not an independent professional.

The California Court of Appeals, First Appellate District, Division Three, reaffirmed "that the doctrine of strict liability, applicable to products, does not extend to the professional services of engineers in private practice."

The term "professional" is being used here to define an individual having recognized technical qualifications (like those of us registered as professional engineers). It would still be wise to cultivate the more modest designation "practitioner," just in case some judge or attorney or other responsible citizen decides to insist on the traditional meaning of "professional."　　　　　　　　　　　　　　　　　　　　　　　　　　　□

Accident investigation

☐ How often is a quality control expert called upon to participate in an accident investigation? Rarely. What's the reason? Is it that quality control experts are purposely excluded? Not really.

What motivates plaintiffs and their attorneys, in many instances, to omit quality control as a member of the accident investigating team? Actually, what the investigators are looking for in most cases can be found without quality control specialists, especially when the investigation is being made on behalf of an injured plaintiff.

The plaintiff's attorney hopes to find that the accident was caused by a defective product, or by a defective part of a product. Not a worn-out part, not a misused part, but a part that was latently defective when it left the plant. Then his client's case is made.

Now, such a determination is essentially an engineering judgment. Furthermore, in the case of any injury-causing accident, the determination can be made on a one-time-only basis. And so plaintiffs' attorneys call upon engineers (mechanical, electrical, hydraulic or whatever) as expert witnesses.

Attorneys for the defense do the same, particularly since the defending attorney hopes for his client's sake that any given complaint would happen one time only.

The consequence of this pattern of *ad hoc* engineering investigations is that individual cases get solved, yet the manufacturing systems which produced the defective parts do not!

The flood gates are open

A further consequence is that the flood of product liability complaints continues to rise. The flood will not be contained until every accident investigation penetrates beyond the defective part itself to the error in the manufacturing system that made the defect possible.

Such investigative penetration requires the quality control expert. It's a matter of training and aptitude. The investigator must be predisposed to see every defect not as a thing in itself, but as a consequence of a systemic error. ▶

Investigators must be sufficiently experienced to be able to speculate shrewdly on what and where the errors might be, so that when he gets into the system he won't just poke around at random. This, again, calls for the quality control professional.

The investigator must be predisposed to suspect that there might have been prior warning indicators of the trouble which subsequently occurred ... and which may now cost the defendant so much. He must then be predisposed by training and aptitude to follow up his suspicions by collecting and analyzing masses of prior inspection and production data. This again calls for the quality control expert. Indeed, the distinguishing characteristic of what may be called the quality control type is reliance on quantitative analysis.

You know nothing 'til you know the numbers

Let no one think that it's easy to be a quantitative analyst, that you can decide to be one overnight or, if you like, to be one on a one-time basis. It's a tiresome business collecting masses of data; it's quite a trick knowing where to look for it. The only way to acquire a conviction of the absolute necessity for quantitative data is to have learned from bitter experience. You have to be convinced that you know little or nothing until you know the numbers.

I don't want to leave the impression that investigations in depth are never made because, of course, they are. The plaintiff's attorney may push for an in-depth investigation if he suspects the defendant had had earlier intimation of the probability of defects, but had done nothing about it. He would then hope to add punitive damages to the compensatory damages. An attorney preparing a class action suit would certainly be relying on the findings of an in-depth study.

One would think that defending producers would always make in-depth studies. Such studies are made; but the rising tide of product liability claims is clear evidence that not enough is being done. The flood of claims will continue until manufacturing systems are cleansed of the systemic errors which produce the defective parts that cause claims. And this won't happen until quality control experts are included in accident investigations. □

On giving evidence

☐ It appears that the most difficult thing to do when giving evidence is to say "I don't know." God knows, there's so much ignorance in the world, you'd think the most conceited of us would admit to a bit of it. But no . . . not when giving evidence or making a deposition.

The phenomenon itself, the reluctance to say "I don't know," and its dire effects were demonstrated by lawyer Wendell Clancy at the quality management seminar AD QUEM II. After some preliminary comments on strict liability and product liability claims, and the amplifying effect of the former on the latter, he organized a mock deposition taking.

"Questionable Quality"

Four participants found themselves burdened with names like "Arbitrary Advertiser"; "Questionable Quality" (Wow!); "Sloppy Sales" and "Crabby Customer" (manager of service). They responded from a prepared script to Wendell Clancy's questions.

By the time all four depositions had been taken, each had implicated the others; between them they had torpedoed the defendant's case! All because of the terrifying reluctance to say "I don't know." Likewise with "I can't remember," a statement that sticks in the craw of most individuals.

After the meeting I joined Wendell and some others in an attempt to measure the alcoholic saturation point for quality engineers. We found it to be slightly higher than the average for the population as a whole, which is to say that quality engineers carry their liquor like gentlemen.

During this edifying test I raised a question with Wendell and I thought you might be interested in his reply. We are all aware that the majority of parts incorporated in mass-produced articles are inspected by sampling. This creates a problem in the event one should be giving evidence at a trial, or responding in a preliminary deposition.　　　　　▶

Be careful how you answer

Assume a case in which a consumer has allegedly been injured by the activation of a latent defect in a part of one of your company's products. The question is put to you "Was this part inspected?"

I suggested to Wendell that a proper reply would be "Well . . . yes and possibly no. 'Yes' because the lot in which this part was included during manufacture was sampled. 'Possibly no' because this particular part may or may not have been included in the sample."

He nearly bit my head off! "No!" he said, "No!" "The only reply is 'I don't know,' because in fact you don't know."

"But it might have been a part of the sample."

"Right, but you don't know, so say you don't know!"

Follow your lawyer's lead

"Then," he went on, "your defending lawyer will question you in such a manner as to bring out the nature of sampling. Much more beneficially to the case than you could do it by volunteering a detailed explanation."

So, dear reader, let me urge you to learn to say "I don't know" and "I can't remember," when such statements are true, before you have to do it in earnest. This reluctance to admit to ignorance or to a lapse of memory is, lawyers have discovered, an almost universal trait. So don't think you're immune from it. In fact, you might try to recall when you last said "I don't know." For that matter, have you ever? □

The statistics of injury

☐ It is an idiosyncrasy of human behavior that we live our lives objectively in the shadow of certain statistical probabilities, while subjectively we disregard them. Indeed, we tend to reject the very idea that certain accidents could possibly happen to us!

We as individuals are confident that statistical probabilities cannot happen to us, yet, as quality control professionals we have to know how they apply to others. Especially when others are the consumers of mass-produced articles. For this purpose NEISS is invaluable.

NEISS (National Electronic Injury Surveillance System), once operated by the old Bureau of Product Safety, is now managed by the Bureau of Epidemiology in the new Consumer Product Safety Commission. The latter is a creation of a Consumer Product Safety Act of 1972.

Keeping tabs on product related injuries

NEISS collects reports on product related injuries from 119 hospital emergency rooms. Keep in mind the size of the sample, and keep in mind also that these are reports on product related injuries which receive hospital emergency room treatment only. NEISS estimated that these reports represent only 38% of the actual total of such injuries.

The remaining 62% of such injuries are treated in Doctor's offices (41%), at home (18%), and by direct hospital admission (3%). Keep in mind "product related injury" does not mean that the product caused the injury . . . only that the product was there. The injured consumer himself may have attacked the product, in the sense that he may have misused it. This problem of where the manufacturer's responsibility ends and the consumer's begins is crucial. It gets tested in the courts every day; the bounds of responsibility are being set by accumulating case law.

NEISS breaks down consumer products into 19 categories which are further broken down into 97 product classes. As an example, general household appliances is a category and fans-electric is a class within the category. Home furnishings and fixtures is a category and power cords is a class within a category. ▶

A report for the month of April 1973 indicates the number of injuries reported in each class or product for that month and gives the cumulative figure for the 10 months of fiscal 1973. That is from July '72 through April '73.

The figures are startling

How many injuries were reported for the 10 months? The total was 149,389. This is a startling total when one considers that it has been accumulated from injuries associated with the most common domestic consumer products. Not included in this total are automobile injuries and industrial injuries.

It is only when one is armed with such figures that one can speak convincingly to the manufacturers of consumer products about the necessity for adequate quality assurance programs.

I thought I would make a Pareto analysis. You remember Pareto? The Italian economist who said in effect: Where many things may happen, for better or for worse, a small fraction will account for a disproportionate part of the whole. In fact, the disproportion is so severe that there are cases where 10% of the things which may go wrong account for 90% of the total of cases. In the case of consumer product related injuries the disproportion is not that severe, but the principle still applies.

Thus, only 6 out of 97 different classes of products account for 51% of the total of 149,389 reported injuries; the Pareto expectation is fulfilled. This doesn't mean that you shouldn't play softball with the kids, or climb the stairs, or ride a bicycle, or chop carrots in the kitchen, or hesitate to look through a window or use a door, but be careful. □

Class of Product	Total No. of Cases for 10 Mos.	Percent of 149,389
Team sports and related equipment	27,998	18.7%
Stairs and railings	17,244	11.5%
Bicycles and equipment	11,972	8.0%
Cutlery, cutting and chopping devices	7,044	4.7%
Windows and glass walls, panels and doors	6,089	4.1%
Doors and associated hardware but not structural glass	5,994	4.0%
		51.0%

The CPSC and sampling

☐ The members of the Consumer Product Safety Commission have a most difficult decision to make: Shall sampling plans be included in safety standards?

The die may have been cast by the time this appears. In any case, let us look at some of the conflicting opinions because, whatever is decided, it is likely to agitate industrial, professional and congressional circles for some time to come.

As to the inclusion of sampling in safety standards, Commission Chairman Richard O. Simpson has declared himself in favor.[1] Senator Frank E. Moss (D-UT), a sponsor of the Act is opposed![2]

The pros and cons

The commission has been holding hearings. Here is what some of the witnesses had to say:

- David Masselli, a member of Health Research Group, a Nader organization, said "they (sampling plans) would insulate the manufacturer in whole or in part from the civil or criminal penalties provided in the CPSAct."[3]
- David Laufer, staff attorney with the FTC (but appearing as a private citizen) put it more emphatically. The inclusion of sampling plans in safety standards, he said, would provide manufacturers with "a virtually iron-clad defense" against government actions.[4]
- James Brodsky, attorney with Consumers Union, said that the use of sampling plans "would gut the Act's effectiveness."[5]
- William H. Rickwell of ANSI, speaking in support of sampling, said that in any case the producer is liable for injury caused by his product no matter whether sampling is in the safety standard or not.[6]
- Abbot & Mundel have entered a brief on behalf of ASQC which recommends that sampling plans be included, but that the sampling plan be applied to a more severe measure of the safety characteristic than the specified standard.[7] ▶

The problem is that the CPSAct provides protection for each purchaser of a product covered by a safety standard. The opponents don't see how the promise of the Act can be fulfilled if sampling plans are included in safety standards. It's not only that there may be defectives in sample-accepted lots, a likelihood acknowledged by the inclusion of sampling in the standard as Commissioner Kushner has said,[8] but as Masselli, Laufer and Brodsky allege, sampling in safety standards could provide the defense with a solid out! One can imagine the defense: Your honor, we are deeply sorry for the injury the plaintiff has suffered. We must accept the expert witnesses' findings that the product is defective, and was when it left the plant. But the sampling plan in the safety standard allows a proportion of non-complying articles, and this is one of them!

Mandated 100% inspection

What happens if sampling plans are not included? Well, it could be implied that each and every article must be inspected to assure compliance with the specified safety standard.

Does the Act say that each and every article must be inspected . . . or only that each article must comply? The Act does not say specifically that every article must be inspected . . . but we can imagine it being argued that since the Act required 100% compliance, how can a producer *know* that he's met the requirement unless he inspects 100%?

If the commission should rule against sampling, it could be interpreted that producers must inspect 100%. Which would throw many commercial producers into a tailspin. Because it must be kept in mind that we are talking about approximately 4,000 consumer items for which the commission is authorized to develop safety standards. How many are produced annually? Billions! To inspect each of several safety characteristics on each of billions of units of consumer products would be like counting the drops of water going over Niagara! □

1. QUALITY PROGRESS, April '74.
2. ibid.
3. QUALITY PROGRESS, June '74.
4. ibid.
5. ibid.
6. ibid.
7. QUALITY PROGRESS, May '74.
8. QUALITY PROGRESS, April '74.

The ghost at the conference

☐ While reading an excellent piece on recalls by Duane Gingerich, my attention was caught by the phrase: "The slim body of case law leaves these and other policy issues clouded." He made the comment in response to the question, "Should the manufacturer be taken off the liability hook if the plaintiff chose not to respond to a recall?"

This raised the question: Is the total body of case law on this or any other aspect of product liability available? If so, how do we, the quality engineers, gain access to it? I thought I would ask Duane a couple of questions on behalf of all of us.

What is the total number of personal injury cases in which the absence or inadequacy of quality control has been alleged? In how many of such cases were one or more members of the quality control department, specifically identified as such by title, included in the charge along with the manufacturer? What exactly were they accused of? What happened? Was the use of sampling ever an issue?

Sampling and the probability of some nonconforming parts and, therefore, the probability of failure is the ghost that hovers in the background of every product liability conference. It is true that we attempt to remove the probability of failure (minimize would be the better word) by classification of quality characteristics and by sampling only those characteristics judged not critical. But, as we all know, the assurance is not absolute.

The ghost is schizophrenic

The ghost at the conference is kind of schizophrenic, divided against itself. There is the Consumer Product Safety Act of 1972 . . . and there is the economic necessity to sample in mass production. The saintly side of the ghost lifts its hands in benediction and demands that *all* consumers shall be safe from injury in the use of consumer products; the dark side of the ghost smiles and whispers in the saintly ear, "It can't be done. Not at a reasonable selling price . . . perhaps not at any price. What about 98 or 99 percent of the consumers?" "Get thee behind me," snaps the saint and continues to hover over the conference with its halo somewhat displaced.

▶

The Consumer Product Safety Commission did its own "get thee behind me" when the Consumer Product Safety Commission Improvements Act was promulgated in 1976. The Improvements Act prescribed that: "No consumer safety product standard promulgated under this section shall require, incorporate or reference any sampling plan."

So there it is, Duane. The use of sampling (which we do on practically all of the parts and components which make up consumer products, and frequently on the end product as well) appears to contravene the intent of the CPSAct. During the CPSC inquiry in 1974 into the use or otherwise of sampling in safety standards, attorneys Masselli (for Nader), Laufer (FTC, but appearing as a private citizen) and Brodsky (for Consumers Union) were emphatic on this point. "It would gut the Act's effectiveness," said Brodsky. "It would provide manufacturers with a virtually iron-clad defense against government actions," said Laufer. Masselli said that "they (sampling plans) would insulate the manufacturer, in whole or in part from the civil or criminal penalties provided in the CPSAct."

Sampling may, in and of itself, be non-defensible

With such emphatic statements in the public record, it cannot be that plaintiffs' attorneys are not on to the possibility of going for punitive damages on the grounds that sampling increases, or may increase, the probability of injury. But if one such case succeeded, the whole consumer goods producing industry would be in jeopardy!

Every quality manager is in potential jeopardy, too. At any time he may be called to the stand and must confess that he cannot say whether the part in dispute was physically inspected or not, because he inspects by sampling. Which is why I urge managers to make sure that they have management's sanction for sampling.

What then, Duane, are the case law statistics on the use of statistics in the production of consumer goods? And have they confronted this problem and laid the ghost to rest?   □

What do consumers want?

☐ What do consumers want?

Prompt courteous service, that's what!

It is said that an exasperated Sigmund Freud once demanded, "What do women want?" It would have been simple to ask ... but he preferred to ask what they dreamed about. Then, by a process of analysis, *he* told *them* what they wanted.

Thus was created the practice of psychiatry, which gave comfort to many women until Women's Liberation came along, and put Freud down as a male sexist chauvinist! Then Women's Lib began telling us, since we still didn't ask, and now for the first time in history we are learning what women want.

Consumerist advocates, quality assurance specialists and members of regulatory commissions haven't asked consumers what they dream about; but neither have they asked the poor suffering consumers outright what they want. I tried it on a number of friends and acquaintances, admittedly a small sample of the population, but I imagine the answer would be the same all over.

Keep working, or be repaired quickly

"What do I want of autos and refrigerators and electric razors and whatever? Only that they should keep working ... and when they don't, I'd like to get a quick repair without being hassled."

That, with only slight variations, was the common reply. Not a demand for "quality," but only that the common items of everyday use "keep working." The word "quality," as a measure of conformance to specific requirements, doesn't get much use outside of professional circles. "Quality," in the common usage, generally means an item in a given class which is "better" than another in the same class. As for example, a Cadillac when compared with a Chevrolet, or a Rolex compared with a Timex. ▶

What the consumer expects of each is that it shall keep going; and if it doesn't, that the agent or retailer shall respond courteously to the complaint and do something about it promptly. Prompt courteous service; that's what the consumers want. And when they get it, they rapidly forget the temporary aggravation.

What they can't forget and won't forgive is the hassling, the stalling, the wall of indifference and evasion that blocks the consumer when he or she makes a claim under the warranty. Despite the Consumer Product Safety Act and a host of regulations, it's not all that much better now. Just try to get a loan car while warranty repairs are being made!

Prompt courteous service is the answer

In the meantime, fervent efforts are being made in many plants to make a better, safer product. Fine. But let us devote a part of the effort to providing prompt courteous service for the products as they are now.

Why does after-sales service not improve more rapidly? It's obvious that better service would abate the cries of the consumers most quickly, at the least cost.

The answer may be that *service is labor-intensive*. But the thrust of management thinking is for more mechanization and less labor. This policy has been extraordinarily successful in providing masses of items of great utility at competitive prices, but when applied to service it is counter-productive. Not only does it keep the service staff at a low level, but it makes it difficult for managers to appreciate the consumers' desire for service. Managers so motivated are myopic to situations which demand a preponderance of labor.

The situation would get better exposure, and would almost certainly improve more rapidly if quality control were to get into service. Not to take it over . . . but to become more extensively involved in the collection and evaluation of field failure data, including consumers' attitudes and blood pressures! Quality control people have had to learn to have a proper regard for the attitudes of their colleagues in administration, engineering, purchasing and production. They are well qualified to observe and report on the attitudes of consumers. □

Equal time

☐ Consumerism is a product of mass production and the current buyers' market. The buyers of mass produced items (automobiles, kitchen appliances, TV, radios), have become intolerant of defects. Powerful advocates have risen up to speak for the disgruntled consumers. Plaintiffs' attorneys are acquiring a sophisticated knowledge of design-production-quality assurance systems; they know where to probe for possible deficiencies. They go through inspection-production records like Sherlock Holmes (isn't there a more contemporary sleuth?). Heaven protect the poor defendant whose records have gaps.

It wasn't always thus. Once upon a time there was a sellers' market. But that was way back in history, in the late Forties and Fifties. In those days a claim for injury caused by a defective product was based on the alleged negligence of the producer. The producer could usually rebut the allegation and the plaintiff got nowhere. But nowadays (since 1962 in California) the legal principle of strict liability in tort applies and it's the defendant who frequently gets nowhere.

How to cope with consumerism

It's no good regretting those halcyon days. The present is upon us and the thing for mass producers to do is to learn to cope before they're caught. The simple way to cope with consumerism is not to ship defective articles to the market. I know . . . it's not that simple. However, had that been done, there would have been no consumerism. But while defective articles found their way into the market, as thousands of product liability cases bear witness, it wasn't planned that way. The thing to do is to find out why it happened when it wasn't planned, and do something about it . . . learn to cope.

The absolute priority in coping with consumerism is to recognize that top management must be behind the effort. Top management must inform itself as to the nature and magnitude of the problem, and direct that all necessary steps be taken to assure the *quality* of the product. ▶

But top management's interest has been centered on *quantity*. *Quantity* is what mass production is about. The ability of mass production to produce vast quantities of articles at popular prices is the foundation of contemporary affluence.

The solution is *not* to attempt to turn management's attention away from *quantity*. What must be done is to *persuade management to give equal time to quality.*

Management must know the numbers

To come to grips with the problem top management simply has to become familiar with the distinction between statistically measured quality as applied to mass-produced articles, and absolute qualitative quality as applied to a unique artifact. Executives don't have to become statisticians but they must pick up the statistical vocabulary, so that the case for quality, reliability and safety can be given equal time in the highest councils of the company.

So the first step in any program to cope with consumerism is to set up a seminar for management. It helps to get in one of the recognized experts to assist in persuading management to consent to a seminar.

The agenda may vary with the product and the market, but certain items are common to all products and all companies: 1) Consumerism as a socio-legal phenomenon, its nature and causes; 2) case history illustrating what has happened to negligent and indifferent companies (for this purpose *Product Liability and Safety* by George Peters is indispensable); 3) inspection by sampling as an inherently necessary part of the mass production of popularly priced articles and the effect of sampling on quality; 4) after-sales service, how to predict the probable volume of claims and to make appropriate plans.

I want to make the point that *the time has come for quality to be given equal time in the councils of companies producing for the mass market* and the further point that *this cannot occur until the chief executive is involved.* □

Can consumerism survive?

☐ Can consumerism survive? The question is relevant because of the increasing manifestations of what I call counter-consumerism.

The probability of survival for consumerism, or any other social phenomenon, is determined by pre-existing longevity, or essentiality to the system of which it is a part, or both.

As to longevity, we tend to take consumerism for granted like weather and taxes, but it hasn't been around very long. We are familiar with the landmark cases of Henningsen v. Chrysler (New Jersey 1960) and Greenman v. Yorba Tool Co. (California 1962). The judgments in these famous cases set aside the defenses of *privity* (the seller is responsible only to the buyer and not to his wife, or lady friend, or other injured party), and *no negligence* (the court's current attitude toward the defendant being that it's commendable that there was no negligence, but the part is still defective and the plaintiff still suffers).

The legal principle of strict liability

These judgments introduced the legal principle of *strict liability*. Then came Ralph Nader and a flock of consumers' advocates. Then Nixon signed the Consumers Product Safety Act into law in October, 1972, authorizing the formation of the CPS Commission, now very much a part of the Washington scene.

In the meantime, battalions of lawyers, specializing in personal injury as plaintiffs' attorneys, were getting moderately prosperous with the help of the contingency fee system while securing substantial compensation for injured consumers.

The appearance of so many attorneys moved by the sufferings of the injured is in itself a remarkable phenomenon. Never before were lawyers so clearly on the side of the angels!

Consumerism appears to have started about 1960 and to have been institutionalized by the passing of the CPSAct in '72. But why then? It isn't because the citizenry suddenly started getting injured by industrial devices. Industrial devices have managed to injure numbers of citizens

▶

ever since the Industrial Revolution, and they got little or no compensation. Furthermore, it should be remembered that Benjamin Cardozzo set aside *privity* in the case of McPherson v. Buick in 1916! But there was no flood of cases to take advantage of such a precedent, the times were not ready for the elevation of the injured citizen and the matter of compensation to the level of national interest.

Consuming for the sake of consumption

Consumerism requires consumers and there were no consumers! The citizens had to eat, of course, and clothe themselves, and some had automobiles and a few took trips as far as Chicago. But, they were not *consumers.* They did these things because they actually needed them; they were producers first and foremost seeking sustenance and covering and a little entertainment. The class of consumers had not yet been invented . . . because there was no excess to be consumed for the sake of consumption.

But things changed after the war. America found itself in possession of a fabulous producing machine . . . products were pouring out all over. Somebody had to consume them . . . not because they needed them (although on occasion there might be a genuine need) but because they were there. And there just happened to be 180,000,000 somebodies who could be transformed into consumers . . . and the men who knew how to do it were waiting on Madison Avenue.

The American populace became the first nation of consumers in history (not the first consumers, because of course from age to age there had always been a handful of the "idle" rich kept busy consuming whatever small excess was available). A whole nation of consumers!

Consumers had arrived! Created out of sheer necessity. They were vital to the economic health of the country. They were not only a highly visible part of the socio-economic scene, they were a *large* part of it. It was inevitable that consumers and what happened to them should become a matter for national concern; that they should become a recognized part of every congressman's constituency; and that laws would be passed for their preservation and protection.

We may conclude, therefore, that consumerism will survive as long as the economy needs consumers. □

No satisfaction without qualification

☐ There is a popular definition of quality assurance which states that it is "a management function to assure that products provide consumer satisfaction."

Now that seems like a most desirable objective, but there's a catch in it. Human appetite for satisfaction is insatiable! It seems to come with consciousness, that disturbing human ability to contemplate and evaluate one's life and possessions as well as to live it and enjoy them.

So far as we know cattle are content to graze and chew the cud all the days of their lives. It may be assumed that they were, are, and ever will be satisfied. Not so with Man. It must have been a pleasant life for our long distant ancestors up in the trees. There was enough to eat, no smog, plenty of exercise, it was a fine solubrious existence. The dangerous animals and flooding rivers were all below. Consumer satisfaction should have been complete. But was it? Not on your life! They were blessed with consciousness, and they looked at what they had . . . and it wasn't enough. They settled down in the delta of the Tigris and Euphrates and invented civilization, which gave them kings and temples and fine garments and legalized mating . . . and still there was no satisfaction.

The 'Model T' and indoor plumbing

So they spread across the face of the earth and in time they came to America and in the early years of the 20th Century they achieved what seemed to be the furthermost reaches of human desire: The Model T and indoor plumbing.

What more could consumer satisfaction demand? Plenty! Consumers who once thought they were content with the Model T, now complain about the Continental, the Cadillac and the Rolls Royce yet!   ►

History, past and present, provides an overwhelming demonstration of the insatiability of the appetite for satisfaction. It dictates caution to manufacturers and marketers of consumer products. We might define quality control as assuring "consumer satisfaction, provided the consumer will be satisfied with the product as specified and/or advertised, and provided he used it only as it was intended to be used." But that's too "picky," although clear and explicit. Furthermore, it would put a crimp in the style of Madison Avenue; but that's going to happen anyway if there's ever going to be a clear understanding by producer and consumer as to what's being sold and what's being bought.

An aggregate of activities

The latest edition of Webster's New Collegiate Dictionary defines quality control as "an aggregate of activities (as design analysis and statistical sampling with inspection for defects) designed to ensure adequate quality in manufacturing products." That's good with the exception of "adequate" which, like "consumer satisfaction," begs the question. When is "adequate" adequate enough? But if it were to read "to ensure the quality of manufactured product, as specified and/or advertised," it would be unambiguous and would serve as the basis for a quality program comprehensible by producers and consumers.

There's another angle. As between a quality manager and his employer, should the manager preface his quality program with the assertion that it will "assure consumer satisfaction" without qualification. It would take only one complaint to demonstrate his nominal incompetence and to justify his involuntary departure from the company!

There are few, if any, employers who would act upon the letter of the law with such speed, but the point is that such action would be legally valid, given that unqualified assurance. So, as the early Americans raised the cry of "no taxation without representation," let us insist that there be no assurances of satisfaction without qualification. □

Is your quality program any good?

☐ How does the quality manager know when he's doing any good? You would think that every quality manager could give a prompt and detailed reply. But it isn't always so.

Quality managers have little time for contemplation, for trend measurement and evaluation. It is all too easy for a quality manager to spend all of his time putting out fires. Indeed, he may be involved in crises every time one of his inspectors turns around. The potential for "crisis-involvement" in quality management is inherently high. Furthermore, there is an exhilaration to fire-fighting which makes it attractive even while one is protesting that it takes too much time. The fire is right in front of one's eyes, there is a sense of urgency, and congratulations are prompt when the fire is triumphantly squelched.

It's easy to be a fire-fighter

It is, then, easy and pleasant to be a fire-fighter, but the quality manager must take off his helmet and pause long enough to consider the quality program as a whole. Is it doing any good? Is it headed in the right direction? What are the measures of successful quality management?

If the quality manager were to take one measure only, it should be the performance of the product in the field. He should watch returns like a hawk; no field complaint should escape his notice. He may find himself confronted by a mass of data, but it can be brought into focus by a monthly summary to management such as the sample shown.

1.	Number of units returned for warranty repair during the month	_____
2.	Number of units shipped during the month	_____
3.	(1) as a percentage of (2)	_____%
4.	Percent returns last month	_____%
5.	Average percent returns for previous six months . . .	_____%
6.	Cost of repairing warranty units	$_____
7.	Total billing for the month	$_____
8.	(6) as a percentage of (7)	_____%
9.	Warranty $ as a percentage of billing last month	_____%
10.	Average warranty $ as a percentage of billing for previous six months	_____%

▶

This simple report would provide the quality manager with an instantaneous reading on the efficacy of the quality assurance program. Either the rate of return is tolerable, or it is not. Either the trend is favorable, or it is not. The quality manager and his colleagues will consider the summary and take action accordingly. The quality manager stands ready to identify the defects occurring the most frequently, but this should only be done when the level, or the trend, or both indicate that there is cause for investigation. For the sake of clarity and an instantaneous recognition of significance, the summary report should not be cluttered with detail.

Distortions tend to average out

It might be objected that units repaired under warranty in any given month are not shipped in that month, but such distortions may be ignored; they tend to average out in time.

It might be objected that there is no reference to the cost of the quality assurance program. There is no intent to bypass the cost, but we are assuming that the q.a. program is in being. It is in motion; a certain sum of money is being spent and the immediate problem is to find out whether it's doing any good. When we have answered that question, we can look more closely at the cost. But get the quality score first.

If the return rate is small and tolerable, then we can find out if the cost is tolerable too, or whether the cost is too much. If the return rate is high, then we can start a series of investigations which will probe the causes of failure, costs and procedures. Indeed, this basic measure of quality program performance will start investigations which will reach into every corner of the plant.

To report on "returns" is to confront the question: Does the product do what it was meant to do? This is the key question. The answer tells you not merely what the customer thinks of your quality assurance program, but what he thinks of your company as a whole. □

Thirty-four new judges

☐ One fine day in October, I was driving along the freeway with the radio chattering away, alternating disasters with commercials, when I heard something close to home. Governor Jerry Brown had just vetoed a bill which would have created 45 new Superior Court judges, 34 of whom were slated for Los Angeles County.

This was the bill which Jonathon Kirsch had referred to in *New West* magazine. Kirsch was reporting on a particular product liability case in which a construction worker had been severely injured by the "snapping of a faulty cable which dumped him in the middle of the San Bernadino Freeway with one arm torn off (it was later somehow sewn on again) and the other arm pulverized."

Kirsch was concerned that it had taken six years for the case to get to Superior Court, when the court took only three weeks to settle the case with an award of half a million dollars. Except that the case wasn't settled; the defendants are appealing against the verdict and the injured man's lawyer told Kirsch he didn't know when or how the case would finally be settled.

Congestion in the courts

Kirsch went on to report the difficulty in getting a trial date for a personal injury case in California, particularly in LA County because of the extreme congestion in the courts. The average wait in Los Angeles is three years; it's two years in San Francisco and San Diego.

Los Angeles attorneys and Superior Court judges have requested that 34 new judgeships be created in LA County, a request which has been turned down three years in a row by the Board of Supervisors.

When I got back to the office I found the current issue of *Quality Progress*. In it is a report by David Endres on the passing of the Utah Product Liability Act, which having been introduced only in January of this year (1977), passed the Utah Senate and House and obtained the governor's signature all in the month of March. ▶

It sets a limitation on the entering of a product liability claim of six years after the initial purchase, or ten years after the date of manufacture. It also states that "no dollar amount shall be specified in the prayer of a complaint filed in a product liability action against a product manufacturer, or wholesaler, or retailer. The complaint shall merely pray for such damages as are reasonable in the premises."

Time limit on liability

The limitation of six or ten years may be found to run counter to the generally accepted principle of strict liability which says, in effect, that a latent defect is a latent defect no matter how soon or late it reveals itself and injures a consumer. The Utah law will undoubtedly be tested in the courts and then it will be seen what happens.

In the meantime, the Pearson Bill in the U.S. Senate is making slow progress, but it's there. It seeks to remove product liability cases from the courts and submit them to arbitration, and to put a limit on the dollar amount which may be claimed.

These various actions were to be expected. They are part of the interactive play of forces and interests which is the distinguishing mark of the U.S. socio-political system; they might be characterized as counter-consumerism. In any case, I thought these scattered events should be pulled together into one report for the information of fellow professionals in the field of quality. Not only are quality managers expected to strive constantly for product quality, but in this day and age the task devolves upon them to keep themselves and their companies informed on all related matters. □

The consumer bureaucracies

☐ One day recently I decided to catch up with the news. The May (1977) issue of *Quality* had just arrived and there was Chick Walsh fulminating against the proposal to create a National Standards Management Board. It would create a new bureaucracy to take over from the American National Standards Institute (ANSI), an exemplary voluntary group. It's Senate bill S.825 and Chick wants all good men and true to let their congressmen know what they think about it.

Then I picked up the LA *Times* for June 2 and was confronted by the headline, "Carter argues for Consumer Agency." Staff writer Don Irwin quoted the President as telling the representatives of about 200 consumer and business groups that a proposed bill would create a new Agency for Consumer Advocacy to represent consumer interests within the federal establishment.

The proposed budget for the new agency is $15,000,000 which, said the President, quoting Budget Director Bert Lance, is only one third more than the $10,400,000 now being spent on consumer advocacy offices already existing in 13 government agencies.

A mere pittance

It's true that $15,000,000 is a parsimonious budget for a government bureaucracy, but let's see how many bureaucrats it will support. The Consumer Product Safety Commission has a staff of about 900 and a budget of about $39,000,000. All of that money doesn't go to 900 staff members; there are 13 field offices which have to be rented and filing cabinets and paper clips, etc. But if we divide $39,000,000 by 900 we should arrive at a rough estimate of the cost of maintaining a consumer bureaucrat. The figure is $43,333.

Let's apply this to the proposed budget for the proposed new agency: $15,000,000 would support 346 new bureaucrats at the same rate. This would bring the total of consumer bureaucrats at the federal level to 1246.

▶

If we compare 1246 with the approximate 24,000 members of the American Society for Quality Control, we see that we are not yet as outnumbered by bureaucrats as we are by attorneys (see "Outnumbered" on page 153).

However, there must be an office of consumer affairs in every state capital and in thousands of sizable cities. Statistics aren't available on the total number of provincial consumer bureaucrats, but if there were only one to every 100,000 citizens, that would amount to 2,150 for a population of 215,000,000. This is a hypothetical figure, but we can be sure that whatever the true figure is, it is far from zero.

Society as a paradox

The point is not to knock the bureaucrats as individuals, because many of them are nice guys; in any case, it's already been done by Parkinson and Peter. The point is to illustrate and quantify the paradoxical nature of the society developing around us.

The ostensible justification for the proliferation of consumer bureaucracies is a growing national and local concern for the safety of consumers. Fine. But concern is not enough. Among the thousands of federal, state and local consumer affairs officials, there must be a very few who have any specific technical knowledge of what is required to make consumer products safe.

Consumer products are mass-produced. The inertial drive in mass production is for increased quantity, reduced costs and quality levels consistent with these constraints. Keep in mind that safety is a quality characteristic and is subject to the same pressures as other quality characteristics.

Neither bureaucratic threats nor pleas can induce mass production to raise the level of quality and reduce the chance of injury. This can be done only by quality control professionals who are well informed as to the impersonal nature of mass production procedures and whose professional qualification is the ability to reduce the incidence of defects (thereby reducing the probability of injury) without adverse effect on quantity and cost. But quality professionals continue in short supply.

It's as though society were determined to emulate the Army. Do you remember how it used to be said that there were two ways of doing things, the Army way and the right way? In the matter of quality improvement and injury prevention we, the nation as a whole, are doing it the Army way.   □

Outnumbered

☐ "There is one lawyer to every 530 Americans."

So writes Jerold S. Auerbach in the October 1976 issue of *Harper's*. Auerbach, who teaches American history and law at Wellesley College, goes on to say that the ratio was one to 1,100 at the beginning of the century which, even then, was higher than the current ratio of one to 1,600 in Britain. By way of contrast, the present ratio in Japan is one to 10,300.

What's it to us in quality assurance that there are so many lawyers? In the field of product liability where lawyers for injured plaintiffs and lawyers for the defense battle over huge amounts claimed in compensation and where we strive to minimize the probability of injury, we are fantastically outnumbered!

How many lawyers are there altogether? The population is about 215,000,000, so there are about 405,660 lawyers. Say 400,000 at the very least. Current membership of ASQC is about 24,000. But every member of ASQC is not a qualified professional by virtue of being a qualified quality engineer and/or a registered professional engineer. The lawyers are all qualified. Let us say that half the membership of ASQC is qualified and let us assume that at least 5% of the lawyers are practicing in product liability either for the plaintiffs or for the defense. That's 20,000 lawyers to 12,000 quality engineers.

There's 3.3 of 'em out there looking for you!

But wait, many of the quality engineers work for the military contractors and are not liable to product liability. Let's assume that half of the qualified Q.E.'s work on consumer products. We then have a ratio of 20,000 to 6,000 or 3.3 lawyers to each quality engineer. We're likely to remain outnumbered because, as professor Auerbach writes, applicants are crowding the law schools.

How should we relate lawyers and quality engineers to product liability? Lawyers work on the cure when the damage has been done; quality engineers work on prevention. ▶

The effects of product liability are two-fold: (1) the injury to the consumer and (2) the financial "injury" to the manufacturer if a suit for compensation is successful. A successful suit also will injure the company's reputation and reduce the demand for its products.

The injured consumer is not, of course, "cured" by a successful suit, although the effects of the injury are assuaged by adequate compensation; whereas the potential injury to the company *is* cured by a successful defense. Even so, the defense has to be paid for.

Attorneys for the plaintiff and the defending company engage in adversarial conflict. If the defense wins, it will still cost the company plenty. If the plaintiff wins, the amount of the compensatory award may shake the company to its foundations.

It could cost you plenty

Paul Nelson writes in "Quality Progress" that product liability claims approximated 500,000 in 1970 and are estimated to reach 1,000,000 by 1980. Claims aggregated $500,000,000 in 1965; $12.5 billion in 1972 and were projected to increase in 1976 to the fabulous sum of $50 billion! At the time of this writing, information isn't available as to whether they made it.

We have to keep in mind that the plaintiff doesn't always win those $ million awards publicized in *Time* and *Newsweek*. The plaintiff may settle out of court for a fraction of the original claim (10% being a typical figure) or he may lose. But if awards aggregated only 10% of the figures quoted above, they would still amount to a staggering sum of money.

What can we do to persuade management to spend a little on prevention before many more companies go broke? After all, they know these figures as well as we do. They experience them directly; they suffer from them.

It has been said that an ounce of prevention costs less than a pound of cure. But whoever said it couldn't have been an American. The national temperament is to take a risk and to figure out afterwards how to save the day if the risk doesn't work out.

In the meantime, we must keep training quality engineers in case management decides on an ounce of prevention. I wonder if there's any validity in that ratio, an ounce to one pound, one to 16. Just imagine getting 1/16th of 10% of $50 billion to spend on preventive quality assurance! □

(Editor's note: Changing trends in liability awards indicate that government contractor immunity is waning.)

The iron ulna of our lord the king

☐ This is a story of standards, simplicity, complexity, injuries and product liability claims.

It was decreed in the year 1305 in the reign of Edward I that the unit of length should be the yard and that the reference standard should be the "Iron Ulna of our Lord the King."*

The yard was defined in medieval times as the distance between the center of the body and the tips of the fingers of an outstretched hand, a distance of approximately 36 inches. Try it on yourself. If you measure 36 inches, you've got about the same build as Edward I; you have something in common with a man who was no mean monarch.

Edward went on a Crusade; he finally conquered Wales (except it's never agreed to stay conquered); he battled Wallace and Bruce, the Scottish champions; and, he rarely missed a year without a foray into France. He wanted so much money for war (does that sound familiar?) that Parliament objected and he had to agree not to attempt to raise money for war without the consent of Parliament. This is what the colonials had in mind when they raised the cry of "no taxation without representation" in 1775. And he authorized the use of a nice simple metal bar as the standard of length.

Measure to a metal bar

A metal bar, tucked away somewhere in London, was still the reference standard when I was at school. It had been modified by Henry VII in 1496 and again by Elizabeth I in 1588. Incidentally, that was the year of the Spanish Armada. It seems strange that while Sir Francis Drake was battling the Spaniards in the Channel, Elizabeth back in London was fiddling around with standards of measurement. But then Elizabeth was always a bit on the persnickety side. She bickered over the sum of money to be spent on potatoes for the sailors who had just saved her kingdom. Such is the gratitude of sovereigns! ▶

The authorities had another go at the standards in 1855 when it became the Imperial Standard Yard. It was not until the sixties that the "Iron Ulna of our Lord the King" (not Edward's bar, but still a metal bar) was abandoned in favor of the yard specified in terms of the meter.

Now the meter is defined as 1,650,763.73 orange-red Krypton wavelengths and the yard reference standard is no longer a metal bar but 1,509,458.3 orange-red Krypton wavelengths. Just imagine trying to tell that to Edward I; for that matter, try telling it to almost any executive or colleague outside of a chosen few. Edward might have clapped you in jail, but your colleagues can only register bewilderment!

Knowing what it is and how to use it

How simple things were in the 14th century. Neither man nor woman ever used a device, sword or skillet, which he or she did not understand; both as to how it was made and its uses.

If such understanding were required of today's consumers, how few would be qualified to drive an automobile, turn on the TV, aim a camera or switch on a washing machine. Yet, while the products and the methods of measuring them have reached an awesome degree of complexity, the men and women who use them, all of us, remain pretty much what our ancestors were.

Which brings us to a central problem of today—the flood of product liability claims. Why so many claims? Because so many consumers get injured. Why do so many get injured? Surely one of the causes is that we are simple people struggling with complex products.

What should we do? We could urge the engineers to strive for simplicity in design. We could gently suggest that they don't have to demonstrate how much they know by making common consumer products ever more uncommon. We could tell the designers that if it's too complex to be measured with the Iron Ulna of our late Lord the King, we don't want it. But what would that leave us with? Swords and skillets! □

*Historical data in part from "Quality—its origin and progress in defense procurement" by H.E. Drew, C.B. Director General, Quality Assurance, British Ministry of Defense from 1966 to 1970. First published in "The Production Engineer" in January 1972.

Quality on the air

☐ Sunday, Dec. 7th, 1975, I was a guest on the Treesa Drury Show, KABC radio, Los Angeles. Treesa Drury is a well-known commentator who specializes in consumer affairs.

Treesa, addressed in this familiar manner by callers and guests, delivered a couple of commercials, made some announcements on consumer affairs, and told the listeners that her guest was a "quality control specialist." She asked me to describe quality control and what it does for consumers; we debated this for a few minutes and then she invited listeners to call in.

What are we and what do we do?

From then on for the remainder of the hour, the calls came in thick and heavy. What struck me was that the callers did not know enough about quality control to put pointed questions. We simply have to let more consumers know we are around and what we do. Somehow we haven't yet succeeded in catching the popular imagination. There are few references to quality control in contemporary fiction; which is a sure indication of popular status. There are many novels in which the hero (or villain) is an advertising man or stockbroker; but I know of no novel in which a quality engineer plays a major part. Yet I would think that quality control is as socially useful as the superb hypnotizing job Madison Avenue does on all of us; and it certainly makes better predictions than your favorite stockbroker!

Most of the questions called in had to do with warranty and service. The consensus among consumers was that warranties are incomprehensible, and that after-sales service ranges from merely bad to outrageous!

Consumers, in general, do not have an exact knowledge of the quality of the products they buy

This matter of service is crucial. Consumers, in general, do not have an exact knowledge of the quality of the products they buy. They are not

►

specification-oriented. They would like the product to outlast the warranty, but whether failure occurs within or outside of the warranty, they are quickly mollified by prompt, courteous service . . . as those few who get it bear witness.

Why, oh why, don't the manufacturers instruct sales agencies to provide prompt, courteous service? It would be a small price to pay for a tremendous increase in consumer satisfaction and, at least, a partial and quite legitimate deflation of the consumer movement.

What's really happening out there?

I told one caller, who was having difficulty finding someone at the manufacturer's to talk sense about his problem, to ask for the quality manager. Q.C. people are far better qualified to respond in such a situation than the public relations individuals sometimes assigned to the task. More companies would be well advised to put quality engineers on consumer-complaint phones. That way Q.C. and the company would get to know what's really happening out there. □

Go tell the Spartans!

☐ In the year 480 BC, the Persians set out to subdue Greece. In the route of the vast Persian army stood the narrow pass of Thermopylae. There the Greeks left 300 Spartans to delay the invaders while the main defense was being prepared. The Spartans fought and died to the last man. Shortly thereafter, a simple stone marker appeared on which was inscribed:

> Go tell the Spartans,
> You who read this stone,
> That we lie here,
> That their will was done.

I thought of this as I listened to Richard Shugrue, a Los Angeles attorney, specializing in defense in personal injury cases. The occasion was the First Annual Industrial Technology Conference, held in March 1978. The conference organized by Long Beach State University and masterminded by Dr. Glen Hayes, drew about 200 industrial engineers, managers, students and consumers.

Lawyers are not dummies

The attorney, whom I had not met previously, was at the podium; I was to follow him. His address was directed at producers of consumer goods. He quoted some of the more stupendous million $ awards. He went on to detail some appalling examples of design error and poor workmanship with which he had become familiar. Incidentally, he spoke on these subjects with considerable knowledge, confirming a speculation of mine that when attorneys for the defense or the plaintiff had to learn the intricacies of design, production, quality assurance (including sampling), they would do so. It would be an unwise engineer who assumed their ignorance.

Attorney Shugrue concluded by appealing to those in the audience in a position to do so to work towards the elimination of defects, and stepped down to vigorous applause. ►

I couldn't possibly have had a better preparation for what I had to say. Quoting liberally from the attorney, who remained in the audience, I launched into a description of the historical and social circumstances which had transformed the injured from objects of piteous concern to relatives and friends, into a matter of high import to every congressman who wished to be returned to Washington. Indeed, to use a word recently fabricated by several of those same politicians, the economy's need for consumers has *prioritized* the necessity to keep consumers safe and sound, and to see that they get adequately compensated when they aren't.

Go tell the producers

It wasn't planned that attorney Richard Shugrue and I should deliver a joint message, but that, in effect, is what happened. And what was the message?

> Go tell the producers,
> You who hear these words,
> That we, the injured, lie silent no more,
> That *our* will shall be done,
> That they should take heed,
> Lest they be undone.

I admit it's stretching the analogy a little, but what does it take to arouse the producers, big and little, to the danger for themselves and the consumers, of attempting to work with little quality and less safety? This thing has been going on since the mid-sixties. It's about time recalls were a thing of the past, a matter of historic interest like the Spartans. ☐

The eyes are not where the hands are!

☐ I was driving west on the Ventura Freeway to call on a client when the radio switched from a perfervid commercial for the latest model of a well-known automobile to news. The news was that another well-known automobile company was recalling 740,000 of its '76 and '77 models for the correction of a potential safety defect.

This set me thinking about the causes of such unfortunate events. Unfortunate for everyone: the drivers who might get hurt; the agents who will be called upon to make the corrections; and the manufacturers who will bear the brunt of the cost.

Automobile production is the very peak and pinnacle of mass production. In an age of rational systems, auto production is the rational system *par excellence.*

Then why the defects: Is it because the popular suspicion that autos are not built to last any longer than the warranty period plus a few weeks is true?

They don't make 'em like that any more

I, for one, don't buy that. Indeed, when I find myself in the company of men and women admiring a "classic" auto of the 1930's and everybody says, "They don't make them like that any longer," I don't buy that either. The "classic" has been cared for and cosseted, the object of tender loving care. Its fellows, produced in the same year, lie rotting on junk piles where they arrived sooner or later . . . mostly sooner.

It isn't true that everything used to last longer. If you're old enough to remember "before the war," you will recall ads for tires which proudly boasted that they were guaranteed for 5000 miles. Five thousand miles! Ask your grandfather what motoring was like in the '20's and '30's. He will tell you that if you completed a 100 mile trip without a flat you were lucky; 200 miles without a flat was beyond reasonable expectation, like looking for pie in the sky. Who in the '30's . . . or '40's . . . or '50's would have guaranteed a battery for life as a famous chain is now doing? ➤

The modern auto factory is a conglomeration of manual ability, of designers in possession of the latest technology, and of sophisticated management systems. How could anything go wrong? Why the defects that cause the recalls?

It is because changes are constantly being made to improve performance, or to gain a competitive edge, or both. The changes may be part of the current proliferation of technology or changes in managerial systems. Both are well-meant and, indeed, are unavoidable in the onrushing tide of technological and managerial experimentation.

Mass production has jaundiced our eyes

Again, why the defects? It is because the eyes that see the design and system changes, looking so precise and perfect on paper, are not behind the hands that encounter the snags and problems they may cause. Furthermore, the eyes behind the hands that *do* encounter the problems have lost their ability to see. The eyes of craftsmen informed by a seven year apprenticeship would have seen at once . . . but this ability has been diminished by the nature of mass production.

We are not going to cast out mass production, which makes it possible for millions, instead of only hundreds, to suffer from occasional failures, or even injury, while enjoying the freedom and the means to travel. But we must find some way of ensuring that the hands of the eyes that see the design and system changes in all their abstract elegance, are brought into physical contact with the snags and problems they may cause.

It's a problem. The contemporary organization excludes such contact almost by definition. But the problem will continue as long as the eyes are not where the hands are. □

Safety engineering and the Murphy effect

☐ The question of safety engineering was raised by editor Chick Walsh and attorney Duane Gingerich in the February 1978 issue of *Quality* magazine. Both urge us to recognize the magnitude of the problem, and belabor us with dire warnings as to what will happen to our employers and clients if we don't do enough about safety. I would like to add something to their prophetic thunder.

Editor Walsh recommends the inclusion of nontechnical personnel in safety engineering teams, a recommendation with which I heartily agree. Attorney Gingerich recommends the creation of a new class of ME's (Murphy's Engineers) in recognition of that immortal skeptic who said that "if anything can go wrong ... it will." I would like to add the recommendation that the designer should not be asked to do the safety engineering on his own design.

At first glance, the designer would appear to be the logical choice. After all, he knows the most about the design, its potential for good performance, and the lack of any tendency to electrify, dismember, poison or otherwise injure the consumer. True or false?

"It's not my job, man!"

False! The designer designs a product to perform a particular function. His goal may be a new and unique product; or, an improved design to beat the competition; or, a design similar to the competition's which can be produced at a lower cost. In any case, he considers safety only in the form of engineering safety factors. So far as the safety of the consumer is concerned, the designer is likely to insist, as Chick Walsh writes, "that it is not his responsibility to protect the stupid and careless user from himself." ►

This is strong language, but it is a fair description of individuals graduated in one of the engineering disciplines. In less democratic countries than the U.S., designers think of themselves as the "aristocrats" of industry and do not hesitate to say so. In the democratic U.S., they make such statements only to each other, to wives and friends, and to their children while the latter are still young enough to listen and believe.

As an EE myself, I recall that I once shared with my fellow engineers some doubt as to the humanity and rationality of the balance of mankind . . . an attitude which, happily, has been considerably modified since I was exposed by quality control to the problems attendant on producing what the designers design.

But there can't be anything wrong—I designed it!

This elite attitude is not the only factor which tends to disqualify the designer for (consumer) safety engineering. There is the built-in reluctance of every creative individual to accept that there is or may be the probability of a defect in his creation or design. There is good psychological justification for this trait of the creative.

The act of creating or designing may be characterized as positive and optimistic; safety engineering is somewhat negative and pessimistic. Gingerich hit it on the head with his Murphy's Engineers. Incidentally, reliability analysts work in a failure-oriented discipline; they know how difficult it is to persuade designers of the probability of failure.

If you're "into" the manufacture of consumer products, make sure you have a safety engineering group, including nontechnical people as recommended by Chick Walsh, and an adequate supply of Gingerich's ME's. The Industrial and Technological Revolutions were made possible, in part, by disregarding Murphy's Law. The rise of consumerism as a consequence of converting the population into a nation of consumers has given Murphy's Law top billing. None of us should forget it. ☐

Quality motivation

☐ Motivation is an impulse within the individual to want to do something. What we have in mind when we plan to motivate a group is to induce in each individual in the group a desire to do a given job the way it should be done.

Now a great deal of motivated behavior is emulative; many of the attitudes we adopt and the acts we perform during most of our lives are done in imitation of examples set by parents, teachers, colleagues, and public figures. We don't act in accordance with precepts but in emulation of example. Our guides and teachers may say "Don't do as I do. Do as I say"; we smile, but we go right on doing what they do!

Product quality is the ultimate measure

The ultimate measure of a quality assurance program is the quality of the product. We are not forgetting schedule and price; but it will be no good meeting the schedule if the product is shot through with defects. It won't matter how right the price is if the quality isn't right.

The problem is, then, to motivate the production operators to want to machine and assemble defect-free products; that is, products on which all measurable characteristics are within the engineering tolerance limits. This is admittedly, "conformance quality," but we are dealing with the hardware and the men who make it. We must assume hopefully that the engineers were motivated to make an adequate design, and that design reviews have confirmed this. The issue in the work areas is conformance. If the product conforms to the engineering drawings, and the design is adequate, the performance will be satisfactory.

What would motivate the operators to want to make parts without defects? The conviction is that that is what is expected of them, that that is what the managers want them to do. Do they have such a conviction? Disturbing though it may be, the answer is not the resounding affirmation one would like to hear.

The production operators don't have such a conviction because they see and hear on almost every day of their lives that the managers are, or appear to be, tolerant of slight discrepancies. Every operator has seen parts, on which dimensions slightly exceed drawing tolerances, accepted by the Material Review Board. He has seen such parts accepted not once but many times. It doesn't matter that every such acceptance is made by

▶

quality engineers, design engineers and customer's representatives in all good conscience; the operators see what they see. The operators learn that slightly defective parts may be accepted in review.

This is a powerful motivator discouraging them from taking time out to check the setup when they see a trend developing toward the upper or lower limit. The operators have a definition of quality founded upon experience; acceptable quality is the quality standards defined by the engineering tolerance limits, plus a bit. Bear in mind that we are not considering gross defects; nobody has any tolerance for them. We are considering only slight discrepancies, marginal defects of which there are so many. But that isn't all.

There is another almost daily experience demonstrating to production operators that slight variations beyond the engineering tolerance limits won't bring the house down about them. The operators witness many debates about quality. The operator may hear his supervisor challenge an inspector's rejection report, accusing the inspector of being a nitpicker! It's important, if one wishes to understand the quality climate in the work areas, to know what this accusation implies. The accuser is not charging that the reported defect is not there; he agrees that it is there but implies that it is, in his opinion, trifling and why bother with it!

The debate may ultimately involve the shop foreman and the inspection supervisor. It may go higher to the manufacturing manager and the quality manager. If it's near the end of the month, the sales manager may thrust himself into the debate to find out who's holding up his shipments. The operators look and listen with great interest. What they see and hear most of the time from most of the managers is a vote for acceptance. I don't mean an actual vote, because of course only the official Board members may vote, but an expression of sympathy in favor of acceptance.

It isn't suggested that the managers are against quality, but they are so emphatically for the schedule that it tends to dominate their thinking. The relentless pressure of the schedule practically dictates the nature and direction of their spontaneous reaction to the question of what to do with slightly defective material. Their attitudes are quite clear to the operators; indeed, clearer to the operators than to the managers, for the latter are not aware of the effect they create.

The official acceptance of slightly discrepant parts, the engineering credibility gap, and the example set by responsible individuals are factors influencing the quality climate in the work areas. It is a complex situation which cannot be changed overnight. Moreover, it is a situation to which so many are so accustomed that they are no more conscious of it than the fishes are of the sea. Its continued study and the search for solutions should be high on the agenda in any quality motivation program. ☐

Ecclesiasticus on motivation

☐ "As the judge of the people is himself, so are his officers; and what manner of man the ruler of a city is, such are they that dwell within."

So said Ecclesiasticus more than two thousand years ago. Ecclesiasticus went right to the heart of the motivation problem: the mainspring of motivation is example.

Monkey see, monkey do

Motivation, the impulse to complete a given task, to pursue a given course of behavior, must take root within the individual. But the individual does not live in a vacuum. He lives in a social environment which constantly urges upon him, either by precept or example, certain modes of conduct. When young he may give thought to the precepts with which parents, priests and pedagogues engulf him. They may engender within him the impulse, the motivation to act as directed. But when the observed conduct of his mentors differs from their normal behavior, then he is likely to follow the examples as he sees them.

In the world of industrial production the same situation prevails. There are the directions, the pious exhortations to produce quality articles ... and the examples set by management. It is from these examples that machinists and assemblers, clerks and supervisors acquire the attitudes which motivate them to act.

We're being attacked from all sides

The need to motivate the entire working force to strive for quality was never more urgent. U.S. products are being challenged from all points of the compass; especially by Europe and Japan. We rack our brains in a frantic search for more and better techniques of design and production.

Do we believe that the European and Japanese success in outselling us in some items, not only around the world but right here at home is due to

►

their superior technology? Surely not. There will be specific instances here and there, but the fundamental problem is mass production of common consumer articles at competitive prices. And the basic techniques of mass production were developed in the U.S.

Nobody knows better than U.S. industry how to do it. But to succeed, we have to want to do it. The wanting, the desire, the will must exist in the entire workforce. Where is this powerful impulse to come from? Who or what is to motivate the workforce? The managers . . . and particularly top policymaking management. Which brings us back to Ecclesiasticus. How is top management to make it clear to designers and producers that, while every effort must be made to keep the costs down, this is not to be done at the expense of the advertised quality? It's not at all an easy question to answer. In essence, the spirit of mass production is quantity. Every man and woman on the payroll knows it. But quantity and quality have to be reconciled.

The boss must back the program

I don't want to go into the various possible solutions at this time, but only to emphasize that whatever program is offered, including those I have prepared myself, it will get nowhere, or not very far, without top management support. In fact, it's more than support that is needed . . . it is support bolstered by conviction.

Top managers who have not been persuaded by modern industrial psychologists may listen to Ecclesiasticus. ☐

Motivation, money and recognition

□ Is money the best motivator? The almost automatic response is Yes! But is it true?

Industrial psychologists say No! Questionnaires responded to anonymously indicate, they report, that what manual operators rank first most frequently is RECOGNITION.

Why should this be? Especially as we are a people who set great store by money. At least, we profess to do so in conversation. An admiration for money, for bigger and bigger wages and salaries, could amost be said to be the national posture. Yet we don't accord the highest rank to money when we are hidden by anonymity.

The explanation appears to be that if one has a typical industrial job or position (machinist, assembler, supervisor), one is likely to be getting a wage or salary that will satisfy the normal expectations. It will provide for a home far enough out in the suburbs to satisfy one's social pretensions; and an automobile to get from there to the plant; and a station wagon for the family; and the customary appurtenances of affluence: TV, riding lawnmower, electro-mechanical can opener, an occasional paperback novel, and a weekly visit to the local movie. The home may not be a palace, nor the automobile a Rolls Royce, but they're adequate. It is this adequacy we confess to in the privacy of anonymity, while loudly asserting in company that we must have more of everything; and money's what we want to get it with.

Two historical events

But why should "recognition" be the most immediate demand? For an answer, we must look back into industrial history when two great historical events had a profound effect on the daily lives of manual operators.

First was the work of F.W. Taylor at the end of the 19th Century, the net effect of which was to separate work planning from execution. The mechanic who had planned how he would go about a given job, and who customarily used his own tools, was now required to follow an instruction step by step. ►

"Do this with this tool, and that with that tool," said the instructions. "Don't think! Don't take time to consider how in your opinion it might be done better. Do it like the instruction says!" The latter statement wasn't included but was clearly visible to the mechanic.

Second was the introduction of the moving assembly line by Ford in 1916. This ultimate technique of mass production necessitated the reduction of the amount of work done by each man to such a small fraction of the end product that it was difficult for the mechanic to believe that what he did was of any importance.

These events may be thought of as methodological tributaries flowing together to form the broad river of material affluence many now enjoy. But the operators, who share in the affluence, also desire recognition.

This strange social phenomenon is one of several contemporary historical surprises. Such an attitude toward material well-being would not have been predicted even as recently as the 1930's. But there it is.

Two basic "musts"

What should motivation program planners do? Many things, but two in particular. Bring the operators back into planning and make sure that each operator understands the importance of the work he or she does.

We have to recognize that many complex products are of such an advanced technical nature that only a few in a given organization are competent to design and to plan production. But whatever plans are made, they (operations sheets, manufacturing route sheets, travelers) usually finish up in the hands of the operators.

It is highly improbable that every detail planned in the front office will be the best way to do everything. This is where the operators' participation should be invited.

An ECR (error cause removal) program already exists in some plants. It will serve the purpose, but it will be more effective if it is renamed CORRECTIVE PLANNING PROGRAM, for this is what it actually is.

Wise managements will promote seminars at which the company's designers will explain to groups of operators what the end product is about, and what the various components and subassemblies do for it.

This is what may be called recognition by inclusion. It is different from the overt recognition attempted in "human relations" programs (which is not to disparage such programs).

You may be assured in the most sincere tones that you are "in," yet not believe it. But when you're invited to submit corrective planning, and when you confer with the designers on the nature of the end product and the exact significance of the various components, then you know you're in! At least, you're well on the way in! □

The message in the medium

☐ Quality motivation is in a McLuhanesque tangle. In his pronunciamento, "The Medium is the Message," Marshall McLuhan analyses 26 communication media under such provocative titles as: Clothing—Our Extended Skin; Telegraph—The Social Hormone; Radio—The Tribal Drum.

Practically everything on the social scene becomes a medium of communication. For example, clothing may speak louder than words. A management conference participant in San Francisco may wander off to Haight-Ashbury in hope of mingling temporarily with the hippies. But while protesting his sympathy, his clothes shout "I'm a square." They wouldn't even pass him the LSD!

Relevance for quality motivation is that ... while common media for communication between management and operators are written instructions, bulletin board announcements, and exhortations on the PA system ... the most powerful voice to operators is the environment in which they work.

The message the operational environment medium shouts at operators is: "I am a complex production system of which you are merely a part. What d'you think you, as an individual, can do to improve product quality? Do you know what the part you're making will do in the end product? Do you even know what the end product is? If you don't know that, how can you begin to think about improving quality!"

Get it out the door!

Moreover, environment whispers insistently, "Get on with it! Get it out the door!" The whisper rises to a shriek toward the end of the month.

Thus, the most effective communication medium ... call it operational voice ... delivers a message counter to well-meant appeals of quality motivators. ►

Typically, quality motivation campaigns appeal to operators to behave like craftsmen. But what is a craftsman? In exercising his skill in a particular trade, a craftsman would expect to give some thought to planning; he would normally select materials; he would not hesitate to question the design, and possibly rework it.

As an example, it took a Middle Ages' craftsman a year to make a suit of armor. The knight would rely upon the craftsman's knowledge of the best design for flexibility at the joints; to know the best material, and to get it.

Moreover, the knight would not be constantly bugging the craftsman for delivery, beating him about the head with the schedule. Indeed, the knight would be prepared to delay his departure for the Crusades until the job was done to the craftsman's satisfaction.

If motivation is to succeed

Now, is this what quality motivation programs have in mind? This intense interest in the task? This unqualified devotion to the quality of the product? In essence, YES!

Is this what the chief medium of communication between management and operators is saying? NO!

Can the two be reconciled? Today's operators are potentially as capable as their medieval ancestors; they want to share in corporate effort for quality. Thus, if quality motivation campaigns are to succeed, appeal for quality through craftsmanship and messages conveyed by operating environment must be compatible.

Motivation, for operators as for everyone else in the organization, must ultimately come from within. This can be best engendered by knowledge of the end product and its function. Only such knowledge can promote an appreciation for, and a recognition of, the need for specified quality standards. ☐

Ballots on motivation

☐ Early in March, 1969, the Channel Cities Section of ASQC and Buenaventura Section of IEEE ran a seminar on "Motivation for Production of Quality." Organization of the event was a remarkable demonstration of how close to professional excellence a group of committed amateurs may approach; indeed, I don't know what more could have been done by professionals.

Panel participants were Captain O.F. Dreyer, USN, C.O., NSMSES, Port Hueneme; Captain N.D. Champlin, USN, recently appointed Chief of Quality Assurance, DCASR, Los Angeles; James Rossi of Planning Research Corporation, Los Angeles, and this writer.

Awards: Group vs individual?

Success of the event was demonstrated when the panel undertook to answer questions. They were showered with pointed inquiries. Typical was the question whether groups or individuals should be recognized and awarded.

This author, in favor of group awards, was vigorously countering a seminarian's arguments supporting the awarding of individuals when Captain Dreyer clinched the group award view by citing that the Sailor of the Month is the sailor nobody wants to go ashore with!

How they voted

A most interesting aspect of the program was that the seminar attendees (engineers and managers) balloted throughout the day on various questions. In response to the question: *"Would they work if they didn't have to?"* the score was 49—yes and 20—no.

I should explain that "they" were the production operators, inspectors and clerks who ultimately execute all of the plans and designs made by managers and engineers. It is "they" who make and inspect and keep records about the physical product itself. It is "they" whom we hope to motivate to pay meticulous attention to blueprints, production instructions and inspection check lists, and to do it like it says—unless they think there's a better way. In which case, "they" must feel confident to make recommendations to management, without fear of reprisal, and with the knowledge that every recommendation will be evaluated and recognized. ▶

The score, in favor of work, reflects the continued sway of the Protestant Ethic. I think it would be fair to say that our current affluence is largely a product of the Protestant Ethic; but we have yet to find out whether those who make affluence also can enjoy it.

What about money?

In response to the question: *"Is money the chief (or best) motivator?"* the answer was a resounding negative! 51—no versus 14—yes.

For the moment all I want to emphasize is that this was a secret ballot in which every vote was anonymous. Nobody was under compulsion to pay lip service to such cliches as "Money isn't everything." Assuming, that is, that you consider it a cliche.

McGregor's theories of management

This writer outlined McGregor's contrasting theories of Management. "X" type management is concerned primarily with getting the product out on schedule, pushing the people as hard as necessary to this end. The "X" type is also called authoritarian or "tough" management.

On the other hand, "Y" type management pays considerable attention to operators, inspectors and clerks in the belief that when they are involved the product will still get out on time with less defects. The "Y" type is sometimes referred to with pejorative intent as "human relations" type management.

In response to the question: *"Is 'X' or 'Y' type management likely to be more effective?"* the largest majority of the day was scored. 60 for "Y" versus 10 for "X"!

The status of ZD

A ballot on the question: *"Do you believe Zero Defect programs have been successful?"* provoked the response 39—no versus 29—yes. The response, which is not, I suspect, untypical, suggests that some ZD programs may need to be revitalized.

Finally, following some comments by Rossi and the writer on the Japanese Quality Circle and on the status of work, income and motivation in the Orient, the question was put, *"Do you think the idea of the Japanese Quality Circle is likely to catch on in the U.S.?"* The response was 39—no versus 29—yes.

You'll agree that these scores are quite enlightening. They are an indication of the attitudes of engineers and managers which will tend to shape and color the motivation programs they design and promulgate. □

More ballots on motivation

☐ Several months ago I reported the results of ballots taken during a seminar on Motivation for Quality. The seminar was held during March '69 in the Oxnard district of California; sponsors were local sections of ASQC and IEEE. Since then I've taken more ballots in Chicago and Phoenix. I thought you would like to see how the results compare.

In Chicago the occasion was AD QUEM—I, where I spoke on "The Design and Management of a Quality Motivation Program." In Phoenix, last month, the ballots were collected at a Seminar for Motivation sponsored by the Phoenix Section, ASQC.

As you can see from the tabulation, the results are remarkably consistent. While the proportion varies in favor of "yes" over "no," or of "no" over "yes," depending on the question, in no case is the direction of the vote changed. The attitude of the participants, demonstrated by their votes, is highly favorable to the development of successful motivation programs. Successful because the votes reveal a sympathetic attitude toward the "they" of the first question. "They" are the machinists, assemblers, and inspectors who physically manufacture and inspect the product; "they" will exercise care, or not; "they" will produce quality hardware (to the extent their efforts determine the quality), or not, according to the degree they feel motivated to do so.

Therefore, it is important that a majority of the participants (managers, engineers, and technical specialists) feel that "they" would work even if they didn't have to. This is to say that they want to work, they want to be occupied and not idle, they want to be socially useful.

The majority at Oxnard, Chicago, and Phoenix expressed the belief that money is not the chief motivator. This must always come as a shock to anyone who started making a living BA (Before Affluence).

The majority voted overwhelmingly in favor of "Y" type or "human relations" management over authoritarian "X" type management. This augurs well for the success of motivation programs in which such individuals participate.

Are values changing?

It is interesting that a majority thought motivational efforts should be directed at groups and not individuals, and that awards should be made to groups. One might have anticipated that the majority would vote otherwise in a country where the admiration for individualism is so high; but there is an increasing regard for the value of groups in and out of industry.

The consistently negative vote on the success of Zero Defect programs surely indicates the need for review and possible revision. It must be

▶

remembered that many of the participants have a close-up view of such programs.

There was a bare majority for the belief that the Japanese Quality Circle is not likely to catch on in the U.S.

The way things ought to be

It is permissible to speculate that some of the participants voted for the way they believe things ought to be: In the matter of Y type management over X type, for example; or on the question of the value of money as a motivator. Even so the votes remain an indication of current management attitudes, attitudes which have changed considerably from the Thirties and Forties, attitudes which will have considerable influence on the success of motivation programs. □

BALLOTS ON MOTIVATION

Question	Location	Yes	No	Per Cent of total
1. Would they work if they didn't have to?	Oxnard	49	20	71% Yes
	Chicago	—	—	—
	Phoenix	30	26	53% Yes
2. Is money the chief motivator?	Oxnard	14	51	78% No
	Chicago	18	112	86% No
	Phoenix	13	31	70% No
3. Do you believe Z.D. Programs are succeeding?	Oxnard	29	39	57% No
	Chicago	25	105	81% No
	Phoenix	19	29	60% No
4. Do you think the Japanese Quality Circle is likely to catch on in the U.S.?	Oxnard	29	39	57% No
	Chicago	—	—	—
	Phoenix	17	24	58% No
5. Is (McGregor's) X or Y type management likely to be more effective?	Oxnard	60(Y)	10(X)	85% (Y)
	Chicago	98(Y)	31(X)	76% (Y)
	Phoenix	45(Y)	10(X)	82% (Y)
6. Are motivation campaigns likely to be more successful when directed at groups or individuals?	Oxnard	—	—	—
	Chicago	75(gr)	55(ind)	58% group
	Phoenix	29(gr)	17(ind)	63% group

Comments on a motivation survey

□ The EOQC Newsletter for November '74 reported a survey by the Bemis Company of its employees, business students in college, and high school students to determine their feelings about work-motivating factors. There were some surprising results: money scored high; "quality of supervision" scored low; "company policies and administration" scored nowhere!

The following table shows the average ranking of 10 motivating factors (1 is first choice; 10 is last).

		Bemis Employees Both Sexes	Combined Student Groups
1.	Recognition for a job well done	3	6
2.	Wages or salary	1	2
3.	Quality of supervision	6	9
4.	Liking the work itself	2	1
5.	Friendly co-workers	8	5
6.	Responsibility I am given	7	4
7.	Good working conditions	9	7
8.	Chance for growth and advancement	4	3
9.	The company policies and administration	10	10
10.	A chance for achievement	5	8

Employees put money first; the students put it second. These scores are a corrective to the growing belief, or the desire to believe, that there are several things employees like better than money. It's no crime to like money; top executives, when surveyed, typically rank financial rewards first. "Not," they said, "that we can't live on $50,000 a year, or $90,000, or whatever. But what motivates us is recognition, and there's no recognition like more money." ▶

The scores on "Quality of supervision"—6th for employees and 9th for students, are a surprise. One works not so much for the company as for one's immediate superior. He may be competent or fumbling, helpful or disinterested, compatible or antagonistic . . . but whatever he is, he has to be lived with 8 hours a day, 5 days a week. Quality of supervision is a critical motivating factor. Although students may not be aware of it, the employees should know from experience.

Western Electric revisited

Low scores of 9 and 7 on "good working conditions" seem like an echo of the Hawthorne Experiment in the Twenties. Are the scores of 10 and 10 on "Company policies and administration" a condemnation of them? Or are the employees and students simply saying, "Don't know. What are they? Never heard of them."

It would have been reasonable to expect a sharp difference in response between employees and students; but this was not the case. They were never more than 3 points apart on any factor.

If items, 1, 2, 4, 6, 8 and 10 are rated as "individualistic" (the individual is considering himself), and if items 3, 5, 7 and 9 are "social" (the individual is considering the group), we find the total score for the 4 "social" factors is equal to 64 (average score = 16), while the total score for the 6 "individualistic" factors equals 46 (average score = 7.6). Keeping in mind that low scores indicate the employees' preference, the message that emerges from this survey is that employees and students alike place factors favoring the individual substantially ahead of social factors. This is an important indicator which, if kept in mind when planning motivational programs, will add a touch of realism. □

Attitudes, quality and cost

☐ An attitude may be defined as a powerful non-verbal communication; on occasion it may be heard far more clearly than the words issuing from the speaker's mouth. Attitudes and changes of attitude have shaped the course of history. Kings have lost their heads because the people lost their reverential attitude. Governments tremble and ministers of state are filled with apprehension as they fearfully study the polls reflecting the public's attitude.

What about attitudes, quality, and cost in the world of industry? In the first case, we may note that they are commonly spoken of as cost and quality by those who have the authority to rank them; which is already a strong attitudinal clue. The cost constraint is all-pervading. It sinks into the consciousness of every operating manager and technician. It motivates them to look not for the best solution, but for the one that fits the cost structure. The euphemism is to say that one is looking for the "optimum."

Cost-constraints shade our solutions

The adopted solution may indeed be the best solution, the best at the price, but the manager or technician does not necessarily know this. He has not been seeking the best solution, but a cost-compatible solution. His imagination has been delineated and directed by an attitude of which he may not be aware.

It is not implied that the manager or technician should not keep the cost constantly in mind. After all, he is being guided by a simple rule to which we all subscribe: the most quality for the least cost. But his thinking is circumscribed, and the adopted solution is characterized, by the prime importance he attaches to the cost. There is a vast difference between seeking the best solution for quality and paring it down to fit the cost, and studying only such solutions as fit the cost. ▶

Another attitudinal clue is management's tolerance for the constant questioning of inspection rejection notices. Practically all operating managers indulge in this pleasant sport. A brand of coffee was once advertised on the billboards by the hedonistic imperative: INDULGE YOURSELF. It is as though the same tolerant invitation were understood by all men of authority in the operating areas. On occasion, the defect is so gross as to silence with shame the protest of the perpetrator, but normally there will be a challenge.

Let's all play "Challenge The Rejection Notice"

As a consequence, large quantities of discrepant material are submitted in review and some of it is accepted. The inspectors, who see their work thrown out of the window as it were, become discouraged, and by imperceptible stages become tolerant of marginal discrepancies. Production reacts to the lowered acceptance standard and a general decline of quality is precipitated.

What radical solution might be attempted? Is it ever possible to improve quality and reduce cost at the same time? It all depends on the attitude of management.

It would be possible to improve the quality, and to reduce scrap and rework and the cost of inspection if top management lets it be known:

- that constant challenges of inspection rejection notices would not be tolerated.
- that the main drive in material reviews must be to find out why Purchasing bought or Production made the discrepant material or parts.
- that a member of top management would sit in on, say, one of four reviews.

When it was known that top management was as likely to sound off furiously against Production for making defective material as against the "nitpicking" inspectors for detecting it, the quality would improve rapidly.

It is not that producers deliberately make defective parts, or that they are not concerned for the company's welfare. On the contrary! The situation is that they do what is tolerated. They tend to believe quite logically that what is tolerated is what is wanted. For too many years they have heard too many inspectors condemned as nit-pickers, and too few producers condemned for making what the inspectors found. Management's attitude is manifested by such acts.

Management's attitude is the true dictator of operating policy and the ultimate determinant of the quality of the product. □

Economic man?

☐ We made a survey of current articles on quality assurance and found that about half were exhortations to reduce cost. These earnest sermons were addressed to everyone in the q.a. business: managers, analysts, statisticians and inspectors. We found ourself wondering whether cost reduction can be achieved by individual effort or by such appeals.

The individual may fulfill his or her assigned task within the prescribed time, thereby supporting the cost structure at the planned level. But while there can be no cost reduction without such disciplined execution of the schedule—whatever the schedule may be—this is not necessarily cost reduction. The individual may exercise care to perform his or her assigned tasks correctly. This again is not necessarily cost reduction, although there can be no cost reduction without such conscientious individuals.

What, exactly, is cost reduction?

Cost reduction is a plan; a management plan. Cost reduction plans are brought into existence because in a given situation it is believed that costs are too high, or it is suspected that they may be. The belief or suspicion is most likely to take root in the mind of someone at the management level. Only at this level can the various factors: cost, selling price, administrative charges, etc., be brought into perspective for comparison. The man in the stokehold can only shovel coal vigorously. He can't know that the effort is being wasted because the ship is on the wrong course. And even if he suspected it, what can he do? Stop shoveling and bring the ship to a standstill, hoping that in the confusion the pilot will hit upon the right course?

Making plans for cost reduction is a function of management. It is the fact that some reduction of costs can almost always be effected, but only when there has been a careful preliminary survey from the management level and when a specific plan has been drawn up. The plan must include

▶

one or more radical changes: It may introduce sampling where there was none before; or reduce the overall number of operations; or simplify one or more operations; or revise standards of acceptance—particularly visual standards which are notoriously difficult to define and which by some perverse logic of their own tend to get more and more severe if not controlled. And there is always the "paper."

Pare down the paperwork

Documentation has a natural tendency to multiply. Documentary records require signatures and this is flattering to the signers—I mean to all of us; none of us is proof against this kind of vanity. Documentary records preserve events and actions which otherwise would vanish from the memory like smoke. This is gratifying to individuals and departments who see some part of their daily lives rescued from oblivion by widely distributed reports. It is understandable, therefore, that documentation should multiply. Economies can be effected, but only by objective planning.

Now, if cost reduction is a job for managers, why badger everybody about it all the time? It is a depressing experience for engineers and inspectors trying to do a good technical job to be constantly needled about cost reduction. Management must create the environment in which good technical performance contributes to planned cost reduction.

Furthermore, appeals to everybody to work at cost reduction implies that everybody is economically motivated, that all men are economic men. History demonstrates that this is not objectively true and most individuals know as a matter of daily experience that it isn't subjectively true either. Which makes it the more surprising that we continue to make such appeals and probably explains why they fall on deaf ears.

Appeal to the right people

It is impossible to organize a rational cost reduction plan without solid support from quality assurance, but the appeal must be for quality and not for cost reduction. Appeals addressed to everybody on the payroll to make an individual effort for quality can be highly successful, as the current "Zero Defects" programs demonstrate. But to appeal to everybody to work at cost reduction?!

The rule should be: Motivate production operators, inspectors and engineers to perform at a high level of technical excellence and let management planning make sure the cost is right. □

What's on the mind of the inspector?

☐ What's on the mind of the inspector? I suppose the copy book answer would be, "Quality, the quality of the parts he, or she, is inspecting." But it isn't true. Or, rather it isn't likely to be true until certain steps have been taken to make it so.

What's on the mind of the inspector is the constant prodding and questioning of expeditors from production control and purchasing, exclamations of shock and disbelief from production supervisors, agonized inquiries from the sales department.

Expeditors are insatiable: "Why this?" "Why that?" "Why, everything?"

"Why don't you inspect these brackets? The line is held up waiting for them!"

"Why did you reject those parts? They look usable to me!"

"Why did you put those shafts into material review? Can't you make up your own mind!"

"Get this monkey off my back!"

A production supervisor, already harassed by an "unrealistic" schedule, by the late arrival of raw material, by the breakdown of a critically needed machine, is in no mood to smile amiably on receipt of a rejection notice. What he ought to do is to congratulate the inspector on his sharp eyes, saying, "I'm so glad you found this defect in these urgently needed parts. I can't see the defect myself, but I'm sure it's there if you say so." He's much more likely to say . . . "!!XXBB."

It's tough to be in the sales department and to have to tell the customer that parts cannot be shipped today despite yesterday's fervent assurance that they were practically on the way! After all, they had arrived in final inspection when the promise was given, and who was to know that the nitpicking inspectors would reject them? ▶

It is not suggested that expeditors should not question, or that harassed production supervisors should not sound off, or that salesmen should not make heart-broken appeals; but it is suggested that the inspectors should not be on the receiving end of questions, outbursts and appeals!

Don't let the work environment influence your inspector

When an inspector is wondering what he will say when the expeditor wants to know, Why? Why? When?—or how he will respond if the foreman of the milling section sounds off again—or how he can keep the people from sales off his back—he doesn't have much time to think about quality. He's going to become confused and distracted. The more it appears to him that he is being left to bear the brunt of questions and complaints alone, the more confused and distracted he will become. The quality suffers as defects are missed in the confusion; indeed, the inspector may develop a subconscious bias in favor of letting borderline defects go by to alleviate the environmental pressures.

To assure the quality of the product, the quality manager must know that what is on the minds of the inspectors is quality. The inspectors must be looking for defects with no subconscious motivation not to see them. The prime task of quality control supervisors is to create an environment in which the inspectors can work without interference; the supervisor himself, or an appointed assistant must absorb all inquiries and exclamations.

The creation of a working environment favorable to quality would include other time-saving and confusion-minimizing features. For example, the inspector shouldn't have to chase around trying to find the latest drawing change. He should have a sufficient knowledge of, and faith in the calibration system to be sure that any gage issued to him is accurate.

It's good management to ask what's on the mind of the inspector (or of any other functionary in an operational situation) and to investigate to what degree operation behaviour squares with the conventional or copybook answer.   □

Motivating the skeptical producer

*Skeptic: from the Greek skeptikos; thoughtful,
reflective, one who doubts.*

☐ We don't mean to suggest that all producers are skeptics or that being skeptical is an essential qualification for producers. But as everyone knows who has spent time in a machine shop or on assembly lines, production personnel have a decidedly skeptical attitude toward the engineering drawings. They just don't believe the specified tolerance limits are firm or, rather, they are skeptical about them. Production supervisors aren't silent on this point either, but what they have to say rarely gets through to top management.

What makes them this way? Experience. About 20 years of experience. For about that long, production supervisors and operators have had it drummed into them that the drawings don't mean what they say! For 20 years, they've witnessed reviews of discrepant material at which the question was debated as to whether parts varying slightly from specification should be used, reworked or tossed in the scrap barrel.

And they use the discrepant parts

Frequently, although not every time (but often enough to leave a strong impression on the minds of producers), the decision was to use the parts. Furthermore, the heart of the decision was an engineering judgment that the parts, although not inside the tolerance limits set by the engineers, could be used without adversely affecting interchangeability and without adverse effect on the performance of the end product. These were formal reviews attended by engineering and quality control personnel and, frequently, by a representative of the customer. Each review was, in effect, a review of the design by the design engineer, for only he was competent to decide whether a nonconforming part would or would not affect the performance of the end product.

Thus, it has appeared to the producers that a decision to use parts outside the specified tolerance limits was a confession by the engineer that he had set the limits tighter than was necessary. ▶

When the producer has seen this happen many times, he learns. If he's a machinist, his reaction is to think twice before resetting a machine just because the parts are crowding the high or low limit. In this condition, it's likely the machine will soon be cutting parts outside the tolerance limits, but he's learned that such parts have a chance of being accepted in review anyway. In fact, he may recall similar parts that were accepted with a small discrepancy the previous week. It seems foolish not to give it a try.

"Load 'em up!"

Jobs may be assigned to machines by production planners or the shop foreman. No matter who does it, the tendency is to load machines to the limit of capability. This practice increases the probability that marginally discrepant parts will be made, but planners and foremen want to get the most out of the machines and there's always a chance discrepant parts may be "bought" in review.

But that isn't all. Inspectors learn too. It would be an unobservant inspector who hadn't caught on to the fact that rejected parts don't necessarily stay rejected; they may be accepted in review. He learns from experience and arrives at the conclusion that it would be a waste of everybody's time to reject parts which he feels convinced would be accepted in review.

Producers and inspectors have come to believe that the designers do specify tighter tolerance limits than they need for satisfactory performance of the end product. Designers have been known to confess that this is so, but whether it be so or not, many producers and inspectors believe it.

It isn't suggested that material review decisions are ever arrived at except in good conscience; nor is it suggested that marginally discrepant parts should not be reviewed. But we must recognize the effects on producers and inspectors, and we must also recognize that producers and inspectors are not to be condemned for learning from experience.

The skepticism of producers and inspectors is a potent influence on quality and cost. It cannot be dismissed by edict. It will decline only as producers and inspectors have reason to believe that the drawing limits are firm; that they represent a true maximum permissible tolerance. □

"I only work here!"

☐ When you hear one of your operators say, "What's it to me—I only work here!," you have a motivation problem. Indeed, you have a demotivated individual; and where there is one there may be more.

"What is the man's problem?"

Well, he feels excluded.

"Excluded from what?"

From any real participation in the work he does day after day.

"What more does he want? I mean, who does more than he does; he does the actual work!"

Yes, and that's the trouble. He does the work, but someone else plans it.

"Somebody has to plan it."

True, but does the operator have to be excluded entirely from the planning?

"It would be a hell of a mess if everybody got into the planning!"

It's a bit of a mess the way it is. Look at the money we spend, and the kind of quality we get.

"You think it would be better if the operator had a hand in the planning?"

Sure!

"What do I have to do?"

You can start by involving the operator in planning for corrective action when the rejection rate is high. You can keep him informed about the quality performance by graphic displays big enough to be seen, and clear enough to be understood at a glance. There's a lot you can do, but first, you must believe that the involvement of the operator is both necessary and worthwhile; then you will do what has to be done from conviction.

You might reasonably ask why the operators should be motivated, or for that matter, what is motivation? Motivation is what inert materials and automated devices don't require; but operators are human and they do. As an illustration, when you see a stone dislodged from the face of a cliff start falling you know it is responding to gravitational pull; you don't assume that it has taken thought before making the plunge saying, "Ah, this will show them!"

But if an individual should jump off the same cliff you would assume he had taken thought about it, that he felt compelled to do so. You might disagree with him, but the point is that you would credit him with having made a plan. The stone and the man both do the same thing, but you assume that the man was motivated.

You are familiar with the separation of planning and execution introduced by Frederick W. Taylor at the turn of the century and generally referred to as scientific management. Now, one of the effects, though not the intention, of the separation of execution from planning has been to equate the operator with a stone.

Production operators are human, too

"Scientific management" assumes that the operator will plunge into the prescribed task without motivation. It assumes, or rather, disregards the vital fact that the operator feels a need to give some thought to the task, he must convince himself that this or that is the best way to do it. That is, he must feel motivated; he must because he's human.

Management might wish that the man, in return for wages or salary, would perform like an automaton; indeed, the man himself might wish that for the 8 hours a day during which he must earn a living he could function without thought, without reflection. But he can't; he's stuck with his human heritage.

Thus, the separation of execution from planning motivates the manager (who is given the opportunity to do what all humans inherently need to do), while it demotivates the operator. I say "demotivates" because the human individual appears to be incapable of indifference. If the individual does not feel motivated, then he tends to feel demotivated and excluded.

Studies made by industrial psychologists and sociologists all concur in the conclusion that the sense of participation is a powerful and necessary motivating influence, both as it allows the individual to make a constructive contribution, and as it gives him the sense of being included, of belonging. Such individuals are worth more to themselves and to the company. When they participate in the pursuit of quality, the company's resources are engaged to the full. ☐

Motivation and the 'hippy'

☐ Is there any connection between motivation and the "hippy?" There might be . . . so let's take a look.

As applied to the quality profession, motivation programs are concerned with industrial behavior . . . which is but one example of human behavior in general. It may be assumed that behavior in one area of human activity is, at least, an indicator of what may be expected in other areas. This being so, it might be worthwhile to look at that completely unanticipated phenomenon, the "hippy" movement among college kids.

By "kids" I mean children born during and since WW II . . . and, of course, I don't mean yours. But they're somebody's sons and daughters, and those somebodies are all decent citizens: managers, engineers, technicians, professionals . . . all moderately prosperous, all having nice homes in the suburbs. That is, they, the parents, are like us; unless you aren't old enough to have made it into Squaresville.

The land of milk and honey

Now, Squaresville is the land of affluence. The affluent are far from being disgustingly rich, but they are more than merely "comfortable." Not only have they chosen to live in the suburbs, but they've paid for a view lot and can see across the neighbor's roof to the smog-shrouded mountains beyond. There's no question about having an automobile; the question is: how many, and should they be Mustangs, Aston-Martins, or Cadillacs? The house may be a thing of elegance or an architectural abomination, but it will have a patch of lawn out front and a pool in back. Television sets will drool, or rock, or "controversialize" in several rooms.

Affluenza (the Square's wife) will wear a Carnaby Street mini skirt if she dares, and tight capris if she dares not. (The length of the mini skirt presents an interesting problem in economics; the price is inversely proportionate to the length, and it's only the consequent astronomical price that prevents them from shrinking to almost nothing.)

There's no question about the kids going to college; the only question is where? Vacations abroad are so common for so many as to have created a new industry: the travel agencies. Almost every traveler has an expensive camera, and hardly anyone has read the operating instructions. But it doesn't matter, because cameras aren't primarily for taking pictures, but are bought and gifted as a function of affluence. ▶

Significant social phenomenon

Such is the land of affluence. It is inhabited by two distinct groups: the parents and the kids, the providers and the beneficiaries. And the beneficiaries are rejecting it! At least, many of them do; a sufficiently large fraction is rebelling to make the rejection a significant social phenomenon.

Why should a large fraction of the beneficiaries of the first affluent society in the history of the world reject what so many have striven for so long to achieve?

We don't know. Is it that affluence itself, in some totally unanticipated manner, is burdensome? Or is it that the gift of so much demands gratitude . . . and gratitude is a sentiment we are reluctant to express? Or is it that we are genetically programmed for adversity and are, therefore, repelled by affluence? We have yet to find out and the answer's going to be important for the future. How, for example, are we going to react to the abundance promised by automation?

What's the relevance for motivation programs? In the Thirties or Forties it would have been reasonable to assume that material benefits would command gratitude and provoke an appropriate response. The promise of material benefit would have been a sufficient motivator.

The best motivator

Since then, a number of studies made by industrial consultants and psychologists, studies in which machinists and managers answer a string of questions anonymously, have indicated that money is not first on the "What I Want the Most" list. Recognition is the most desired, and therefore the best motivator. But what kind of recognition?

To make production operators feel that they are recognized, that they belong, has been the goal of many human relations programs. The programs have been characterized by a kind of uncritical tolerance. Results have been sometimes disappointing and well-intentioned managements have wondered why. It may be that individuals programmed for adversity are suspicious when things are too easy and, as a result, respond cautiously; it may be that to be properly motivated they need an obstacle or, at the very least, criticism.

We don't know, but we have to learn. Contemporary experience is shattering assumptions that few would have questioned prior to WW II. We must build motivation programs on valid assumptions about human behaviour. ☐

The perils of affluence

☐ "Any questions?"

"Yes. How do we motivate our employees?"

"Well, individuals can be motivated to do many things. What do you want to motivate them to do the most?"

"To be there."

"To be there?"

"Yes, to be there. To be on the job. Not to be absent!!!"

That was it! They had pinpointed one of the major problems confronting industry today: absenteeism.

I had been invited to design a seminar on the management of small businesses. The theme I developed was that the small business is not merely a smaller version of the large corporation and should not be managed as though it were.

At our meeting, an interesting debate ensued around the plague of absenteeism. Comments and opinions were shooting every which way. It was obvious that the routine remedies had all been tried without permanent success. So I asked, "What do you do about the chronic absentee?"

"Fire him," called out one owner-manager.

But what if he is one of your best men?

"No, you don't," called out another, "not if he's one of your best men, you don't." There were sounds of general agreement with the second speaker. Their employees are skilled manual workers; they are getting to be a rarity in our upwardly mobile, increasingly white collar society. Skilled manual workers are hard to replace.

"When do they stay out?" I asked.

Half a dozen voices called out "Fridays and Mondays" to the accompaniment of general laughter.

"What do you think would stop it?"

Voice from the back, "A good stiff depression!"

"Let's hope not," I said, "but you've put your finger on the problem. You've found the clue."

"How come?"

▶

"Not only are we not in a depression, with everybody fighting for a few available jobs, but since the war we've been in a state of affluence unprecedented in the history of the world. It's 'receded' a bit recently but many are still affluent. And that includes your skilled workers. They're affluent, too."

"Does that give them the right to take time off?"

"It isn't a question of 'right.' It's a question of what might be called 'living in the spirit of the times.' TV, radio, magazines, newspapers and pop concerts all cry out that the times are good. So live it up! So that's what well-paid blue collar guys do. What are they going to do with that small power boat if they don't hitch it up to the Buick and take off for the nearest lake for a long weekend?"

"What about our schedules?"

Look to the averages

"That's the real problem. But since you haven't succeeded in eliminating absenteeism entirely and neither have the big corporations, you could look at the situation realistically. What are your average absentee rates?"

Various figures were called out from the floor, ranging up to 4%.

"Okay, since you know your average absentee rates, why don't you base schedules on expected average attendance? Let's say you have 54 producers. That should give 8,640 hours for a month of four 40 hour weeks. But if you average 3 absentees on Fridays and Mondays, you're going to lose 48 hours a week and 192 for the month. That's 2.2% of the total. You could build the schedule on that basis."

"Couldn't we make it up?"

"You could hire more people. But it costs money to hire. And you take the risk that it might rain on Friday and everybody comes in and you're overloaded. You could make it up with overtime. You might be able to absorb the overtime premium into the sales price. In any case, the thing to do is not to give yourselves monthly headaches by making schedules based on the assumption that everybody's going to be on board nice and early every day just like it was before affluence descended upon us. Do everything you can to minimize absenteeism; keep precise records on it and make rational schedules."

There is a remarkable reluctance on the part of management, large and small, to recognize that affluence is a part of the ambience permeating many industrial plants; that relatively well-paid manual workers are susceptible to it, too. You don't have to be knocking down $90,000 a year to be able to take Friday and Monday off; you can do it nicely on some of the wages currently being paid to skilled manual workers. □

Japanese quality control

☐ The quality of Japanese products confronts us at every turn. Indeed, the high quality of Japanese articles is rapidly becoming a by-word in the market. This is the more surprising because prior to World War II almost the exact opposite was the case. It was said that Japanese products were "cheap copies" of European or American models. The word "cheap" applying not only to the price—but even more so to the quality.

This was probably a gross libel, but many believed it—and it is what people believe that matters.

What happened to hoist such a poor reputation to almost the top of the quality scale—if not the top? Well . . . the Japanese really got down to the production of quality articles.

"But," you might say, "who doesn't? Competition compels everybody to strive for quality." Yes—but it depends on what you strive with.

QC was first and foremost

What the Japanese did was to attack the problem with formal QUALITY CONTROL. Quality control was applied comprehensively, not piecemeal. Quality control was applied as a stringent discipline guiding the actions of all from assembly operators to general manager. Quality control was adopted enthusiastically, not reluctantly.

The degree of enthusiasm was made manifest by the spontaneous formation of Quality Circles among production operators and first line supervisors. This remarkable phenomenon broke out in 1962 and has, since then, expanded to truly amazing proportions. The best and, I believe, the first account of the Japanese Quality Circle to appear in the U.S. is Dr. Juran's article in the January '67 issue of *Industrial Quality Control.*

As Dr. Juran writes, it is not only the managers and engineers who are familiar with Quality Control's statistical techniques, but the operators too. The operators have been instructed in the analytical approach; Pareto and Ishikawa are as familiar to them as film stars. ▶

How and why did it happen? In the first case it must be recognized as an historical event of major importance, like the advent of F.W. Taylor in the U.S. And it is sufficiently recent to be able to trace the course of events. In the years after the war, two outstanding advocates of the systems approach, of statistical analysis and of formal quality control were invited to Japan. These, known to all of you, were W.E. Deming and J.M. Juran.

They listened . . . and became enthused

They were listened to by Japanese businessmen and managers—at first with careful attention—and then with enthusiasm. Seminars for managers, engineers, and technicians were organized and enthusiastically attended. Japanese industry took off on the rapid climb to its current pre-eminence in quality.

Don't let it be thought for one second that it is stated or implied that Deming and Juran were solely responsible for the spectacular Japanese quality performance. But I doubt if any responsible industrialist in Japan would deny the significance of their contribution.

Now, what did Deming and Juran do? Well—they lectured, and seminared, and expounded on quality control and statistical analysis and the systems approach. And the Japanese listened and absorbed all that was said.

But the Japanese could have read all about it in books. Many are available. By means of books they could have acquired all the necessary information. But to be informed is not necessarily to be *moved*.

That is what Deming and Juran did—they moved the Japanese—they imbued them with the "idea" of quality control. Once the Japanese "dug" the idea of formal quality control, the rest was (relatively) easy.

What the story illustrates is the great value of prior advocacy, the motivating power of the "idea." And the moral of the story is that every quality manager should see himself as an advocate of the idea of quality control. Those brilliant plans, those scintillating applications of statistical technology will receive little attention until those on high, who alone can authorize their adoption, have been prepared by prior advocacy; until, in marketplace English, top management has been sold on the idea. ☐

A training course for supervisors

□ I was called on recently to develop a training course for the supervisors of a company which mass-produces appliances. "The quality is falling off," said management. "What we would like you to do is to tell the supervisors how to motivate the workers to do good work."

The quality manager had statistics which demonstrated that the quality was indeed falling off, although not catastrophically. I didn't question the assertion that the workers were short on motivation, because this is an almost automatic response on the part of management . . . and, of course, it might be true.

Is there dissension in the ranks?

Did the supervisors think there was a morale problem? There was scattered assent, but no rousing confirmation of management's opinion. Towards the end of the meeting I asked each supervisor to take a sheet of paper and complete the sentence: "To reduce the defect rate in my department I should have . . . " There was no limit to the number of needs each man could list.

To reduce the defect rate in my department I should have:

	Score
Better job instructions	18
Better tooling and equipment	11
Better interest in job	10
An active Q.C. program	8
Rewards for good work	7
Improved schedules and planning	7
Better supervision	6
Better communication between depts.	5

There were 19 other "needs" for a total of 27 with low scores of 1, 2 and 3. The total number of scores was 109.

Thus, only 8 out of 27 different needs accounted for 72 scores, or 66% of the total. The first 3 alone accounted for 36% of the total. The Pareto analysis with all 27 needs and scores was blown up poster size and from then on it became the agenda. ▶

The first complaint happens far too frequently. Job instructions are usually written by production or industrial engineers, competent individuals who can always explain what they have written. That is the trouble, that they need explaining.

Rolling right along

At subsequent meetings, the industrial and production engineers came in to defend their instructions. There were some noisy and productive debates. Indeed, from here on out the course went along like a house on fire. The tooling engineers joined us and the tools were anatomized. The quality manager and his supervisors stood up to defend the Q.C. program. It was a good program, but it turned out that the supervisors didn't read the reports circulated to them (they said they didn't have the time). This is a common complaint and is true enough. In a busy factory, the first line supervisors have plenty to do without reading reports. It was agreed to have poster size defect charts displayed in each section.

The 7th item, "Better supervision," was not a case of the supervisors beating on themselves; it was what they wanted from their supervisors! The debates about the schedules were hot and heavy because of the nearly universal practice of over-optimistic scheduling. One of the planners said that no individual could do his best unless the goal was just beyond his reach . . . and some of the supervisors agreed with him! The problem for them was how much beyond?

Increase the inherent interest level

When it came to "better interest in the job" I put it to the group that the interest had to be provoked by the job itself, that individuals could not be prodded by motivation schemes to take an interest in a job which was, by its nature, essentially boring. We agreed that, while mass production pours out tons of goodies, it does so at the expense of creating many boring jobs. Management and the industrial engineers agreed to give some thought to the restructuring of jobs to increase the inherent interest level.

There's a special atmosphere which can be generated in a seminar and when you can get it going behind a Pareto analysis you have the combination for maximum information exchange and learning. With everyone moving along in the same groove, it took only six months to cut the scrap and rework rate by almost 60% for substantial $ savings.   □

What supervisors look for

☐ "Name categories of performance you would utilize when reviewing a subordinate." This was one of a number of questions in a mid-term test put to students of a course, "Problems in Industrial Supervision." The course is given at one of the many colleges in the Los Angeles area. The "students" are all adult employes and most are first line supervisors. I thought you might like to see the results.

Why do "Attendance" and "Attitude" occupy the first two positions at the head of the Pareto array? Would you have expected such a result? Why not "Quantity" and "Quality" which are, after all, what the entire manufacturing effort is all about. I think the students are telling us something about conditions on the line. Their responses indicate clearly what they require of the line workers so that they, the supervisors, can complete their own assignments.

Be there—and be cooperative

Why do they value attendance and attitude so much? Because, presumably, they find themselves in their daily lives as supervisors, confronted by too much absenteeism, lateness and by uncooperative attitudes.

Absenteeism and tardiness seem to be on the increase. Why? Because more and more businesses, institutions and bureaucracies are adopting personnel policies which protect employes from arbitrary supervisory action. There is no immediate penalty for being absent or late. A determined supervisor may accumulate a record on an employe which may, in time, bring down some punishment on the head of the employe but, in the meantime, the employe continues taking long weekends starting Thursday evening, and is not too much concerned when caught in a traffic tie-up on the freeway. The uncooperative attitude may be deliberate exploitation of protective personnel policies, or it may be no more than a relaxed response to the same policies. ►

It was to be expected that "Job knowledge" would rank high. However, even this score may bear witness to a desire for well-trained employes which supervisors find is not fulfilled as frequently as it might be. This, again, might be a consequence of personnel policies, both local and national; policies which are an expression of the national sentiment for equality of opportunity.

And look at the bottom of the list

The scores at the bottom of the list are equally significant as indicators of conditions on the line. Perhaps what the supervisors are saying is that initiative is fine, and so is the ability to communicate, but let's get the job done first . . . and to get the job done, what the supervisors want most is that their subordinates should be present and on time!

Again, it may be that the low scores for "initiative" and "ability to communicate" are an accurate reflection of what is wanted or, rather, of what is not wanted on mass production lines. Mass production, whether of hardware or clerical products, requires that the workers follow instructions, period!

Would executives have anticipated such results? Not too many, I suspect. "Initiative" and "Ability to communicate" are holy words in front offices, and so they should be. The executives may have far worse attendance records than any of the people on the line, but then, as they would say, they aren't working for the company only when they sit in that office. One cannot argue from a knowledge of conditions in the front offices as to what conditions are, or should be, on the line. The only way to find out is to ask supervisors.   □

Attendance	28
Attitude	26
Job knowledge	22
Quantity (work performance)	21
Quality (also referred to as accuracy)	21
Getting along with people; adaptability	9
Regard for safety regulations	5
Appearance	5
Use of time (this, perhaps, might have been classed with quantity)	5
Initiative	5
Ability to communicate	2

Supervisors rate motivating factors

☐ What do supervisors think about motivation? The question is particularly relevant because management assigns first line supervisors the responsibility for motivating the manual work force.

Motivational programs originated by management are launched with a fanfare and then left to the supervisors to put into effect. In most instances, supervisors are not asked whether they are in sympathy with the program, or whether they think it may or may not succeed, or how they would do it if it were up to them.

While reviewing the final examination papers of a group of supervisors who had taken a course in "Industrial Management," I was struck by the response to a question on motivation. 32 of the 34 taking the course were supervisors in charge of groups varying from 4 to 78 people.

The question on motivation was: How would you rate the following as motivating factors? Recognition; the human environment (attitude of supervisors, etc.); money; self-satisfaction (a feeling of accomplishment). Explain why you put the first item first.

The scores for first place were:

Self-satisfaction 12
Recognition 11
Money 9
Human environment 2
                                       ──
                                       34

Who's motivating whom?

What shook me was the score of only 2 out of 34 for the "human environment." Keep in mind that these men and women were supervisors. They were the missionaries management would rely upon to spread the word for motivation. Yet the almost unanimous negative response to the "human environment" as a motivating factor seems to indicate that first line supervisors don't identify with management! ▶

In effect, 32 out of 34 did not see themselves as administrators of motivation programs. They replied as though they would be on the receiving end. This despite the fact that the title "supervisor" most of them held was written into the question.

The slow progress, or downright failure of many motivation programs is undoubtedly due, in part, to the fact that first line supervisors aren't "with it." Motivation programs are something imposed by "them" (management). They are not prepared and promulgated by "us" (the supervisors and their fellow managers). Which raises the question of what should be done to make first line supervisors feel and act like a part of management; but that's another question. For the moment let's realize that it's a very real problem.

Self-satisfaction through recognition

The remaining scores are interesting because of the contrast between self-satisfaction and recognition on the one hand, and money on the other. Self-satisfaction and recognition may be more closely related than is first apparent. It is not usually a private experience, although it sounds that way. It may be private for those exceptional individuals who achieve self-actualization in the style of Abraham Maslow, but most of us enjoy self-satisfaction more if colleagues and supervisors agree that we have just cause for it. Recognition greatly enhances self-satisfaction. If self-satisfaction and recognition are linked together, the joint score becomes an overwhelming 23 out of 34.

The score of only 9 out of 34 in favor of money as the prime motivator confirms a reported trend away from cash money. The trend is toward socio-economic fringe benefits and psychological rewards, one of which is recognition . . . which is in short supply because the supervisors who could hand it out don't see themselves in that role. □

Is the Umwelt good for your quality?

☐ Umwelt may be translated from the German as the "perceptual world." I came across this phrase in "The Parable of the Beasts" by Bleibtrue. It's an account of the response of animals to the world as they perceive it . . . and of the perceived world as a determinant of behaviour. It's a fascinating book, but I shouldn't get into quoting from it or I'll never get around to quality . . . yet quality is what it's about . . . the quality of behaviour, and its dependence on the world as perceived. Anyway, it's in paperback and I recommend it to you.

I thought we might examine the perceptual world of industrial machinists and assemblers in the hope of finding a clue as to why there's so little quality when there are so many cheers for it; so little quality, that is, if one judgest by the rising tide of product liability claims, and the increasing number of recall campaigns.

Don't blame it all on the operators

The machinists and assemblers aren't by any means solely responsible for quality, or for the lack of it. They don't design the product, neither do they select the parts and components, nor do they plan the operations they are required to execute . . . but they *are* expected to machine parts to close tolerances, and to put the product together all tight and secure.

The "world" of the manual workers for eight hours a day is the machine shop and the assembly lines, plus expeditors, supervisors and managers. Does that world, as they perceive it, encourage dedication to quality? If machinists and assemblers in mass-production plants from Connecticut to Colorado to California and forty-seven other states were asked what was expected of them, would they answer "quality?"

A mighty shout of "QUANTITY! QUANTITY! QUANTITY!" would roll from coast to coast as though it were a battle cry . . . as indeed it is. No perception could be so blunted as not to be aware that quantity is the first requirement in that "world." ▶

What do machinists and assemblers hear from the supervisors morning, noon and night? "Keep it moving!"

What do they hear from the expeditors? "More! More! More!"

When managers descend upon them from the front offices what do they want to know? "How soon?" And "Why not sooner?"

Quantity is what mass production is all about

Now, it isn't a crime to go all out for quantity. Quantity is what mass production is about. Those vast quantities are the foundations of affluence. Affluence is the chief product of mass production. So nobody's knocking quantity. But we have to have quality.

It is generally agreed that a majority of the causes of poor quality are attributable to management; but if all of these were eliminated, the quality would still remain in jeopardy if the perceptual world of the manual operators remained unchanged.

It is true that management raises those cheers for quality . . . and in all sincerity. It is true that beautiful motivation programs are developed in carpeted conference rooms, hushed by soundproofing and cooled by air conditioning. And it is true that posters full of pious pronouncements for quality are tacked up on the walls. But the "umwelt" of the machinist and assembler doesn't change; what he perceives is still that QUANTITY is king.

It may be that the quiet conference room is not the right place for evolving motivation programs. Do the would-be motivators, however sincere, have any intimation of the perceptual world of those they would motivate? As for the posters, they lose their appeal somewhat, when they serve as background to an angry supervisor demanding "Get a move on! Get the lead out!"

A balance of quantity and quality in the mass production of consumer articles has to be achieved, not only for domestic reasons (the increasingly quality-sensitive mass consumers), but also to assure America's success in the face of international competition, especially from Japan and a resurgent Europe. And we can do it. It's just that we've been going hell for leather for quantity since World War II and have failed to recognize the side effects. □

"A part of the Maine"

☐ *"No man is an Island, intire of itself; every man is a peece of the Continent, a part of the Maine."* Thus spoke John Donne in the 17th Century. An absolute statement about the human condition which stands alone and unassailable; which is "intire of itself." It has been quoted thousands of times by writers, public persons and psychologists concerned to demonstrate that we are all dependent, one upon another.

I remind you of Donne's well-known axiom because I think we should ask ourselves whether quality assurance managers, engineers, technicians, and inspectors feel themselves to be "a part of the Maine."

The question is always relevant in so far as a number of quality assurance activities are indisputably critical and, as a consequence, quality assurance people may be identified exclusively as critics. As "critics" they may be excluded from "The Maine" by their colleagues. Indeed, they may exclude themselves!

Are you a part of the group?

It is this latter consideration that concerns me. The matter was brought to a head by something I heard at a recent conference. This was a one day seminar on quality management at which I was one of the speakers. The luncheon speaker was a prominent financial executive of a leading aerospace corporation. As I settled back to listen I was pleasantly surprised to hear, not the customary protestation of devotion to Motherhood and Quality, but a well informed and critical evaluation of quality assurance and its place in the corporate body as a whole. But I was shocked when I heard him say that he believed many quality assurance people suffered from a case of "institutional inferiority."

Later in the day I inquired what had given him such an opinion. He replied that he had acquired it from direct contact with quality assurance managers and engineers. He had, he said, found them to be rather apologetic, not sure of their exact function, and skeptical as to the degree to which they were accepted by their colleagues in the organization. ▶

I didn't attempt to counter his statement. What was there to be said? He was recording an impression. But I did ask: "Do you find them effective despite this attitude?"

"Oh yes, but they would be more effective if they were more confident."

It was with this problem in mind that I recalled John Donne and his much-quoted lines. When one is confronted by such an attitude as that reported by the aerospace executive, it is not enough to say to quality assurance practitioners:

"You shouldn't feel doubtful about your value. You are absolutely essential to the proper functioning of the organization. Now you keep that in mind and act with vigor and conviction." Attitudes aren't changed that easily, although it helps to receive positive assurance.

The point about John Donne is that he said it for all of us, and he said it in those sparse, penetrating Elizabethan phrases. Phrases? They are more like arrows!

We are all brothers, one to another

Each of us is "a part of the Maine," and none more so than quality assurance engineers, managers, inspectors. No man is an unbiased judge of the quality of his own work, nor of the work done by people he has supervised, nor of the work produced according to plans he has made. No man and no people, ever!

In the case of a single work of art it might be agreed that the artist's subjective evaluation is the last word—but it won't do the artist any good if his word is indeed the last word, and no one speaks up to say "I'll buy it." But consumer goods, soft and durable, and hardware, commercial and military, must be made to objective specifications.

A manufacturing organization without inspectors is like a head without eyes, a body without a nervous system. The problem is to perform the critical function without alienating one's colleagues.

But this is merely to say that the task is difficult. The critical function is as essential now as it was when the critic John Donne was holding forth in Elizabeth's times, and when the prophets were thundering against sin in Biblical times, for they were critics too. Isaiah, Jeremiah, John Donne, and every quality assurance engineer, manager, and inspector is each and everyone "a part of the Maine." ☐

We can't turn the clock back

☐ There is moaning and groaning throughout the land about the decline in productivity. Actually a decline in the rate, but it causes the same distress. The President leads the chorus and we all join in.

It's not only the productivity, it's safety and quality too. A poll of consumers taken by Consumer Response Corporation in '78 revealed that 44 percent knew of at least one product they considered hazardous—in '79 the figure was up to 56 percent!

"Where are the craftsmen?" we ask. "Why aren't the operators motivated to do good work?"

What is a craftsman? A craftsman is, or was, a man who achieved the status of journeyman after an apprenticeship of seven years. When he hired into a company, he brought his own tool kit. As a machinist, he would have a specialized knowledge of milling machines or turret lathes or whatever. If he worked in sheet metal, he himself might design the holding and bending jigs and fixtures. It was sufficient to give the craftsman the blueprint and raw material and leave the rest to him.

Furthermore, he made the whole part. If the part were not the end product, he knew what function the part would perform in the end product. The sweetly running steam engine, the pump that never leaked, the bearings that ran cool were the joint product of the craftsman and fellow craftsmen. The signature on each part was each craftsman's special skill, and every part fit like a glove.

Those days are long gone

But craftsmanship is not a part of mass production. It's too slow and too costly. It's true that as the Industrial Revolution forged ahead in Britain during the 19th century, the mechanization of labor, combined with craftsmanship, greatly increased productivity—but nothing like the fabulous increase created by American mass production methods. ▶

What happens to craftsmanship in mass production? F.W. Taylor's radical changes in manufacturing methodology separated the machinist and assembler from participation in the planning. The planning is now done by industrial engineers. Henry Ford's moving assembly line necessitated breaking the product down into small fractions; the worker could not possibly feel that the screws he tightened or the joints he soldered had any effect on the performance of the end product. A worker was emotionally "deprived" of interest in the work by exclusion from planning and intellectually "deprived" of technical interest in the end product by *fractionation*. His time and motion studied, told what to do and when and how to do it, he felt like a robot.

Furthermore, Taylor's *separation* and Ford's *fractionation* did not require skilled workers. On the contrary, they were designed for semiskilled and unskilled workers who, it was thought, would tolerate the robot-like existence because of the relatively good pay.

It's the "Joe the Plumber" show

We cannot, today, in all good conscience demand of the unskilled and semiskilled operators that they become craftsmen. Apart from the fact that the seven-year apprenticeship system is a part of bygone history, the possession of manual skill carries no social status. If a plumber should appear on TV, it would be for comic relief.

Starting with Taylor, we have developed a fabulously productive system compounded of front office planning, machines, and industrious, semiskilled, manual workers willing to endure a somewhat robot-like existence in return for good pay. It worked as long as the manual workers could be motivated by pay—as they certainly could be by five dollars a day in 1916. It worked for larger sums in later years, but not any more.

As for craftsmanship, if the entire work force turned into craftsmen overnight, what would we do with them? They couldn't all be toolmakers. They would cause havoc on mass production lines by their disregard for time schedules and instructions, which conflict with their estimate of what is good for quality.

It is the declining productivity rate in mass production we are concerned about, not the hand-crafting of a few specialty articles which sell precisely because they are too expensive for the run of the population.

We have to rethink the situation from the way it is; we cannot solve it by trying to put the clock back. □

The communications crusade

☐ Communication is all the rage. On the market place and in academic halls, in machine shops and management conference rooms the cry is for more and better communication. It's a crusade and everyone is joining up.

If you have a proposal to present to a superior and if it has to do with communication, it has a better chance of acceptance. If it proposes to "promote," "improve," "enhance," "integrate," "consolidate" or "clarify" communications it will get a hearing. Why? Is there indeed a communications problem? The universal reply is "Yes!"

The fundamental problem in communications is the subjective nature of knowledge; it is inherent in the human condition. A speaks, B hears, but what B hears is not necessarily what A meant to say. Jack says "I love you"; Jill hears "Will you marry me?" The president of the company declares at the monthly staff meeting, "Quality is our goal." The department heads hear, "Quality not quantity. To hell with the cost!" Or, in another vein, the president reminds the staff, "We're in business to make a profit." The attentive managers hear, "Quantity is what we want. To hell with quality."

The pyramid effect on communications

The subjective nature of knowledge and its effect on communication is universal, applying equally to the quality scene as to romance and politics. But there is a communications problem which applies particularly to industry. This is the effect of the hierarchical management structure. In the traditional organization, A has authority over several B's; each B over several C's, and so on down the line. It is a pyramid in which each man sees beneath him several or many, and above him only one. Implicit in this management structure is the belief in the mind of each individual that he knows better than those below and that, in turn, his own ability is surpassed by the man above.

The organizational pyramid has a particular effect on communication. Imagine that an incident occurs in, say, the machine shop which leads the supervisor to feel that something should be done to prevent a recurrence. The supervisor is at level D. He must report to C. He assembles the facts in his mind and arrives at a conclusion as to what should be done. But the moment he thinks of making a recommendation to C he begins to

▶

speculate on how the facts would have looked to C, and on what C would have concluded. Bit by bit he modifies his recommendation until it is what he thinks C would want to do. It is not totally different from his initial evaluation of the incident, but it is not the same. He reports to C. C prepares to report to B.

What has happened to the communication? It has been modified or distorted by supervisor D's attempt to rethink it with the "superior" mind of C. It is further distorted by C's immediate reaction, which is to assume that D, the subordinate, did his best but may have missed the significant point. C rethinks the communication and prepares to report to B. But how would B see the situation and what would he do about it? C rethinks the communication with B's "superior" mind and reports. B listens tolerantly with half an ear, knowing that C has done his best but is handicapped by his limited view of the scene. B rethinks the communication from his own point of view and rethinks it again with the mind of A. He reports to A. A gives the communication a final rethink and issues an order like closing the New Jersey plant, or authorizing the use of green smocks by girls on the assembly line!

The required attitudes

It should not be thought that organizational subordinates are being accused of subservience or their superiors of arrogance. These attitudes are required by the organizational pyramid. It would not survive without them. It, like every institution, survives in the belief of its members. It would be foolish to strive for a higher position on the organizational pyramid if you thought those above were idiots. Those who succeed must feel that they know better and those who have yet to succeed tend to concur.

So much for the subjective nature of knowledge, which is general, and the effect of the hierarchical management structure, which is industry-wide. What about quality communications? They meet yet another obstacle. Usually founded on adverse inspection reports, quality communications are by their nature unpopular. Nobody wants to know when things have gone wrong. Not that anyone wants to suppress the information, but everybody in the chain of communication wishes it hadn't happened. Not the production foreman, not the factory superintendent, not the general manager who sees monthly billing jeopardized, and certainly not the contracts manager who must get on the phone to the customer and make one more apology.

Further on, we'll explore the subject of how to communicate in quality assurance, but it was necessary as a preliminary, to outline the communications complex of which quality communications are a part. □

Science fiction

☐ Try this test: open any book on management at the index and check for "quality control." Try it on several management books. What luck did you have?

What started me on this was a question about a book on management systems. What did I think about it? Did I think it would tell the reader "everything a manager should know to be successful?" This modest claim was printed on the jacket. I flipped over the pages and, sure enough, there were gorgeous organization charts and long dissertations on marketing, design, purchasing, production and service. Functions were subdivided into almost microscopic fractions; what was expected of each fraction was spelled out in lengthy detail. I mean, there didn't seem to be anything missing—except I hadn't come across a single reference to product quality or quality control.

To make sure I hadn't missed anything I checked the index:
- Under Q—nothing about quality or quality control!
- Under I—nothing about inspection!
- Under P—nothing about product quality!
- Under S—nothing about statistical techniques for any purpose whatever!

Living in a dream world

So I read a number of sections with more care. On procurement, for example, the Purchasing Manager floats through the day like a dream, sending out invitations to bid, comparing prices, calmly directing the activities of his subordinates. No day is ever disturbed by the shocking news that Receiving Inspection has rejected 19% of those parts just in from wherever! No urgently-needed shipment of raw material is ever rejected, thereby wrecking the schedule and precipitating chaos! No Monthly Quality Summary ever draws the attention of top management to the fact that, say, 7% of all purchased materials inspected during the month was found to be defective! ▶

Likewise with the Production Manager, except that he has to be at the plant, instead of fishing or practicing archery or whatever, life is largely a bed of roses. Batch after batch of finished parts all to specification and all completed on time! No lousy inspectors sabotaging the beautifully-planned operation by finding shaft diameters undersize, and hole diameters oversize! Not even a machine shop supervisor driven to the verge of apoplexy by inspectors who dare to reject parts that are only slightly different from the specification!

This experience prompted me to check the index in a number of other books on management. Out of 26, only 7 indexed "quality control!" The remaining 19 made no reference to product quality, or quality control, or inspection, or statistical techniques!

They know not whereof they speak

Why do they do it? Why do so many authors presume to tell industrial managers what to do, while making no reference to quality control?

Of course, one could say that some of the authors are academics who, as the saying goes, have never had to meet a schedule and have never, therefore, been harassed by such operational problems as defective purchased material, defective machined parts, failures on final function test.

But even if one had never been inside a plant, the media (newspapers, radio, TV) are full of complaints about the poor quality of consumers' products, complaints frequently tied in with comments on quality control. The law of the land requires that contractors to the military have an adequate quality control system.

Or do these authors think that the detection and correction of defectives can be left to the man who bought them or made them? Do they think that the principle of conflict of interest will cease to operate when a producer under schedule pressure is called upon to inspect his own work?

How then can one classify books which profess to be concerned with industrial management but make no reference to product quality and quality control? I suppose one must think of them as science fiction, attempts to portray a utopian future from which defectives and the probability of their occurrence have been forever dismissed. Anyway, you might check through your own management books and see how many are concerned with operational reality, and how many are science fiction. □

Psychological effects of quality

☐ A knowledge of the psychological effects of quality action is essential to the success of a quality control program. Indeed, it might be the most important ingredient.

A quality manager's plans may be administratively and technically correct, but if the psychological effects of their application are not recognized and provided for, the quality program is likely to be shattered by the storms it provokes.

Who is affected by quality control action? People in purchasing, production control, manufacturing and sales.

Consider a typical incident: A consignment of urgently needed parts arrives at receiving inspection. The parts are already ten days behind schedule; they are vital to production control; the assembly foreman will have to send a score of girls home if he doesn't get them; the sales manager can't delay delivery of the end product any longer.

But you can't reject them!

The inspector gets out his gages, inspects the parts, and rejects them! Purchasing, production control, assembly and sales are stunned! "Are you sure you've got the right drawing change?" "What am I going to do about those girls?" "You've fixed us good! You've really knocked the schedule!"

It doesn't matter that the parts were already ten days late on arrival; what matters is that the parts finally arrived and quality control rejected them. Purchasing, production control, assembly and sales are dismayed; their plans, their expectations have been knocked awry by this quality control act. Aroused by disappointment and by the indisputable problem which has been created for them (they have to reschedule and explain the further delay to top management), sweet reason takes a back seat.

The fact that the parts are indeed defective as charged is out of sight. The dominant fact is the act of rejection. The guilt at this moment attaches to the inspector, not to the defective parts, or to the supplier who made them. ▶

We are reminded that when in ancient times, a messenger, spattered with blood and sweat, arrived from a distant battlefield to report defect, his account was received with rising anger, and then he was beheaded as the bearer of bad tidings! They can't set up a guillotine in receiving inspection to behead the inspector, but they can get angry with him, and they do!

In the machine shop, on the assembly lines, in final test, the potential for such incidents is ever present. Like the problem at receiving inspection they get solved one way or another. But whether they are solved in a manner conducive to continued working harmony between the operating departments depends on the quality manager. The single most important step he can take is to recognize the problem, and give it some thought. Once he has acknowledged that the quality control act having the most impact on his colleagues is the rejection of material, and that this is never going to make them happy, and that it shouldn't be expected to, then he can take steps to mitigate their distress.

In anticipation of such incidents, he should establish good communications with his fellow managers. He should avoid being known to them only as the man in charge of the people who reject their purchased supplies, their machined parts, and their assemblies. Then, when a schedule-disturbing rejection must be made, there will be some possibility of an unheated dialogue with the victims.

Easing the pain of rejection

The quality manager should instruct his line supervisors to be alert at all times to the presence of urgently needed parts in their sections, and to see that they get prompt attention. He should see that information about a rejection of urgently needed material does not reach the victim by a routine rejection report. His supervisor, or he himself in an exceptional case, should phone in the information, having already confirmed that the rejection is a true report, having already set up a review with the engineer, or being prepared to offer the services of an inspector if production will work overtime on the rework.

By such actions, the quality manager will temper the violence of psychological reaction. He will, moreover, create a managerial atmosphere in which his colleagues will be more inclined to listen to his recommendations for the introduction of process control, for the more careful selection of suppliers, etc.

The chief thing is to recognize the problem, and not to put it aside by saying that such competitive individuals as purchasing agents, manufacturing managers and sales directors should remain calm and sweetly objective when confronted by catastrophic rejections. □

On seminars

□ It is a paradox of human behavior that, while we seem impelled to group together in organizations, we construct organizations which tend to inhibit communication. The vertical organization is excellent for the transmission of orders and directives from the top down; but is a poor transmitter of feedback. The departmental structure puts constraints on lateral communications.

It's not difficult to see why. The vertical line of management makes each individual a subordinate to his superior, and a superior to a number of subordinates; except for the chief executive at the apex and the operators at the base. Subordinates must perforce take heed of what comes down from above; but superiors usually pay little attention to what subordinates say. There is an assumption on the part of the superior that he knows better than the subordinate; and this is quite likely to be true.

"Don't listen to anyone else!"

The obstacle to easy lateral communication is the reluctance of department heads to have their subordinates influenced by the attitudes and opinions of individuals in parallel departments. This can be understood when it is kept in mind that the department head is responsible for the guidance and direction of scores or hundreds of subordinates; he wants to be sure they are doing it his way.

It is possible to regret and bemoan the behavior of people within the constraining delineations of organizational rank and function, but in the meantime the channels of communication must be opened up. This is what the seminar can do. I mean the seminar attended by about 10 to 15 members of an organization, and conducted by an "outside expert." Expert suggests a man who will conduct the seminar as a course in his particular expertise. Obviously the seminar leader must have expertise in one or more of the disciplines employed by the organization in the conduct of its business. But this is not what gives him his value as a seminar leader. His most valuable adjunct is that he is not a member of the organization.

▶

As such he is objective as far as the problems of the company are concerned; he has no vested interest in any particular plan or project. This provides him with the ability to take an unbiased overview of the company's problems. In his presence, the normal constraints on inter-level and inter-departmental communication will be relaxed. He is nobody's boss; and nobody's subordinate. He is on a level with everybody, he is equally approachable by all.

Furthermore, protocol can be forgotten and questions can be put bluntly to the seminar leader. Once they are out and on the table, the debate may proceed calmly or vigorously. The seminar leader moderates and will know how to cool it if it gets too acrimonious.

There is another valuable feature of the seminar and that is its effectiveness as a method of inquiry. Francis Bacon wrote, "If a man will begin with certainties, he shall end with doubts; but if he will be content to begin with doubts, he shall end with certainties."

Certainties obviate doubts

It's not possible to engage in the daily rigors of management without some certainties. A manager cannot operate when in doubt. He may, of course, have doubts ... but with whom can he discuss them? His superiors? Not likely. His subordinates? Equally not likely. A friend in another department? Possible, but not very probable. So he dismisses the doubt (which may have been well founded) and falls back on his certainties.

But certainties which must be maintained in formal daily contacts, like the rigidities of protocol, may be left at the seminar conference door. It is permissible in a seminar to admit to a little doubt. It's a salutary experience to step down occasionally from the pedestal of certainty, and to float around in exploratory doubt.

The seminar is a supreme communication device. It was never more needed than now, when every company producing for the contemporary market of activated consumers should review the quality of its products, the adequacy of its quality assurance program, and the similarity between product and advertisement. □

Selective inattention

☐ Selective inattention is what you're guilty of when you listen to subordinates with half an ear. Don't say you don't do it. If you're on the organization chart with a title, manager of this or that, it's more than likely you do it every day.

Don't be shocked. It's almost certain you're not conscious of it; if you were you wouldn't do it. It's an example of "situational behavior," behavior motivated by attitudes you adopt without conscious thought when placed in certain situations.

When the situation is one of formal authority in an organization, the attitude you adopt or, more correctly, which adopts you (it comes with the position), is the assumption that you know more and better than your subordinates. Which, indeed, is often the case.

This attitude on the part of managers motivates them to listen with half an ear, which blocks communication with subordinates. As a consequence, valuable information about microcosmic problems encountered in the attempt to execute the manager's macrocosmic plan is lost.

Listen with both ears

What's the remedy? In the first case the manager can make two admissions to himself. 1) That it is, or may be, the case that he listens with half an ear to subordinates. 2) That it is, or may be, the case that his subordinates experience some difficulties in the detailed execution of his overall plan.

And then what? Then try listening with both ears. It's not easy. It's much more difficult to listen than to talk, despite the common wisdom and the many courses in communication based on the premise that it is more difficult to say what you mean than to hear what is meant.

In time your subordinates will recognize that you are really listening to them. What you learn may very well transform your operation from a well planned effort hounded by frequent petty breakdowns, to a well planned, smoothly executed exemplary operation. ▶

"Get that expeditor out of here!"

A quality manager using both ears might learn that the reason for the excessive proportion of defectives getting into stock past receiving inspection is not due to incompetence or poor eyesight but to the fact that expeditors pester the inspectors all day long, inducing in them a tolerance for marginal defects to get the expeditors off their backs.

Anyway, think about selective inattention. Repeat it to yourself like a mantra. In time, the idea of selective inattention and the possibility that you just might be guilty of it will become familiar and will no longer offend you. Then, as we say in quality control, you will be ready to take corrective action.

What is your mantra?

A mantra, as you must know if you've spoken to anyone under thirty recently or if you saw the Maharishi on TV, is a secret word whispered by the guru in the ear of the initiate to induce in the latter a state of transcendental meditation. In this condition, the initiate acquires the wisdom to see the problems of daily life reduced to their proper size and not to worry. There are those who scoff and those who believe. One of the believers who appeared on TV with the Maharishi was Hollywood actor Clint Eastwood. How would you like to be the Clint Eastwood of quality control?

If you want a positive mantra, try repeating "Listen! Listen! Listen!" This will translate you to that higher plane of existence where you will *know* what those above and below and around you are trying to tell you. Seeing clearly, perhaps for the first time, through ears now wide open, you will become a power in the organization. Just listen. □

Communication by Ringisho

☐ Communication has always been a problem. Prehistoric man found it necessary to zapp a female with a club to persuade her to share his cave, to cohabit and bear children. The club seems to be a peculiar communications device: nevertheless it was obviously successful, since the race did multiply and we are all here.

The club has lost its popularity, but communication problems still remain. Indeed, from all that one reads, hears on the radio, and sees on TV, the problem is worse than ever. It is said that the generation gap has made communication practically impossible between parents and children (not that this is anything new, if you remember what happened to poor King Lear); students say they can't understand professors (which raises the question whether or not they want to); and the Watergate scandal is a communications tangle for all seasons.

Up the organization

Furthermore, as every organization man knows, it's difficult to communicate up the organization; and it's equally difficult to communicate across departmental lines. Communication up tends to be blocked by selective inattention, a reluctance on the part of superiors to pay attention to what their subordinates have to say. Attempts at lateral communication run into vetos imposed by competitive departmental managers.

But the Japanese have found a way to communicate across and up by the RINGI system (the "g" is hard as in rig). It works this way. An individual somewhere in the pyramidal organization, but not at the top, gets an idea. It may be an industrial engineer, a supervisor, a clerk, anyone who may wish to recommend a change of procedure. He prepares a RINGISHO. The ringisho is a specific recommendation as to what should be done, if the recommendation is accepted. ►

Send it on its way

The initiator now prepares a list of individuals who may be affected in various departments and at increasing levels of management, culminating in the top man. He starts the ringisho off on its journey. So it progresses across and up the organization. At each step it may be rejected by a recipient and returned to the initiator, but typically it will continue on its way collecting approving signatures. By the time it reaches the top man it is loaded with approvals. The top man may veto the recommendation but rarely does so. To do so would be to challenge the judgment of many subordinates. The ringisho is approved and is put into effect.

The beauty of the ringi system is that it enables a member of an organization to obtain a hearing for an idea from colleagues in different departments and at different levels of management. It's a way of working around and up the organization without offending protocol.

Could we use it here?

Communication by ringisho is the more remarkable because it's a feature of Japanese industrial organization. It would be reasonable to expect a rigid regard for protocol among a people with Japanese cultural background. Indeed, there *is* a meticulous regard for protocol in Japan, and yet the ringi system exists and flourishes. As a consequence, the Japanese employee may have a better chance of communicating up the organization than his opposite number in the U.S., where we profess not to care for protocol. We live and learn. ☐

The Peter Principle and communication

☐ You all know the Peter Principle.* It's the one that states "in a hierarchy every employee tends to rise to his level of incompetence." And then, according to Peter's Corollary, "In time every post tends to be occupied by an employee who is incompetent to carry out its duties." Shocking, isn't it?

But if it's so shocking why do we think it's so funny? Why do we quote it with such glee? I suppose because it seems to fit our organizational superiors and ranking colleagues so exactly! Well ... some of them anyway.

But seriously, if the Peter Principle is a valid proposition, how does the work get done? Professor Peter and Raymond Hull have the answer. They postulate that there shall be sufficient time and enough positions to allow everyone to rise to his or her level of incompetence. But there's neither sufficient time nor enough positions ... and so most positions are occupied by competent individuals still waiting for an opportunity to rise to their levels of incompetence!

A motive for better vertical communication

It's a provocative idea, but what does it do for us? Well ... it might provide us with a motive for better vertical communication. In an article, "Communicate! Communicate!" published in February '71 by the Hitchcock Publishing Company magazine *Woodworking & Furniture Digest,* I examined the many barriers to communicating up the organization and concluded that first among them was the superior's failure to listen carefully to subordinates. The failure to listen was attributed to the superior's assumption that he must, by virtue of his elevated position, know more than any subordinate, and could therefore afford to listen with half an ear. This assumption is generally acquiesced to by subordinates because it's how they feel about their own subordinates. The article concluded that rapid improvement in communication could be effected, if superiors at all levels would only listen to their subordinates. ►

Now, that was and is, I believe, a good recommendation, but it lacked something. Something that would motivate the superior to put aside his assumption of superiority, and to listen to subordinates not merely in conformance with recommended procedure, but because he might miss out on vital information if he didn't.

This is what the Peter Principle provides. The wise superior, familiar with the Peter Principle, now knows that some of his subordinates may be competent to do their own jobs and his too! From which it follows logically that each superior should listen attentively to his subordinates.

Don't hold your breath waiting for it to happen . . . but can you imagine the consequence? An organization that tried it would be revitalized by floods of information gushing up through normally clotted communication channels! The company would rise to success almost overnight.

Requires modesty and humility

Of course, the utilization of the Peter Principle in this manner would require excessive amounts of modesty and humility from all of us in management. But if it were to happen, what would you, the quality manager, tell an attentive chief executive? That consumerism is powered by a corps of plaintiffs' attorneys; that it isn't going to fade away; and that building a quality product that won't injure consumers is the first order of business? Or that you're strapped for budget and can only afford to keep an inspection finger in the dike, and can't do any quality engineering defect prevention?

Anyway, be prepared to speak your piece in case the implications of the Peter Principle ever strike home. In the meantime listen to your own subordinates, and then you'll be as competent as they are in the event that any of them have not yet reached their levels of incompetence. □

*"The Peter Principle," L.J. Peter and R. Hull (William Morrow, 1969).

Indoctrination and instruction

☐ Managers require indoctrination more than technicians need instruction. If the technicians develop a new technique it will become effective completely, or partially, or not at all to the degree that management supports it. In contrast, if managers have been indoctrinated and have acquired an understanding of a new technique and wish to make use of it, they will clear the decks for the technicians in short time. If it should happen that the technicians have no knowledge of the technique, the managers soon will see that they are instructed. Technicians cannot, unfortunately, see that their managers are indoctrinated; but managers can and do move fast to see that technicians are instructed!

The consequences are that technicians frequently find it difficult to fulfill advanced technical requirements. They find themselves attempting to operate in an environment which is not so much inimical as uncomprehending.

Few managers have been indoctrinated

The advent of quantitative reliability has created many such problems. Reliability has provided technicians with a means of analyzing complex designs and of identifying those components most likely to cause failure of the whole system. Such identification has already resulted in substantial improvement in the reliability of components and systems. But the potential has hardly been tapped because, while many technicians have been instructed, few managers have been indoctrinated.

It is important to understand why things don't go if managers are not indoctrinated. To stay with reliability, as an example, reliability is not something that can be mulled over by a small isolated group of reliability specialists. It is a happening that, by its nature, involves everybody; if the managers don't dig it, it won't happen.

Since a demand for quantitative reliability appears in an increasing number of specifications for components and complex equipments; and since the technicians must attempt to do something; and since the something they must do cannot be confined to a single segment of the organization; and since the managers all too frequently do not dig it: the effect of the introduction of quantitative reliability is likely to be poor performance on the contract reliability-wise, delivery-wise and cost-wise. If one may be facetious about something so serious, it can be seen that three wise men topside, three well-indoctrinated managers, could switch the rating from poor to excellent performance-wise. ▶

To illustrate the problem let us consider the procurement of high reliability components. Designers and quality assurance engineers in need of components with low failure rates will locate particular suppliers. Quality assurance will work with the supplier and agree on certain quality controls and test procedures to assure the specified reliability.

But the drawing does not change; the dimensions and material are the same. There is an agreement to exercise meticulous controls during production but this does not appear on the drawing.

Purchasing sends out invitations to bid to all suppliers capable of meeting the nominal print requirements. The lowest bidder gets it! And so he should, for he is capable of doing all that appears on the face of the print.

But what's on the print is not enough

The successful bidder may regret it when his product hits the reliability-conscious receiving inspectors, and bounces right back again! Months later the embittered supplier will have learned what to do and the first acceptable deliveries will begin to trickle in.

Designers can and do name the capable supplier on the print but it's customary to add "or equivalent." The "or equivalent" is a bit of a cop out. I mean, what is the purchasing man going to do when there's an "equivalent" supplier in the next suburb as compared with the named supplier who is halfway across the continent and is notoriously slow on delivery?

Again, the presence of reliability deeply affects scheduling. Production Control must allow extra time for the acquisition of high reliability components; extra time for meticulous quality controls in production; extra time for the complex business of reliability failure reporting, analysis, and feedback; extra time for protracted reliability demonstration tests.

The unscheduled delays, which are the consequence of a lack of preparatory pre-indoctrination, all land on top of the production manager! If he isn't driven out of his mind, he's likely to be sour on reliability for many contracts to come.

Now the managers of purchasing, production control, and manufacturing are not about to make radical changes in established procedures at the request of quality control. They will get with it when top management gives the signal, and then they will get with it fast.

The problem is to indoctrinate top management. It is not to instruct, but to create a new point of view compatible with the new technology and its by-products, of which quantitative reliability is one of the most portentous. □

The comprehension gap

☐ It has been said of de Gaulle that "he loved France, but hated Frenchmen." Likewise, it might be said of some industrial executives that they love quality assurance, but hate inspectors.

The industrial executive who loves the idea of quality assurance thinks of it as a kind of benevolent presence hovering over the labors of purchasing men and producers, dutifully making the sign of acceptance on everything in motion from the receiving dock to shipping. Whereas the inspectors, who may be thought of as Saint Sigma's disciples, insist on examining materials, parts, and assemblies before making the sign of acceptance, and then they don't always make it.

Bring them back to reality

The problem is: how to reconcile the idea with reality. What would create in the mind of the executive the idea of quality assurance as a benevolent presence? Well, for one thing, the name itself. "Quality assurance" has a nice, comforting sound to it. There's no hint of the sometimes devastating critic in "quality assurance." It's not as harsh as "quality control," which implies that some kind of control is going to be applied . . . and it may not always be pleasant. It doesn't sound nearly as threatening as "defect detection" (and correction), although that is what it is.

I don't think we should disregard the importance of words and phrases; after all, this is how we communicate. What bugs me is that a kind of comprehension gap still exists between many chief executives and their quality assurance managers. How do we bridge the gap?

Since many of us are engineers and technicians, the tendency will be to develop more and better technology, more and better statistics and metrology. Fine . . . but will that do it? Will chief executives who don't comprehend the significance of the considerable body of technology we already have comprehend more of the same? ▶

Bridging the comprehension gap

It's doubtful, and in any case we shall continue making technological improvements because technology seems to be self-perpetuating. The important thing for quality control practitioners to keep in mind is that the comprehension gap exists . . . and that it is essential for the welfare of their companies and for their professional careers that the gap be bridged. This is the first order of business for all quality managers. Each will attack the problem in accordance with his specific situation, but all should give some thought to semantic barriers to communication.

There is a distinction between "quality assurance" and "quality control." The former designates the corporate commitment to a quality assurance program, and the latter designates specific actions of inspectors and quality control engineers.

You can never love your inspector

The use of a more vigorous terminology is not going to bridge the gap, but it is a step in the right direction. We may succeed in bringing chief executives around from loving quality assurance and hating inspectors to where they might appreciate quality control and tolerate inspectors. You didn't think you could ever get them around to loving inspectors, did you?

□

"Quality assurance is . . . ?"

☐ Bill Schleicher sounded off in a past issue of *Quality Assurance* magazine about the public image of quality assurance. "It isn't good," he said, "and we ought to do something about it!"

I wish he were wrong, but I fear that he isn't. Many of the people, in and out of industry, to whom one might put the question, "What is quality assurance?" would find it difficult to give a clear and explicit answer, which is the best (or worst) evidence of a poor public image.

Why should this doubt exist in the minds of employers, fellow managers, and the public? Because practitioners of quality assurance themselves are not in agreement as to the nature and extent of their role! It will be impossible to project a clear and explicit public image of quality assurance until those who practice it are clear and explicit about what it is.

What's the difference?

Let's consider one of the problems. Is "quality assurance" something different from "quality control?" The terms are used interchangeably by many in industry. As a consequence, it's possible to find a "quality control" or "quality assurance" department responsible for all of the functions assignable to either or both. One may find quality assurance and quality control organizationally united or separated. Quality assurance may be subordinate to quality control and vice versa.

Where should we turn for distinguishing definitions? Let's see what DoD and NASA have to say about them; we aren't compelled to follow their recommendations unless we're looking for military or space business.

Quality control, say DoD and NASA, is a management function to assure that products conform to quality standards. Since the "quality standards" are engineering drawings and specs for the particular product, this definition might be construed as limiting quality control to checking raw material, parts, and assemblies for conformance to drawings and specs. It does not make quality control responsible for satisfactory performance in the field. Indeed, many engineers and other responsible individuals assert that this limited role is all that is expected of quality control. Strenuous efforts may be made to confine the quality control

▶

manager to checking for conformance. The qc manager might say, with apologies to Tennyson:

> Mine not to reason why,
> Mine but to measure and to certify;
> Mine not to question the specification,
> Nor the customer's possible mortification.

However, if the product does mortify the customer, a broad construction is immediately placed on the definition! It will be said that "conformance" to the customer's needs is implicit in the definition; that the customer's need is a quality standard. If the quality control manager goes a bit paranoid at such times, he deserves our sympathy. But it must be remembered that he is the victim of general confusion as to the nature and scope of quality control, to which he himself may have contributed.

DoD and NASA remove all limitations, stated or implied, in their definition of quality assurance: "all actions necessary to assure with reasonable confidence that the product will perform as intended." "As intended" by the customer and, therefore, quality assurance must take steps to assure that the customer's intentions were clearly understood. It should also ensure that the proposed design will fulfill the customer's desires, and that proposed manufacturing plans are adequate. The inspection system proposed by quality control must be appropriate, and that field service and maintenance plans are sufficiently comprehensive.

A place for each

It seems to me that quality control and quality assurance are both useful terms when these definitions are kept in mind. They are, of course, equally applicable to commercial production and military contracting. As I use them, I assign all line actions to Quality Control (inspection, test, process capability studies, supplier control, calibration, etc.) and the coordinating function to Quality Assurance.

"Quality Control: a management function . . ." and "Quality Assurance: all actions necessary . . ." are discriminating definitions and it's essential that they be kept in mind to avoid confusion. But they're not the stuff from which to fashion a commanding public image. That's the problem to which we should all give some thought. Let no one think that it's good enough merely to be good, for if you want to be effective your colleagues will have to know exactly what it is you're trying to be good at.

□

The transformation effect

☐ Let A be a first line supervisor.
Let B be a department manager.
Let C be a general manager.

A is in charge of a group of assemblers. His prime interest is in the product itself, the technical problem associated with its assembly. He's in serious trouble; amplifiers are being rejected from test like crazy. He goes to see B.

"B, we're having a lot of trouble with those amplifiers."

"Are we going to miss the schedule?" is B's prompt response.

End of communication! What A wanted to hear was "What's wrong with them?" He and B would then have entered into an investigation of the technical problem and, hopefully, a solution would have been found. But the crux of the problem for B is the schedule, which dictates his response.

Now B reports to C that "Model X equipments, of which the amplifier is a part, are moving slowly." C promptly responds, "What will it do to the billing?"

He didn't say what I wanted to hear!

B had hoped that he and C would enter into a discussion of scheduling, enabling B to make the point that there was no flexibility in the scheduling, no time allowance for unforeseen obstacles. But the crux of the matter to C is the $ billing which, again, dictates his response.

As a consequence of such encounters, A and A's fellow supervisors assert that "B couldn't care less about the product! Just keep them moving. That's B!"

B and B's fellow managers say somewhat the same about C. "It's no good talking to C about anything but $'s!"

Now what the A's say about B, and what the B's say about C is essentially true. It can be attributed to what could be called the *transformation effect.*

It's easy to construct a transformation tree:

A	Product	Supervisors
	to	
B	Schedule	Department Managers
	to	
C	$ Billing	General Manager

▶

But it's not so easy to know what to do about it. It should be expected that individuals at all levels of the organization will be sensitive to the crucial demands of the position each occupies. Indeed, the tendency is to be obsessed by them to the extent that they are not only crucial for the individual but, in his or her opinion, the prime concern of the organization.

So it appears that the communication blocks caused by the transformation effect are inherent in the subjectivity, the egocentricity of the individual. But even if one looked at the situation objectively from the organization's point of view, the organization would surely wish that each individual should be devoted to his particular task; and devotion, again, leads to myopia.

The hierarchical effect

There is another factor of great importance militating against communication, and that is the *hierarchical effect,* the tendency for A's to defer to B, and B's to defer to C. Deference is not subservience. It is based on the reasonable, and frequently true assumption, that the superior knows more, has a better grasp on the overall situation than the subordinate. As a consequence, A doesn't exclaim to B, "Damn it! *Reply* to me by asking what's technically wrong with the amplifiers. Don't *Respond* by getting jittery about the schedule!"

Likewise, B is not likely to say to A "For God's sake, can't you give some thought to the vital problem of scheduling, instead of everlastingly talking dollars, dollars, dollars!"

That might be the key to better communication: to consider when replying to a subordinate, or to anybody, whether you are *responding* or *replying.* To "Respond," as I am using it, is to respond in the psychological sense of a "conditioned response," where the conditioning agency is the prime requirement of the individual's organizational position. To "reply" requires that one shall actually listen to what the speaker is saying—and what a task that is!

Organizations might try appointing communication facilitators, a kind of ombudsman. Consultants may perform this task on occasion. Certainly in my own practice I frequently find myself in the role of ombudsman, explaining or attempting to explain A to B to C.

Anyway, the problem exists. The transformation and heirarchical effects aren't going to vanish overnight. However, the next time you're approached by a subordinate you might try replying instead of responding. That would help. □

Seeing is believing.   Or is it?

☐ "Seeing is believing" is one of the many maxims on which we were all brought up. Others are: "Look before you leap"; "A stitch in time saves nine"; "A bird in hand is worth two in the bush"; "He who hesitates is lost," although this seems to contradict the one about leaping. Together, they constitute a distillation of the popular wisdom.

But is it true that "seeing is believing?" Let us test it physically and psychologically. Imagine that you're standing at the corner of Main and Elm with your wife, waiting for the light to change. Your wife, looking up Main, exclaims, "Look! There's my mother." You look and there, sure enough, about four blocks away, is your mother-in-law.

Now, at that distance, she would appear to be about two feet tall. But you don't say, "What a short mother you have!" You don't, because you don't believe what you see, although what you see is indisputably a woman two feet tall.

Do they hear what you meant?

What about psychological seeing and believing? The problem is equally complicated. An individual may believe that he has made a clear exposition on a given subject, only to find that listeners have "heard" him many different ways. The listeners have heard the words, but the meaning they attribute to them is a product of their own reading on the subject, and of their own experience in the subject, and of such "prejudices" about the subject as they may have acquired during prior education and incultration.

Expositors run into this psychological phenomenon in all fields of knowledge. It can be said, not that "hearing is believing," but that "believing is hearing"; for the listener "hears" what he is preconditioned to believe about the subject.

Relevance for quality assurance practitioners is that some basic assumptions we make are not shared by our colleagues. Necessity for inspection is postulated on the assumption that no man is an unprejudiced critic of his own work. This is almost the first law of human behavior, but few believe it to be true of themselves.   ►

Thus, when we are "selling" an inspection system we ought to state that this is the postulate on which we are building. We should attempt to gain acceptance for this fundamental assumption. Not to do so is to leave management and operators thinking that inspectors believe that purchasing men aren't trying to find good suppliers . . . or that producers aren't trying to make good parts!

If such miscomprehension is possible in administration of quality assurance, it is even more so in statistical technology. There is very little about statistics that is immediately apparent to "common sense."

As an example, imagine that a lot of parts has been sampled at, say, 4% AQL. Assume that the number of defectives found in the sample does not exceed the acceptance number and that, therefore, the lot is acceptable.

Never make "common sense" assumptions

"Common sense" assumes that what this means is that the lot is 4% defective. Common sense does not prompt the uninitiated to say, "What inspection of the sample has given us, is an estimate of lot quality. Quality of the lot may be by random chance, exactly 4% defective; or it may be better; or worse. The truth is, we don't know."

We assume that what is known to us should be obvious to "any intelligent man." Accordingly we inspect by sampling without explaining the risks. Consequences may be catastrophic for producers, who may find lots better than the AQL rejected; and for consumers, who may find lots much worse than the AQL accepted. Dodge and Romig explained this very clearly as early as 1939, but while we know it, most of our industrial colleagues don't.

Seeing is not believing in qa administration and statistics. Industrial managers and operators see what, from previous knowledge and experience, they believe they should see. Quality assurance practitioners must inform, initiate, indoctrinate their colleagues so that what managers and operators believe they see is what qa knows to be true. □

When all else fails, read the instructions!

☐ You drop in on a fellow manager for morning coffee, or to decide where to go for lunch, or to prepare yet another instruction. And there on the desk, next to the picture of his smiling dependents, is a card with the sardonic maxim, WHEN ALL ELSE FAILS, READ THE INSTRUCTIONS!

You smile, he grins, and the secretary giggles. You tell your favorite story about the detailed instruction you spent so much time on, "D'you think anybody read it? Not on your life!" He tells his story and the secretary undulates off in search of coffee.

It doesn't matter whether I quote this ironic message, WHEN ALL ELSE FAILS, READ THE INSTRUCTIONS! to morose quality managers, or to haggard production superintendents, there is general agreement that that's the way things are. Nobody seems to have subordinates or colleagues who read instructions!

Assuming that, in the main, they are right, an assumption supported by the spontaneity of their response, we might ask whether it's reasonable to expect colleagues and subordinates to read the instructions we labor over?

Is there time to read the instructions?

If the recipient is in administration then we should expect the instruction to be read with care, and acted upon. But if the recipient is in operations, if he or she is immersed in the ocean of frenzied activity and orderly chaos typical of production, then perhaps we ought to re-examine our expectations.

Is it reasonable to expect a production operator or an inspector to study an instruction in a busy shop? I mean to study it carefully, to be sure he has understood it. In the first case, every minute of the day is scheduled for work and none is scheduled for reading instructions. In the second case, even if you attempt to read an instruction the environment isn't favorable; there are things to be done, and reading isn't in the class of things to be done. If you're reading instead of doing something you're liable to be accused of goofing off.

The problem is particularly significant for the quality manager. Others may deviate, perhaps because of the problem of finding enough time to read detailed instructions, but the inspectors are there to catch such

►

deviations. The quality manager has to know that the inspectors have read the instructions he and the quality engineers have developed. Confronted by evidence to the contrary, is he going to quote the sardonic maxim with a wry smile, or will he recognize that it's too much to expect individuals in the schedule-paced work areas to pause long enough to thoroughly understand an instruction? Assuming he arrives at the latter conclusion, then he has an excellent opportunity to do something for communications.

This is a basic communications problem

To get an idea of the magnitude of the problem he might take one section of his command, and count the number of sheets of instructions in the area on a given day. Listing the inspectors in the area, he can tabulate the number of sheets each is expected to read. The quality manager might get copies of the instructions and give himself a reading test. How long does it take him to read them all, or a sample of them? Since he is reading in the peaceful privacy of his office he should multiply the figure by a "turmoil factor" to arrive at an estimate of reading time in the shop. Does each inspector have this amount of time to spare for reading? If he should take the time would he not bottleneck the flow of material?

There is no easy solution to this basic communications problem. Inspectors and supervisors could meet in an off-work area to listen to an explosion on the latest instruction, to question it and to arrive at a common understanding of it, and agreement on how to apply it. Obviously, such briefings must be arranged at times not detrimental to the flow of production. Something can be done with billboards when the instruction is not lengthy. Sampling tables lend themselves to this kind of display.

There are other alternatives, which should be explored and implemented, but the important thing is to recognize the problem. □

The receiving inspection report

☐ What do you want to say? To whom do you want to say it? These questions are just as relevant in quality assurance as in any other field of human endeavor. Indeed, perhaps more so, because quality communications are by their very nature unpopular. They purport to be reports on quality, while they are, in fact, reports on the lack of it.

There is no hiding this fundamental fact and since this is so, we ought to consider how to make quality communications acceptable and effective. Not acceptable in the sense of being popular, but by virtue of being readable and accurate. To be readable they must be pointed; what they have to say must strike the reader at first glance. To be accurate they must lay the blame exactly where it belongs.

Let us take as an example a report on receiving inspection. Let it be the monthly report to management. What is the most pointed piece of information one can aim at management? It is the percentage of lots found defective. If, for example, 1000 lots of purchased material were inspected during the month, what management wants to know primarily is whether 2, 5, 10, or 15% were found defective.

What is the percent defective?

Management wants to know whether things are getting better, worse, or staying the same. Therefore, the report must compare this month's percent defective with last month's. Management wants to know trends. So, the report should be accompanied by a simple bar chart in which percent of lots found defective is plotted month by month.

It may be objected that some lots are large and some are small. Therefore, it may be considered necessary in particular cases to divide purchased materials into two or more classes; when it would become necessary to report percents defective against each class. However, such classifications should be approached with caution, since it does not follow that the importance of a lot is directly related to its size. We have seen the rejection of a handful of urgently needed parts cause chaos on the line, and this is probably a fairly common experience. Even if one considers the nature of the material, it is equally likely that the rejection of a lot of simple contacts may upset the schedule as much as the rejection of a consignment of complex components. To fulfill the schedule, all of the lots, large or small, simple or complex, must arrive on time and all must meet the quality standards. ▶

QUALITY REPORT ON SUPPLIERS
Month of January

1. Total number of lots of
   purchased-direct material inspected   1000
2. Number of lots found defective
   (some or all of the material)   84
3. Percent of total defective. 8.4%
4. Percent defective last month. 9.5%
5. Comments:
6. Three worst suppliers this month:

		Number of Parts Inspected	Number Defective	Percent Defective
a.	Sub-Marginal Corp.	1600	800	50%
b.	Meta-Spec Industries	2000	700	35%
c.	Anti-Sigma Co., Inc.	1400	350	25%

As you can see from the sample report, the three worst suppliers for the month have been identified. This is to point up the fact that there are indeed such unfortunates; unfortunate both for themselves and for the purchaser.

In identifying the three worst suppliers, we have switched to a parts count to get a comparison which is independent of the number of lots. But the question arises: What about the complexity of the parts? Should the less complex parts be weighted to make them comparable with the effort made by the supplier of more complex parts? We have personally tried various weighting systems and, apart from the difficulty of finding a truly equitable system, I now think they tend to overlook an essential feature of quality measurement.

Quality is quality by definition. A simple device has the requisite quality when all of its measurable characteristics are within the specified limits; the same is true for a complex device. Quantitatively, each is a "quality" article when it is in full conformance with the applicable specification; neither has more "quality" than the other. Of course, qualitatively, one product may be considered "higher" quality than another (a Cadillac than a Chevrolet, for example) but in the field of quality measurement we must stick to conformance or lack of conformance to the specification.

Thus, it is possible to put together an inspection report on purchased material, which is both readable (pointed) and accurate (lays the blame where it belongs) by concentrating on the crucial question: Did the supplier make the effort he was paid for?   □

Quality, the key to profit

☐ Well, is it? The statement falls so glibly off the tongue. But is it true? If it is true, what is quality control's contribution?

What does it take to make a profit? An organization, some money, a product, and a market. Which is of greatest import?

Good men are available, if you look for them. There's plenty of money for those who can convince investors a profit can be made. The current market is beyond the wildest dreams of our Victorian forefathers. Thus, the crucial requirement is the product . . . but it must be a good one!

A "good" product is one that does what it's advertised to do. If a razor, it must take off whiskers without taking off skin too; if a refrigerator, it must keep the beer cold; if a walking doll, it must really walk.

The customer, be it DOD or a housewife at a sale, BUYS ADVERTISED PERFORMANCE . . . that is, QUALITY. That's what the company sells, and that's what it has to keep right on selling to make a profit. It is the specific task of qc to assure management that only quality items are released to the market; to assure that they conform to advertising, catalog, blueprint or specifications.

Tolerances vs capabilities

An ever-present potential danger, and frequently the biggest factor contributing to poor quality, is the conflict between engineering tolerances and production capabilities.

Engineering tolerances are arbitrary in that they are dictated by the necessities of design. This is understood by all. But production capabilities are equally arbitrary . . . and this is not so widely known.

Quality control's use of the word "capability" must be understood. If it is stated that capability of a process is ± 0.0010 in., this is not to say that this is the best the process can do . . . it doesn't mean that the process couldn't produce pieces with a tighter tolerance. This is how the word is commonly understood, unfortunately . . . and the result is a misunderstanding which blocks communication between qc specialists and their colleagues in parallel departments. ▶

What is actually meant is that the process has an inherent tendency to "spread" ±0.0010 in. Or, again, that when the process is varying only from "chance" or "natural" causes it will spread ±0.0010 in.

This explanation may introduce another problem in communication. It presupposes a knowledge of variability and its presence in all the repetitive production processes; and such knowledge is not universal.

Typical example

Let's say engineering tolerance on a dimension is ±0.0005 in. Let's imagine the capability of the process on which the part is made to be ±0.0010 in. Provided the operator sets-up on the nominal, the process will make many parts within the limits of ±0.0005 in. Indeed, it may make some parts no more than ±0.0001 in. from nominal, and it may by random chance, right on nominal. But it will also make a substantial number of parts in excess of ±0.0005 in. up to ±0.0010 in.

Any qualified qc engineer can tell what percentage of parts can be expected to be outside (and inside) tolerance limits . . . that is, he can predict the yield.

Since the process is going to spread to the limits of its "capability," it is obvious that maximum yield from any process will be obtained when process "capability" is equal to or less than the engineering tolerance. But whatever the relationship between engineering tolerances and process capabilities, a reliable prediction as to yield of good parts can be made when process capabilities have been determined.

This can be done by statistical techniques of production process analysis known to every quality control specialist.

To make a profit, a company must make and market a "quality" product; it must be able to predict the percent of quality pieces. Quality control assures the one, and can provide the other. Thus, the product, production, profit (dependent on the ability to predict the yield), and quality control are all locked in together.

The optimum

☐ Imagine that you, the quality manager, are at a staff meeting; the proposal is made "to optimize quality." Such a proposal would be likely to win your instant approval.

Again, imagine you're the production manager and the proposal is made "to optimize costs." "Good" you might say, "Let's go."

But would either of you be right? I mean, would either of you be approving a policy that would work out the way you thought it would?

Well, what does optimum mean? What is the optimum? Webster's Seventh New Collegiate defines optimum as "best; most favorable; greatest degree attainable under implied or specified conditions." We might say then, that in an optimizing exercise, one variable is to be optimized, while another interacting variable is to be held constant (the specified condition). Again, "optimize" is frequently used as though it were synonymous with "maximize."

Just what is the optimum?

Does this mean that the quality manager sees the quality as a variable to be maximized while the costs are held constant? Does he mean to commit himself to a policy which states, in effect: As much quality as can be attained, without exceeding the specified maximum cost, will be enough. Surely not!

Does the production manager mean to maximize costs in the effort to attain a fixed or specified level of quality? Of course not. Because, of course, the "most favorable" is not necessarily the maximum. To optimize costs is to minimize them. Does the production manager mean then, that he will minimize costs while holding quality at a specified level? Would that he did!

It appears that the quality manager should favor a policy which optimizes (minimizes) costs while holding quality at a specified level. While the production manager should favor a policy of optimizing (maximizing) quality while not exceeding specified cost. This brings us to the crux of the matter. ▶

All roads lead to consumerism

As all roads once led to Rome, nowadays all roads lead to consumerism. The policy of optimizing quality for a fixed maximum manufacturing cost, has been the de facto policy in many commercial mass production organizations. Far too frequently, specified maximum costs have been inadequate to attain advertised quality. Companies are now paying the price as they stagger beneath the blows of angry consumers and their advocates.

What's to be done? Well, producers have to decide which variable is to be fixed and which is to be optimized. Recent experience has shown that what must be fixed is the advertised quality (performance, durability, safety). This is the starting point. Producers of consumer goods must make sure that their executives know exactly how much quality has been advertised ... that is, they must know the advertised quality in quantitative terms.

We must produce as advertised

The advertised quality determines the minimum cost level. Various other costs and the desired profit are added to arrive at the selling price. At which point, a company may find it has priced itself out of the market!

So ... it may decide to produce less quality, and advertise accordingly; or get more efficient in production and reduce manufacturing costs; or reorganize to attain greater over-all efficiency. But whatever is done, the advertised quality cannot be considered as a variable to be optimized; the quality is the "specified condition"; not to be maximized or minimized; just to be produced ... as advertised. □

Technicians and economists

☐ At the XVth Conference of the European Organization for Quality Control, (EOQC), held in Moscow in 1971, 84% of the papers were presented by technicians, as opposed to only 14% by economists. "Others" accounted for the remaining 2%. At the XVIIth Conference, held in Belgrade in 1973, the breakdown was 82% technicians, 13% economists and 5% others.

So reports Dr. Bronislaw Oyrzanowski, Professor of Economics at the Jagellonian University, Krakow, Poland, and Chairman of the Committee for Quality Control of the Polish Economic Society. The articles appear in the Summer '74 issue of EOQC Journal.

Dr. Oyrzanowski's point is precisely presented in the juxtaposition of 84% and 82% technicians versus 14% and 13% economists. The "mix" is out of balance. The overwhelming proportion of technicians tilts the scale heavily in favor of the technical point of view with too little regard for the economic whole, of which technical expertise is only a part.

The percentages are out of balance

What is the relevance of these figures for managers and consultants in industrial production? In the first case, would the same disproportionate ratio of technicians to economists prevail at the national and regional conferences of ASQC? I think so. I know that when I check through the programs looking for papers concerned with organizational and social interface I am somewhat amazed by the preponderance of papers on technical subjects.

In the second case, does the same disproportion exist in the organizations where we work and advise? No! No! A thousand times no! And that is the problem.

The problem is that in industrial and governmental organizations the paramount concern is for economics, as indeed it should be, since economics is a large part of what life and work are about. Which means that technical proposals are listened to with economic ears; they are evaluated in an economic context. ►

Now, we in quality control have to learn how to interface with the economic organizations of which we are a part. I don't mean, of course, that we are completely ignorant. If this were the case, we would have vanished long ago. Even so, we don't multiply fast enough. There are about 57,000 sizable manufacturing corporations in the U.S., whereas the current membership of ASQC is only about 24,000. There are, of course, quality control practitioners outside of ASQC, but these 24,000 are the "official" quality control population. For each sizable corporation, we have less than half of a quality control man or woman! And nobody for the smaller outfits.

What to do about it? To interface with the economic organizations we serve, we must learn the language and recognize the distinction between technical and economic considerations. We are not going to learn the language when we spend so much time talking to each other as witnessed by Dr. Oyrzanowski's ratios. We must attend management and business seminars and we should certainly do some reading in economics. As for the distinction between technical and economic considerations, let me conclude by presenting an example. Whereas the selection of a sampling plan is a technical task, the decision to inspect by sampling is an economic task. Moreover, the economic decision should precede the technical implementation.

Know the economic consequences

But in most plants the economic decision to sample has been thrust upon the quality control supervisor. I suppose because he was frequently the only one who could read the sampling tables or was at home on the slippery slopes of the OC curves. He himself has generally accepted the burden of this major economic decision. As a consequence he may find himself commended for the immediate economic gain of reduced inspection costs . . . but he is being increasingly condemned as more and more companies realize that they have, or may have, non-complying products in the field. A couple of simple axioms will help to remind the technician that he operates in an economic environment. (1) Look at the economic consequences before you leap to put a technical procedure into operation. (2) Insist on the approval of top management before you use sampling for final product acceptance. Make sure that marketing and field service know the consequences of sampling. □

Planning versus performance

☐ What's so sacred about the planning? Why does the planning always get off scot-free at the monthly *post-mortem?* Why do the operating managers get clobbered for falling short of planned goals while the planners just sit there enjoying the show? Why don't we ask instead whether there was ever any possibility of meeting the planned goals?

It's not easy to answer these questions but before we try, let us attend one of those monthly meetings called by the chief executive to see what went wrong in the previous month.

We, the department managers, gather in the conference room and kid each other about who's going to get it this time. After the chief makes his entrance, orders for coffee are taken. Cautious conservation prevails while the secretary fills these orders. Most get what they asked for and the meeting comes to order.

Here we go again!

The chief may make a general attack: "Alright guys. What happened?" Or he may pick on Marketing: "What happened in the Midwest?" Or on Production: "I see that we missed the schedule again." Or on Purchasing: "Why did the cost of supplies exceed our estimate?" and so on.

The questions, the charges, the accusations are aimed at performance. The operating managers attempt to explain their shortcomings. They don't challenge the planning. It's almost inconceivable that Marketing would reply: "What happened is that Planning overlooked the fact that there's no surf in the Middle West, so they didn't buy surfboards!" Or that Production should assert "That schedule was utterly unrealistic. There's no way we could have made it! No way!" Or that Purchasing should respond: "That estimate was an arbitrary figment of the imagination of the geniuses in Planning and Cost Accounting. Any similarity between it and current prices is purely coincidental."

Yet these statements may be true. The reason they aren't made is that managers are oriented in their thinking to recognize that performance may

▶

be inadequate, but not that the planning might be impossible. Indeed, the attitude is manifested in the framed statements one sees in so many offices: "The difficult we do immediately. The impossible will take a little time!" These optimistic slogans hang around gathering dust while the difficult sometimes takes forever, and the impossible remains impossible.

The attitude is further confirmed by the frequency with which "problems" in management seminars and text books are presented as errors of performance. Rarely, if ever, is it suggested that an "inadequate" performance may be evidence that the planning was beyond the capability of the organization.

The Pangloss Syndrome

The modest admission that the "impossible may take a little time"; the practice of setting over-optimistic schedules; the reluctance to recognize that performance may be as much a measure of the realism of the planning as of the competence of managers and operators, all fit nicely into what may be called the Pangloss Syndrome. Dr. Pangloss in Voltaire's "Candide" remained an inveterate optimist despite all experience. He infected Candide with his blind optimism and poor Candide barely escaped with his life.

However, the times are changing, the state of the economy has compelled Washington bureaucrats and industrial executives to ask, "How did we get this way? What did we do?" Even in such dire straits there's a reluctance to speak of the "planning," but the planning, or lack of it, is what these questions have in mind.

In this new managerial climate, chief executives are going to want to know, not only why performance fell short, but whether the planned goals were ever attainable. Quality managers should make sure that their data collecting and analysis capability is in good shape, in preparation for that incredible day when they will be asked "What do the figures tell us about the planning?" □

After-dinner speaking

☐ After-dinner speaking should be done after breakfast. In that way, the audience might absorb and benefit from what the speaker has so carefully prepared.

After breakfast, the members of the audience are not exhausted by a day's work, nor partially plastered. Not that I think it's a crime to be partially plastered. Indeed, you might feel that a man has a right to "tie on a few" after a hard day's work. But it doesn't improve the ability to appreciate a good argument presented by the speaker.

It's interesting to speculate on how after-dinner speaking came into vogue. I suppose it started way back in the dawn of history, when our ancestors spent a lot of time hunting and fighting. At the end of the day, they would gather 'round a roaring fire on which an ox, or a boar, or the leg of a dinosaur was roasting. There would be heavy drinking and the women might be hovering on the fringe of the feast, ready to rescue thoroughly smashed warriors who fell into the fire. At least, I suppose they rescued them. But what a marvelous opportunity for an aggrieved wife to let a temporarily smashed husband stay in long enough to singe beyond salvation!

I'll have a mead and tonic

Anyway, the ox is finally roasted and torn apart by the famished warriors and washed down with mead or moonshine, or whatever. The satiated, smashed warriors, many of them still relatively conscious, loll around the fire.

This is the moment they've been waiting for. The bearded bard rises to his feet, and in a furious rush of words recounts the day's hunting or fighting, telling how the fierce animals or the fiercer enemies were overcome; and what great heroes they are; and what great heroes their ancestors were; and how the Gods look down on them with utmost admiration and approval!

Homer must have been one of the first after-dinner speakers. Not that I mean to infer that the Greeks were heavy drinkers, but I expect they took a few. Anyway, you can see that there wouldn't be much of a question and answer period after such an event. When a poet tells you what a marvelous man you are, what's to question? Whereas, the contemporary after-dinner speaker is likely to present a provocative argument that demands many questions and answers. ▶

Typically, the chairman will allow one or perhaps two questions, and then close the meeting because, after all, it's now 9:30 or 10:00 pm and it's been a long day for everybody.

These thoughts were provoked when, recently, I was the after-dinner speaker at a company management club. There were about a hundred people present from every department of the company. I had been asked to trace the connection between market price and quality control.

What is the real issue?

So I developed what I believe to be the most important issue at this time for all companies mass-producing items for the vast consumers' market. Which is:

- That the prices of popular items of considerable technical complexity are made possible only by mass production methods and inspection by sampling.
- That sampling creates the probability of some defectives.
- That the probable rate of defectives should be known by all responsible members of the company, particularly by sales executives.
- That the estimated defective rate should be made the basis for an adequate warranty and maintenance program.
- That the warranty and maintenance program should be executed promptly and without grudge.

Well, I got most of this across. There were a couple of questions and the meeting closed because it was 10:00 pm and everybody, including me, wanted to hit the freeway and get home.

However, I received many questions by phone the next day, and because of the interest in the subject shown on this and other occasions, I'm organizing seminars, especially for non-QC managers, many of whom are not aware of the consequences of sampling.

But to get back to after-dinner speakers; I don't really think that it's going to be switched to after-breakfast, but it could be switched to before-dinner. Then there would be a commanding subject for conversation during dinner. The speaker could join in the festivities and would be available for extensive questioning. I've suggested it at various times and on two occasions it was tried. Both occasions were successful in that the subject matter of the speech was thoroughly explored during dinner, and many more questions were asked in the relaxed atmosphere of the cocktail bar and dinner table. There are questions you can ask with a scotch and soda in one hand that you wouldn't ask if you had to stand up formally and shout across the audience at the distant speaker. Anyway, program managers, you might give it some thought. □

Quality control in fiction

☐ "The president of General Motors was in a foul humor. He had slept badly because his electric blanket had worked only intermittently. Taking the mechanism apart he observed a badly joined connection. Muttering sourly about poor quality control of blanket manufacturers, the GM president took the unit to his basement workshop to repair."

Don't be alarmed. We haven't been spying on GM and its current president. What you have just read is a quote from *Wheels** by Arthur Hailey. The president is fictitious, although GM is real enough.

Not only is it a quote from this fascinating novel (of which the true hero is automobile production, as airport management was the hero of Hailey's *Airport*) but it's the very first paragraph! Quality Control gets shot down on page 1!

How would your boss react?

How would a quality professional expect a well-informed executive to respond? After the first moment of exasperation, he might recall that there's no way to get millions of automobiles onto the market at a competitive price except by mass production methods, one of which is inspection by sampling. He might have muttered, "This must have been part of a lot accepted by sampling. I suppose I'm just one of the consumers selected randomly by chance to suffer from the allowable fraction defective. Oh well. C'est la vie."

D'you think it's likely to happen? No? Neither do I. One could wish that executives and consumers would learn to think along these lines. But, while they are capable of understanding the inexorable risks of sampling as an intellectual exercise, they do not incorporate it into the thinking that directs their daily lives. And neither, I suspect, do we, the specialists. When I get into my car and start the engine and charge onto the freeway, it's not because I've computed the probability of failure for my car and the other thousands that share the freeway with me. I just drive along, confident that I shall get where I'm going. ▶

If we had been at that breakfast table we could have told the fictitious president that what happened to his electric blanket might happen to any mass-produced article and that, furthermore, we could not predict zero probability of failure even with 100% inspection. From which it follows, we would say, assuming that he were still listening, that the only rational policy is to do everything possible within the imposed cost constraints to minimize the probability of defects; and then to be prepared to provide prompt courteous service in the event of failure. To which he might reply, "D'you mean to tell me that we don't give prompt courteous service?" What could we say, except "Go out and try it, but don't let them know who you are."

What does quality control demand

What else happened in *Wheels*? On page 8, Matt Zaleski, assistant plant manager, runs smack into a grievance the moment he steps into his office. As he leaves to find out what it's all about, he glances at the pile of paper on his desk, sure that it will contain more headaches, "material shortages, quality control demands, machinery failures." Does it sound familiar? Those material shortages! But as for quality control, what could they "demand" except that the product be somewhat like the blueprints?

Zaleski's foreman, Frank Parkland, is sounding off on page 17. "You are on our necks every day for production, production, more production; and if it isn't you it's Quality Control who say, build 'em better even though you're building faster." You can see that the author did his homework thoroughly!

By page 180 the new model the designers have been working on is well on its way, and so is Matt Zaleski's ulcer. Plant management now wants him "to increase production yet hold down plant costs and somehow raise quality standards." How's that for an assignment!

Although we cannot eliminate the risks of sampling, we can and should do something about the fairly common impression of quality control as just one more burden on the backs of the already overburdened production people. It would make a good seminar: How to improve quality control's image. Every time I get the chance, I give it a bit of a polish. Let us all do the same and perhaps some day someone will write a novel in which the hero is a quality control engineer. □

---

*"Wheels" by Arthur Hailey; Doubleday & Company.

MBO and system capability

☐ MBO, management by objectives, was all the rage a few years ago. I was reminded about it by an amusing book called *Systemantics.* * The author, Dr. John Gall, a professor at the University of Michigan, deserves to be bracketed with Parkinson, who propounded the law of perpetual bureaucratic growth, and Professor Peter, who assures us that the managerial aspirant may expect to rise to his or her level of incompetence! Dr. Gall's words of sardonic wisdom are that organizational systems don't ever do what they are designed to do!

This will come as no surprise to those who search diligently day by day for any similarity between Standard Operating Procedures and what they see going on around them.

Dr. Gall selects MBO for one of his sharpest comments. The effect of inviting managers to state their own goals, and then to measure them against their own promises, he defines as "administrative encirclement."

Failure rate almost equaled production rate

This brought to mind a quality problem on which I was invited to consult. The product was and is an excellent consumers' item. However, at the time I speak of, the failure rate in the field was almost equal to the production rate. The product, while still in the engineering development stage, earned the admiration of the man at the peak of the pyramid. "Start production at once," he said ... and that was that. His word was irresistible; the result was inevitable.

A plan was outlined which called for the meticulous collection of field failure reports; the Pareto analysis of them; and concentrated efforts by Production to eliminate what were designated Pareto Dominants. Another feature of the plan was the publication month by month of what was called the Gross Quality Statistic. This was the ratio of defective units in the current month to the total of units shipped in the same month, twelve months previously.

In the beginning this was an appalling figure, but in a few months we had it down to 18 percent. At this point in time, the man at the peak took a

▶

course in MBO. Now each department manager had to forecast anticipated improvements in quantitative terms. The quality manager was asked to forecast what ultimate figure the 18 percent would decline to, and when.

It was pointed out that the failure rate would decline until it leveled off at a value which would be a measure of the *System Capability,* the "system" being the entire organization (design, production, quality control, etc.), while the "capability" was an inherent parameter of the system as then constituted. This parameter, the consequence of many variables, could not be predicted with any exactitude.

This argument was accepted, but since all other departments were committing themselves to objectives, Quality Control offered the likely figure of 3 percent to be achieved within the coming year.

Overshot the objective

As it happened, and because of the continued excellent cooperation between Production, Field Service and Quality Control, the failure rate stabilized at 1.5 percent in eight to nine months.

Fine . . . until the cost accountant noticed the discrepancy. We had overshot the objective of 3 percent. He proposed that the number of quality control inspectors be reduced to the point where the failure rate would rise to the prescribed objective of 3 percent!

It was almost as difficult rebutting this ostensibly logical argument as it had been to reduce the failure rate. However, it was done. I thought you might find the incident amusing and, possibly, instructive.　　□

---

*"Systemantics" by Dr. John Gall with drawings by R.O. Blechman; Quadrangle/The New York Times Book Company, 1977.

Why inspect?

☐ It's always been a matter of surprise to me that this question is so rarely asked. Company officials, production executives and engineers have been known to wonder why there should be so much quality control or, indeed, any at all. They also suffer from a certain amount of agonizing about quality assurance, which seems to be filling up all the corners that quality control failed to reach, but the fundamental question, Why inspect?—I mean, why inspect at all?!—is seldom asked.

Purchase orders don't specify what percentage of material may be defective, yet defective material is supplied. How much? Are we talking about 0.1%, or what? Well, it varies with the industry, but 2 to 5% is fairly common, and 20% is not unknown.

Machinists and assemblers aren't hired to turn out defective parts and assemblies, but they do. That is, they make a number of parts and assemblies that have to be scrapped or reworked. They do this about 1 to 8% of the time, depending on the product.

Why do we have all those defects?

Why? Before we try to find the answer let it be understood that everyone is trying to supply and make good parts. Neither the suppliers nor the machinists nor the girls on the assembly lines are goofing off. They regret the scrap and rework as much as anyone. Then why do they make it?

There are three causes:
- Variability
- Technology
- Schedule

Variability is the nightmare that haunts the would-be producers of identical interchangeable parts. Experience has shown time and again that an attempt to make 100 or 100,000 identical parts is doomed to failure. No matter how new the machine tool is, nor how carefully the operation is tended, the parts come out different. There is a perverse tendency to variability! ▶

Now, we all know that Dr. Shewhart and his colleagues at Bell Labs, working on the problems of inspection, quality and economy during the 20's and 30's, developed a set of techniques for the measurement and control of manufacturing process variability. Variability may be an absolute barrier to the production of identical parts, but not to the production of good parts, when by "good" we mean parts within the drawing tolerance limits. All that is required is to keep in mind the natural limits of variability as measured by the Shewhart techniques and not to load the manufacturing processes beyond their capabilities. The rule is that the specified tolerance limits on the part should exceed the natural spread of the process.

Technological change + tighter tolerances = process variability

Why don't we follow Dr. Shewhart's advice and circumvent variability? Or, rather, why don't we do it more frequently? Because of technology. It gets tiresome constantly referring to the accelerating pace of technological change, but it should never be forgotten. It's the most significant portent of the times and if you don't keep your eye on it, you're likely to get left behind. Technological change demands greater accuracy and closer and closer tolerance limits. The demands are constantly ahead of the state of the manufacturing art. Nevertheless, producers must attempt to manufacture what's wanted on the available machines. Therefore, jobs with narrow tolerance limits must be assigned to processes with wider natural spreads, assuring that some defective parts will be made. The output must be inspected to sort the good parts from the bad.

What about the schedule? The schedule affects the situation by virtue of the tendency to variability in production operators. Since people are different, both in their ability to comprehend a given task and in their ability to execute it, it is inherently impossible to set the scheduled pace of production to suit everybody. Whatever the pace, there will be some for whom it will be a burden, creating the probability that defective parts will be made and inspection necessitated.

Thus, variability, technology and the schedule create that modern industrial environment characterized by the extreme demands made upon resources, both human and mechanical. We are, as it were, constantly running ahead of ourselves. It would be interesting to find a moment in history when we weren't, but that is an academic question. The immediate problem is the continued production of discrepant parts, the necessity for inspection, and the development of quality assurance plans alert to the effects of variability, technology and the schedule. □

Who should inspect?

☐ This question comes up at every Quality Control conference. And well it might because the inspectors are required to perform a harsh and necessary task. They are expected to look for defectives and to exclude them from the bulk of shippable product, thereby cutting into the scheduled quantity all others are striving to fulfill. Furthermore, they are required to keep records which, when analyzed by quality engineers, point directly at those deficiencies in the production system which cause the defects. Thus they are required to act as critics of the product and of the production system.

The net result is the progressive correction of systemic deficiencies with a consequent reduction in the number of defects. The ability to meet scheduled deliveries with acceptable product is improved; scrap and rework costs are reduced. But this is not apparent in the short run. All that is obvious in hour-by-hour operations is that the inspectors obstruct the ordered flow of production.

This apparent obstruction is exasperating to production bosses, an attitude with which the sensitive quality specialist can surely empathize. The logical reaction of the production bosses is to seek control of the inspectors; and so it is persistently asserted that the producers should inspect their own work.

Inspectors must be psychologically qualified

Which would be fine if it can be shown that producers are qualified to inspect their own work. I don't mean qualified in the sense of being able to use measuring equipment; because they can do that, or they could be instructed. I mean psychologically qualified; which is the prime qualification for the satisfactory performance of any task.

In the first case, the producers would have to be capable of an unbiased attitude toward their own work. To do this they would have to be different from the rest of mankind. A bias in one's own favor is a universal attribute

▶

of the human being, male or female. Without it, he or she would be defenseless against the frequently critical attitudes of colleagues and even of friends and relatives. Subjective bias is our only armor.

So the producer is disqualified by bias as an inspector of his own work. But, for the sake of argument, let us say that he's not. Let us imagine that there are producers of a special breed utterly without bias in their own favor.

Even so, they would still have to be motivated to care about the quality before they could put forth the effort to make a close examination. Are they so motivated? Not in mass production. Why not?

They're not emotionally or technically involved

Because mass production is a system of serialized repetitive operations which manual operators are required to perform exactly as planned. The planning is done for them, excluding them from emotional commitment. Furthermore, each operation is such a small fraction of the whole that the worker cannot identify with the end product, so that he cannot feel any technical or intellectual involvement. In the absence of emotional commitment and technical involvement, there is no motivation to care for the quality.

Motivation is an impulse from within; but it must be stimulated from without. The objective situation must prompt the individual to respond with emotional and technical interest. The objective situation in mass production for the line worker is negative on both counts.

It appears, therefore, that human nature being what it is, and mass production being what it is, the producer is not qualified to inspect his own work. This is not to say that producers are not qualified to inspect. Competent producers are frequently transferred into quality control and make excellent inspectors. It all depends on whether your bias is hurting, and whether you are emotionally committed and technically involved; inspection requires both.

It is relevant to comment on the fact that mass production is the basis for the affluence to which the line workers make such a heavy contribution, and in which they share. It might be thought that this would act as a stimulus to quality motivation. Apparently it doesn't. We may live objectively in a social macrocosm; but we exist subjectively in a series of microcosms, one microcosm at a time.   □

"When in doubt, stamp it out!"

☐ I suppose you've heard it said that when an inspector is in doubt about the quality of the parts he's inspecting, he rejects them automatically! It's quite remarkable how many in industry believe this. And yet it isn't true!

The belief in the inflexible inspector, stern and unbending, unwilling "to give the company a break," is an article of faith that may never die.

Why not? Well, because in the first case there may indeed have been some isolated examples to support the assertion. But the overwhelming case for its survival and perpetuation is that it provides such a beautiful alibi! It allows the unfortunate producer of rejected parts to believe that the parts would have gone through if it weren't for this objectionable quirk of inspectors.

Covering their bases

It should be understood that beautiful alibis survive because they are believed to be true. But why should they be believed in so readily? Because, in general, they support what the believer believes about himself. In our particular case, the myth of the hardnosed inflexible inspector survives because it supports the believer's reluctance to accept that he could have made defective parts, or that he could have made so many.

But what do the inspectors say? "WHEN in DOUBT, STAMP it OUT!" You must have heard it. Just in case there are readers who aren't familiar with the phrase "stamp it out," the stamp is the inspector's acceptance stamp. When he finds a consignment of parts in conformance with the specification, he stamps the "paper," that is the accompanying control document. He may be required to stamp the parts themselves too, but either way he "stamps it out."   ►

But the inspectors do pass questionable lots

Why do inspectors quote to each other such a cynical code? Because it epitomizes what many feel is expected of them. It is possible in mass production that an appreciable percentage of the parts manufactured may be "on the borderline." That is, they appear to be just outside the specified tolerance limits; just under the lower tolerance limit in the case of an outside dimension; just outside the upper tolerance limit in the case of an inside dimension. But there may be some doubt about it. The inspector who conscientiously rejects such borderline cases is likely to find himself in the middle of a big hassle. Doesn't he know the schedule's "to hell and gone a'ready!" What's he getting uptight about! Nitpicker! It's a hassle, and who wants it? So, say the inspectors, "WHEN in DOUBT, STAMP it OUT!"

But times have changed and we are all, inspectors and producers alike, confronted by consumerism. Manufacturing organizations must know the exact quality of products they ship to the market. Indeed, it might be wise for producers to urge inspectors to act as they have for so long been unjustly accused of acting. "Inspectors," they might say, "when you're in doubt, for heaven's sake, reject! Then we can find out where the quality really is." □

Anatomy of an inspection report

☐ Do you find that inspection reports answer all reasonable questions, or do you have to conduct an anatomy? Inspection reports tend to be cryptic because they employ a special terminology known, in general, only to initiates; an example is "AQL." But the cryptic nature of the terminology is not peculiar to quality control; every technical specialty has one. The problem I have in mind is the inspection report which is not clear even when examined by a quality control specialist.

Let's take an example. You're supplying Metalunar with part #7470B. Your last shipment to them of 2,000 pieces has just been returned. Your friendly sales manager is on the verge of hysteria; the production control people are wailing against the wall of receiving inspection.

But while the girls in sales endeavor to calm their distraught boss, and the expeditors assuage their grief, you, the inspection supervisor, must do something.

What are they telling me?

What you have to do will be dictated to some extent by Metalunar's rejection report. What did their inspector write?

>   *Part: #7470B*
>   *Quantity: 2,000*
>   *Defect: 1.250 in.   ± 0.002 in. oversize*

That's all the Metalunar report says . . . and it leaves in doubt the following questions:

- How much oversize?
- How many are oversize?
- Did Metalunar sample? If so, what was the AQL, sample size, and acceptance number?
- How many defectives were found in the sample?
- The part has, say, five dimensions. Were the other dimensions checked and found OK?

You don't know. But let us attempt an anatomy of Metalunar's report. It is probable, though not certain, that they sampled . . . for if the lot had been inspected 100%, the entire lot would not have been returned. Good pieces would have been retained, and the balance of defective pieces shipped back.

It is probable, though not certain, that the remaining dimensions are satisfactory because it seems the reasonable thing to do to complete the inspection before shipping the lot back. But the report doesn't say so, and we must bear in mind that what is considered reasonable varies considerably.

A complete report would have left no questions

There would have been no questions to ponder over had Metalunar's rejection report stated:

> Part: #7470B
> Quantity: 2,000
> Defect: 1.250 in.   ±0.002 in. oversize to 1.255 in.
> 1% AQL (MIL-STD-105D)
> Sample: 125
> Acc. #:   3
> Number of defectives in sample: 7
> Remaining dimensions acceptable
> Lot returned for screening.

At first glance, it might appear that this is a lengthy report. For example, "MIL-STD-105D" might have been omitted on the assumption that both supplier and customer were agreed to draw sampling plans from 105D; but was it agreed? If agreed, then the sample size and Acc. # might have been omitted on the further assumption that the customer and you, the supplier, are agreed on single sampling at inspection level II.

Even the phrase "remaining dimensions acceptable" might be omitted if it's agreed between you and your customer that the stated cause for rejection is all that is wrong with the parts, that all other dimensions and features have been checked. But do these agreements exist and are these assumptions warranted?

When inspectors don't fill in available blocks on preprinted reports, or when they write bare reports like Metalunar's inspection above, it's not, in general, because they hold the instruction in disregard, but because they've been told too many times to "Keep it moving! Don't take all day writing an essay!" Such admonitions delivered in the interest of sectional efficiency sometime contribute to inefficiency in the overall system, the ultimate recipient of the report being very much a part of the system.

It's an interesting and possibly instructive exercise for a quality manager to cruise through his inspection areas, to pick up rejection reports at random, and to check whether he can understand them without the aid of the inspectors who wrote them. Try it.   □

On the line with the inspector

☐ What's it like to be an inspector? What's it like to be out there in the midst of the battle for quality, inspecting parts and assemblies, stamping off the acceptable and hanging rejection tags on the defectives?

The question hit me while reading "The Face of Battle."* The author, John Keegan, is an instructor at Sandhurst, the British West Point. He was going along nicely, instructing future officers, until one day the question occurred to him, "What about the soldiers; what keeps them in the line in the face of danger?"

So he studied three great battles (Agincourt, Waterloo and The Somme) and found that what encourages the soldiers to stand and fight is the presence of and the example set by the officers. Simple? Well . . . yes, but it's not the conclusion you would arrive at from a general reading of history. From the latter one gets the impression that Caesar "fought" the Gauls; that Wellington "fought" Napoleon at Waterloo; that the Revolutionary War was fought and won, not by those ragged soldiers with feet wrapped in sacking, but by Washington in that flowing cloak. The implication in Keegan's simple statement is that it's the soldiers who win (or lose) battles and that officers (and managers) should never forget it.

Thrown into a cage of lions

What's it like then to be an inspector? It's a difficult job. He or she works in a hostile environment. Nobody's going to shoot at them, but their lives can be made quite uncomfortable. Producers do not jump for joy when a rejection tag is hung on parts or an assembly into which they have put so much effort. On the contrary, they are likely to start an argument and if that gets them nowhere, they appeal to the production supervisor. Then the inspector is confronted by a ranting individual with more rank and what is he to do? Appeal to the audience? They're all producers! He withstands the attack this time, but the next time he's going to think twice, especially if the deviation is, say, no more than a thousandth of an inch above or below a tolerance of plus and minus five thousandths. If the measurement appears to fall smack on the upper or lower tolerance limit (on the borderline) he's not going to think twice.

▶

As Dr. Juran** points out, the treatment of borderline cases will have a profound effect on product quality as it affects the attitude (quality consciousness) of the production work force. The disposition of borderline cases cannot be left to the inspectors; they must not be compelled to make the decision by default.

You must isolate your inspectors

The quality manager must take steps to protect inspectors from the ranting of irate production supervisors and the constant prodding of expeditors. Ranting and prodding may be necessary in mass production, but the inspectors should not have to bear the brunt. The quality manager can arrange with his fellow managers that all inquiries and comments shall be addressed to him or his supervisors. It will be the more effective if the arrangement is made the subject of a management procedure.

The quality manager should deploy his troops so that every inspector has quick and easy access to a quality assurance supervisor. It may be necessary to increase the ratio of supervisors to inspectors for this purpose. As a general rule it may be said that the ratio of supervisors to workers in all categories should be determined, among other considerations, by the frequency with which problems may occur. The frequency's high in inspection . . . ask any inspector.

The quality manager himself must see and be seen by the inspectors. The inspectors must know that they have a representative in management. Each inspector must find himself or herself in the physical presence of the quality manager at least once a month; more frequently would be better. This can be effected by meetings to discuss problems, or instructional seminars, or by the manager's presence on the line. Let it be remembered that the quality, the degree of conformance to drawings and specifications is in the hands of the inspectors; the manager and supervisors are there to plan, to instruct, to solve difficult problems and to provide moral support.

□

*John Keegan; "The Face of Battle," Vintage Books, New York.
**J.M. Juran: "Quality Control Handbook," McGraw Hill.

The decline and fall of inspection

☐ Decline? Yes. Fall? Well . . . no; but had it not been for Zero Defects campaigns, inspection might have declined beyond the point of no return. The continued incidence of defects in missiles and spacecraft finally convinced us that we had to do something. Defects were often trifling in themselves but devastating in their effect on end-performance.

Zero Defects campaigns appealed to production operators for a return to craftsmanship, and quality control got a grip on inspection before it went down for the third time. We know what had happened to the production operators who, obviously, had to build the defects in before they could be missed by inspectors. They, the producers, had forgotten how to be craftsmen during the long years in mass production. But what happened to the inspectors—that they apparently lost the ability and/or the desire to find defects and reject them?

We can only speculate, because the revival of interest motivated by Zero Defects programs has already changed attitudes to such an extent that it may soon be difficult to recall what the recent past was like.

Prevention, not inspection

I think that the decline of inspection was a by-product of quality control's heavy emphasis on prevention. The shift in emphasis from "inspection" to "prevention" can be attributed to two main causes. In the first case, it is manifestly better to attempt to prevent the production of defective pieces than to inspect for defects when parts have been completed. In the second case, the tool for prevention is the set of statistical process control techniques developed by Dr. Shewhart and his Bell Labs colleagues in the late 20s.

Ever since then, quality control practitioners have sought professional recognition by attempting to add to the body of statistical knowledge, and by publishing reports of successful programs of prevention. ▶

But you should not neglect inspection

Thus, common sense and the desire for professional recognition have acted powerfully to keep the quality manager's attention focused on prevention. That this should lead to neglect of inspection was not the intent, but it was nevertheless, a typical example of human behavior. Indeed, the tendency to think "either/or" was strongly reinforced by the common practice of putting "prevention" and "inspection" in opposition. We would say, "Inspection is after the fact; while prevention gets in there before the defects have been produced!"

This was a completely valid argument and it was repeated so often that quality managers who still gave any thought to inspection began to feel like professional delinquents. Inspectors received less and less direction until they felt they were adrift in an administrative vacuum. As interest in them declined, the inspectors' enthusiasm declined and the probability that defects would be missed was greatly increased.

Then the Zero Defects rocket went up and in its bright light the lack of craftsmanship and of meticulous inspection was startingly illuminated. Attention was refocused on inspection, direction was sharpened, the inspectors' search for defects was pursued with renewed zeal. Now, the product is better, the cost is less and all's well that ends well. □

Zero defects and the vanishing craftsman

Motivate: To provide with a motive; to impel; to incite.
Motive: That within the individual, rather than with-
out, which incites him to action.
(Webster's Collegiate Dictionary, 5th Edition)

☐ Zero Defects programs are spreading like wildfire. It's reported that hundreds of industrial organizations have engaged in them. The Department of Defense and the National Aeronautics and Space Administration are keenly interested. Most of the companies with such programs are contractors for DoD or NASA, or both, but the movement is not confined to military and space contractors. It is spreading throughout the industry.

An outstanding feature of ZD programs is the emphasis on motivation. Posters flourish, dedication ceremonies bringing managers and machinists, customers and suppliers together are very impressive; the interest and enthusiasm are comparable to the "E for Excellence" campaign of World War II. This being the case, who is to be motivated?

Motivation is the method

Well, everybody, but in particular production operators. It's the machinists, sheet metal fabricators and assemblers who are to be motivated. Why? Because the advent of space exploration and the demand for one space vehicle to orbit the Earth, another to take pictures of the Moon, and another to make the incredible journey to Mars has compelled a sharp revision of manufacturing methods.

One or four or nine space vehicles cannot be mass-produced. Brilliant engineering and meticulous planning are required, but the quality of the article which carries our hopes into space depends ultimately on craftsmanship; and we don't have enough craftsmen!

It is no accident that there are so few craftsmen. We developed mass-production and made them superfluous. This is not said to deplore mass-production, but the demise of craftsmanship was a logical concomitant and must be recognized since it is relevant to Zero Defects programs and their probability of continuing success. ▶

The scarcity of craftsmen is not all. A question which must be considered is whether the production operators want to become craftsmen? There is no doubt about their ability, for they are the sons and grandsons of craftsmen. But production operators—like the program managers and members of DoD and NASA—have been molded, and their attitudes formed by the same powerful cultural influences. The culture manifests itself in an individual in many ways, but particularly in the tendency to believe that certain occupations confer social status and proof of success.

Nobody wants to be a craftsman

Manual work of all kinds is low on the status scale, and craftsmanship is manual work. Indeed, to say that manual work is low on the status scale is putting it mildly. It might be nearer to the truth to say that manual work is held in contempt, certainly in such a degree of disregard that many presently engaged in it reconcile themselves to their lot by the knowledge that their sons are at college qualifying to be managers or engineers. Those influenced by the cultural imperative to acquire white collar status are not opposed to craftsmanship, as such. Indeed, Italian shoes, English sports cars and German cameras—all believed to be the work of dedicated craftsmen—are universally admired; it's just that we don't want to be the craftsmen who made them.

As a consequence, production operators are apt to wish success to ZD programs as heartily as management and government officials, while tending to subconsciously resist the motivation to excel as manual craftsmen. "Resist" may not be the right word; it is rather that the cultural indoctrination has done its work well and truly, and production operators cannot learn overnight to admire and to wish to be what they have disparaged for so long.

Zero Defects programs have achieved considerable success, but the success will only be permanent if we give some thought to reinstating manual craftsmanship as a status symbol, and excellence therein as an object of social approval and admiration. □

A place in the sun

☐ It is interesting to study the flood of journalistic comment and encomium, of applause and condemnation for Zero Defects; and to find so many quality assurance practitioners among the critics. Yet ZD has created an industrial environment highly favorable to qa. Indeed, ZD has helped give qa a place in the sun.

The qa specialist is now at liberty to apply all that he knows to achieve Zero Defects, or to work in that direction. Having been shunned, or merely tolerated for many years, he is now the star. Everyone wants him to succeed.

It used to be difficult to get a budget for quality engineering; one could get something for inspectors, but for staff engineers, little or nothing. Whereas in the highly favorable environment created by ZD, the quality manager is likely to have a budget thrust upon him.

People are listening now

Much that the critics say is true. Indeed, statistical quality control procedures were specifically designed to identify and measure the behavior of the process as distinct from the operator. The simplest analysis of inspection and test data was likely to point to inadequate production facilities and/or poor management if these existed; but what a job it was to persuade anyone to listen!

In the favorable atmosphere created by ZD, the qa specialist can go to work with a will. If he identifies causes for error other than production operators, his recommendations will be given proper consideration. If anything, he will find the response uncritical since the state of mind created in all ranks by Zero Defects campaigns is predisposed to accept recommendations for quality improvement. We have been a voice crying in the wilderness and now we have been brought in and seated at the head of the table. ZD involves everybody and everybody is waiting to be pointed in the right direction. ▶

The comparison between driving into one's garage without an error in a lifetime, and the tendency to commit errors on the job has been drawn too far. In any case, since it is always the wife who shatters the walls of the garage, the comparison could only apply to the smaller section of the workforce.

But is ZD just so much hoopla?

Is there too much ballyhoo? Who's to say? There is a lot of history to show that if large numbers of people are to be persuaded to move in a certain direction, or to adopt a new point of view, it must be done by fervent speeches, by the creation of an emotionally charged atmosphere in which there is an impulse to dedication. On the more fortunate historic occasions, the emotionally dedicated have striven for a rational goal. Surely the goal of Zero Defects is a rational goal, for it is nothing less than the success of space exploration and the lives of the astronauts.

What about the cost? Well, there have been some remarkable successes reported, especially by those plants who report ZD program economic benefits as "costs avoided." There have also been some fairly heavy promotional expenses and it might be difficult to determine the net gain to the industry. One thing we can be sure of is the favorable environment created for quality engineering and analysis. We know that it is in the nature of qa analysis to identify both the quality and the cost and we can be equally sure that as qa practitioners move to take advantage of the ZD environment to improve quality, the techniques they employ will keep quality and cost in proper balance.

It might be said, "Why didn't they give us the money first, instead of spending so much on promotion?" But that isn't the way things are done. The thing to do is to plunge in and do all we can for quality and for the rationalization of manufacturing and managerial procedures—while the sun shines. ☐

What does the quality engineer do?

☐ What does the quality engineer do that inspection doesn't? To simplify this frequently debated point, it could be said that the quality engineer is looking at the production process while the inspector is looking at the parts produced by the process. The quality engineer's task is to measure the "inherent system capability," while the inspector sorts good product from bad.

And just what is the system?

The "system" is the manufacturing complex: planning, tooling, procurement, and production. Design has not been included because there must be a defined area in which an effort is being made to achieve a specified goal. The goal is to manufacture a product in conformance with drawings and specifications. It must be assumed that these limitations are adequate until proven otherwise. The quality engineer may arrive at the conclusion that the tolerance limits are too tight, causing such high rework and scrap as to make unprofitable the manufacture of a particular product. This would precipitate a top level debate among engineering, production, quality assurance, and general management to decide whether to modify the design, to radically improve the production capability or, possibly, to drop the product. But this cannot be done until the manufacturing complex has made a production attempt and the degree of success has been measured.

The "inherent system capability" is the stabilized rate of rework and scrap arrived at after completion of the learning period. To determine the system capability, the quality engineer will collect and analyze masses of inspection reports and will issue weekly (or monthly) summaries. These summaries will tabulate quantities inspected, number of defectives, and percent defective. Percent defective will be plotted period by period. The analysis will include the identification of those defects which occur most frequently. The quality engineer will investigate them and make recommendations for correction.

In time the percent defective stabilizes. ▶

We can produce at a fairly constant loss

The quality engineer is then in a position to say to management, "Well, that's it. The manufacturing system is capable of producing this product with a fairly constant loss of 4 percent."

"Does that mean we can't cut down on the 4 percent?"

"No, we could cut it down, but it might be expensive. It has to be decided whether it's worth it. This is a measure of the ability inherent in the manufacturing system as it now stands: the skill of the operators and of the managers; the capability of the equipment; and the effectiveness of procurement. If we want to cut down to, say, 2 percent loss in scrap and rework, we will have to make a radical improvement in one or several of the factors."

"What, for example?"

"We could make a substantial investment in new equipment; we could put on a vigorous training program for operating personnel."

"And if we don't?"

"We can hold the line at 4 percent manufacturing losses. The question is whether we can absorb it and still make a profit."

The quality engineer has many duties but right up in the forefront of them is the measurement of the inherent capability of the manufacturing system. This is what the quality engineer's employers should demand from him as the basis for important marketing and manufacturing policy decisions. The conscious pursuit of this task will keep the quality engineer on course no matter how multifarious the daily distractions may be. □

Corrective action for corrective action

☐ Is it true that the writing of corrective action reports has become an empty ritual? The allegation is made so frequently that we must assume there is some justification for it.

One of the hazards of formalized reporting is that the procedure tends to acquire equal importance with the substance of the report and, on occasion, continues to flourish even after the substance has shrunk to almost nothing.

What was corrective action meant to do? To promote quality improvement and cost reduction by presenting manufacturing supervision (in one's own plant or a supplier's) with evidence of repeated failure to make good parts, and to request corrective action.

Is it doing it? The answer, in many cases, is yes and no. Yes, because corrective action requests are being written and presented in great numbers. No, because in too many cases they are not provoking the expected response; they are not noticeably improving quality and reducing cost.

Is it worth keeping? Absolutely! It is the feedback essential to a continuous, rational control of quality and manufacturing costs.

Should it be revised? Let's give that one some thought. The principle needs no revision; the implementation is the problem. We tend to write too many corrective action requests. We tend to shoot off a C.A.R. regardless of the nature of the defect, the proportion of parts defective, or the frequency with which the defect has occurred previously.

A report is not always required

Let's assume hypothetically that we find inspectors and supervisors holding the belief that every rejection calls for a corrective action request. We'd better read our procedures to check exactly what they say. If it's possible to interpret them in this manner, we'd better tighten the phrasing to remove the ambiguity. Indeed, we might add a paragraph specifying when a corrective action request is not to be made.

Let's also make sure of a planned follow-up and the careful analysis of inspection records so that it's possible to say, "Here are ten suppliers whose work has improved considerably because of pressure for corrective action," or, "Scrap and rework have been reduced from seven percent to three percent over the last six months because requests for

▶

corrective action have pointed directly to manufacturing processes badly in need of overhaul and improvement."

If follow-up has been poor and if the inspection records cannot be tied in to the corrective action procedure, let's take some corrective action.

Sometimes it turns out that there are too many cooks. I recommend that one individual be made responsible for implementing corrective action procedures. C.A.R. analyst can keep inspection reports in constant review. It is he who can decide when previous inspection history justifies the issuance of a C.A.R., or when the proportion of defectives in a lot of parts manufactured for the first time is so high as to demand immediate investigation. It is he who can follow-up and compare inspection reports before and after. It is he who can prepare a monthly summary report to management for the quality manager's signature. In a large organization, the analyst may need assistance. In a small organization, it may be a part-time occupation for a nominated individual. In any case, the issuance and follow-up of corrective action requests and the necessary coordination should be somebody's business, not everybody's.

Make the C.A.R. a separate document

Next, we might have a look at the C.A.R. form itself. I find that it's more effective if it is a separate document, not merely a blocked space on the inspection rejection form; although it may be the second or third copy of a multi-copy inspection rejection report. In such cases, a detachable C.A.R., bearing part number, etc., a description of the defects, the number of parts inspected and the number defective, goes to the analyst. The C.A.R. form should be austere, not cluttered with so many informational boxes as to discourage the reader. But, the request made by the analyst should be sufficiently detailed to make it quite clear as to why the request was issued. Some inspection rejection reports are so parsimonious as to approach the cryptic, translatable only by recipient 007 (fiction's James Bond). Such sparseness is particularly objectionable in correction action requests.

There remains a question of how many copies of each C.A.R. should be sent around? *Again, the common practice is to send too many.* The option should be left to the analyst. He should involve only those people who are immediately affected. I doubt if the manufacturing VP wants to be "turned on" every time a C.A.R. is issued, or for that matter, the quality manager, since he has supposedly placed the job in responsible hands.

Finally, it is recommended that the quality manager—briefed by his analyst—call top management into conference once a month and summarize what has been done and what $-amounts have been saved. □

Classification of characteristics

☐ Why are designers so reluctant to classify characteristics? Well, let's look at it from the designer's point of view. Let "Hatch" be the designer and "Gage" the inspector.

Gage: How're you getting on with the classification of characteristics?

Hatch: Well, let's say it's in the exploratory stage.

Gage: Does that mean you haven't done anything?

Hatch: Not exactly. I've been thinking about it. I want to ask you some questions.

Gage: Right. What d'you want to know?

Hatch: You want me to go over the drawings and mark each characteristic "C" for critical, "M" for major, or "Mi" for minor?

Gage: That's right.

Hatch: When I've done it, what will you do with the information?

Gage: I'll inspect criticals 100%, and sample majors and minors.

Hatch: What kind of sampling plans might you use?

Gage: Oh, perhaps 1.5% AQL on majors; 4% AQL on minors.

Some defectives will slip by

Hatch: Doesn't inspection by sampling create the probability that some defectives will get by?

Gage: Sure. That's what the numbers are about. They let you know the probable percentage of defectives in lots accepted by sampling.

Hatch: Are those numbers firm? Are those the maximum percentages of defectives each plan might let by?

Gage: Well, no.

Hatch: You mean it might be worse?

Gage: It might be.

Hatch: Come on, give. How much worse?

Gage, who plans to inspect by attributes, if he can only get Hatch to cooperate, opens Mil-Std-105D (military sampling tables), and finds the operating characteristics curve he wants.

Gage: We shall do single sampling and if, for example, 200 parts are being sampled at inspection level II, the sample size would be 32 and the rejection number would be 2 for the 1.5% AQL. If there happened to be ten defectives in the lot, that lot would have about a 50-50 chance of being accepted.

Hatch: But that's 5% defective! Why would a 1.5% plan accept it?

Gage: That's one of the risks in sampling. I told you the 1.5% was not the worst possible. ▶

Hatch: All right. Now, what about the 4% plan? How bad might a lot be and still be accepted?

Gage turns to the appropriate O.C. curve.

Gage: Well, if a lot 11% defective were sampled, it would have a 50-50 chance of acceptance.

Hatch: You mean that there might be 22 defectives in a lot of 200, and the sample might not catch it?

Gage: Well, like the O.C. curve says, there's about a 50-50 chance it might not.

No guarantee as to magnitude of error

Hatch: I see. Now tell me something else. When these defectives get by, would you know the magnitude of the error? Would you know how much outside the tolerance limits they might be?

Gage: Well, no; not exactly.

Hatch: You mean you wouldn't know?

Gage: That's right.

Hatch: So you're asking me to classify characteristics major or minor so that you can inspect by sampling. You admit that some defectives may get by, but you can't tell me how many, or the magnitude of the error?

Gage: Well, that's going to extremes!

Hatch: But that's the way it is, isn't it?

Gage: All right, but what d'you want me to do? Inspect every characteristic 100%?

Hatch: That's not for me to say. If you decide to sample, that's up to you.

Gage: But I can't sample until the characteristics are classified.

Hatch: Then do it yourself!

Gage: But you're the designer. You know what's critical and what isn't.

Hatch: Right, and I've already indicated that by the tolerances I've put on the drawings.

Gage: Then why can't you go one step further and classify?

Hatch: Because my design depends on parts conforming to the tolerance limits. It doesn't seem to me that what you propose will guarantee that!

And so it goes. Sometimes the designers can be persuaded to classify; sometimes, quality control engineers do it; frequently it doesn't get done.

The decision to classify in order to sample some characteristics must be made by management. Shall it be done? If so, who is to do it? Design, manufacturing, and quality are all involved in the tangle of technical and administrative issues raised by classification. □

Quality consciousness

☐ We hear a lot about quality consciousness. We, the quality assurance fraternity, constantly urge it upon our colleagues in the organization, especially upon production managers and supervisors.

What do we expect them to do about it? Do we expect them to forget the schedule and concentrate on quality? Don't be ridiculous. That's heresy! I don't mean, of course, that it's heretical to concentrate on quality, but it is beyond belief for production to forget the schedule.

What then? Well—perhaps we should urge production managers and supervisors to give equal weight to quality and quantity.

OK. So what do they do about it? Do we then expect the managers to say to the supervisors, who will say to the operators, "Meet the schedule! But only with good pieces!"?

But they try to do that now

But they do that already. Even if they don't say it, it's implicit in the instructions. The Work Traveler states the quantity and everyone understands that every piece should be good. And that, of course, is what the operator sets out to do; but all too often it doesn't work out that way.

When a substantial number of defective pieces is made despite the good intentions of production managers, supervisors, and operators, what should they do about it? Should they slow down and measure every piece so that a correction may be made the moment a dimension goes outside the tolerance? They could, but this would murder the schedule and everybody would be in trouble.

To arrive at a solution, we must recognize a fundamental characteristic of mass production. I'm concerned with mass production because it's the foundation of that "affluence" that some nations now enjoy—and all strive for. If we were crafting a few exotic items it would be a different problem altogether. ▶

The basis of mass production is the ongoing schedule. Everything is keyed to keeping the schedule. A serious breakdown in the schedule causes chaos. Time is not normally allowed production operators for critical examination of, and reflection on, the quality of the millions of parts they make.

Inspectors perform the critical function

The "critical" function is performed by quality assurance inspectors. What might be called the "reflective" function is performed by quality assurance engineers. They collect and analyze many inspection reports to determine quality trends and to pinpoint those processes which produce the most defectives.

These facts suggest a description of quality consciousness as it might, most desirably, manifest itself in production personnel:

- Prompt and cooperative response to in-process inspection findings by production operators and line supervisors.
- Prompt and cooperative response by industrial, production or methods engineers to the need for process improvement as indicated by quality assurance engineering statistical analyses of inspection/production reports.
- An awareness on the part of managers of the phenomenon of inherent variability in repetitive production processes, prompting them to request that process capability studies be made.
- The promulgation by managers of a production policy dictating that no job be assigned to a production process unless the drawing tolerance is greater than, or at least equal to, the known process capability.

Well, there it is—an attempt to give substance to the sometimes amorphous concept of "quality consciousness." ☐

How much quality is enough?

☐ The phrase, "Don't buy more quality than you need," implies that one can know when one has enough. How do you know when you have enough quality? Well, what is quality? It is conformance to the quality standard, and the quality standard is the engineering drawings referenced in the purchase order.

A "quality" part is one on which all of the measurable characteristics are within the drawing tolerances; a "quality" product is one made up from such parts. Can you have too much conformance? That is, can you have too much quality? If every one of the characteristics measured smack on the drawing nominal, would that be too much? No. It would be a miracle, but it would not, by definition, be too much quality!

Could the axiom, "Don't buy more quality than you need," mean "Don't buy Cadillac quality when Chevrolet quality will do."? This is what is usually implied, but it creates a problem, too. "Cadillac" and "Chevrolet" are used here as measures of quality in the popular or qualitative sense. But we are bound by quantitative measures of quality, according to which a Cadillac and a Chevrolet, each of which, if in complete conformance with its appropriate drawings, are articles of like "quality."

There are differing levels of quality

The quantitative difference between a Cadillac and a Chevrolet is perhaps in their performance, which is implicit in their designs and the selection of materials, etc. The performance—the design objective—is spelled out exactly in the drawings and specifications and is not negotiable. The quality, as measured by the degree of conformance to these same drawings and specifications, is not negotiable either. Or is it? It appears that we cannot have more than complete conformance, but could we have less? Could we specify less than complete conformance? Yes, providing that the engineers and quality controllers are willing to classify the characteristics and to assign levels of quality at something less than complete conformance. These are the "levels" of quality, determined quantitatively, such as 1% AQL (acceptable quality level), 2.5% AQL, etc.

▶

However, buyers make little use of this method of specifying the quality level. Indeed, since the majority of purchase orders don't specify the quality level, it is implicit in the P.O. that what is required is complete conformance or zero % AQL!

Since neither the performance, nor the quality as we have defined it, is negotiable, and since buyers do not usually challenge the design or the necessity for conformance, what prompts the constant repetition of the warning, "Don't buy more quality than you need."? It must be the frustrating experience, shared by all buyers at one time or another, of being caught between two groups of inspectors who cannot agree that a consignment of urgently needed parts is or is not acceptable. This leads to accusation of "overly critical" inspection, or the belief that some inspectors demand "Cadillac" quality on every occasion no matter what is specified. Such conflicts, which occasionally develop into thorough-going Donnybrooks, are not rare; they happen frequently enough to keep alive the belief that there is such a thing as too much quality, and that many inspectors spend all of their time looking for it.

The problem is the variability of acceptability

The core of the problem is not in the definition of quality, which moves out of the controversial area if it is defined quantitatively, but in the definition of acceptability. Once the blueprints have been exchanged between buyer and seller, can it be assumed that any two inspectors will come to the same conclusion about the degree of conformance of the subsequently manufactured hardware? This is a common assumption, but it does not take into account the all-pervading phenomenon of variability as it affects inspectors; and their measuring instruments; and the tendency for equally conscientious and competent inspectors to make different interpretations of the same statements on a drawing or specification; and the difference in results which can be determined when the same dimension or functional characteristic is measured by two different methods.

The solution appears to be the acceptance inspection and test procedures authorized for use by the buyer and seller and referenced in the P.O. This makes it possible to define a "quality" part or product as one found to be in conformance with the engineering drawing and specification when inspected and tested by the authorized method. Some thought could be given in such an inspection procedure to the effects of inspector and instrument variability. Should an estimate of the magnitude of the effect be deducted from the seller's tolerance; or added to the buyer's tolerance; or split between both? And what price adjustment should be made? □

What is quality?

☐ What is quality? The quality control practitioner's answer is "conformance to specified requirements." We may say that quality, or a quality article, is that which satisfies the customer. All well and good, but then we must ask: What do we have to do to please the customer? And the answer is "manufacture a product on which all of the measurable characteristics are within the specified tolerance limits."

It may be that the customer's requirements were challenged during negotiations and some may have been changed. But ultimately there is a corrected specification. The corrected specification is IT—the standard of acceptance. Quality articles are those which do not exceed the agreed tolerance limits. Quality is conformance!

We might tack on the adjective commonly associated with conformance and say quality is "mere" conformance. But if quality is mere conformance, why do we find it so difficult to persuade people to make parts of which we demand merely that they conform to specification?

Why is there so little of it? Or, rather, why is there not more of it? Might it be that quality and conformance are not equated in the minds of the producers or, for that matter, in the minds of those who speak so powerfully in favor of quality?

What does the dictionary say?

Let us see what a dictionary of psychology* has to say about quality.

> QUALITY: A fundamental aspect or attribute of
> sensory experience, differentiating one experience
> from another, within the same sensory field, or a
> non-quantitative character, and independently of
> all aspects of a quantitative character.

It's a bit of a shock! It's true, of course, that psychology is not concerned directly with industrial products, but it is concerned with the behaviour of people, and people make industrial products. It is probable that the psychologist's definition corresponds to an understanding of quality acquired by all of us in our earliest years. ►

If we ask what quality is in the traditional sense, what are the implications of the word "quality" as we acquire them during our early inculturation? The answer would surely be: the ability to excel. But to excel is to be different! Quality is that deviation in the direction of excellence which distinguishes the individual, or the work of the individual. One's son or one's daughter, for example. The "customized" automobile. The essential pitch made in all advertisements is that the product is "different."

Consider what we are likely to do when we've made a sufficient sum of money from the manufacture of industrial products. We collect objects of art. And what do we demand most of all? Uniqueness! Difference! Indeed, we may treasure a particular painting, or a piece of sculpture, or an Indian pot for an error which is felt to set it apart from all others. There is only one like this in all the world; it is forever different, and it is ours!

Consider how shocked we are when some misguided individual makes replicas of art, exact copies which appear to conform in every detail. We don't want him or his products. We destroy the one and jail the other.

Their definition and ours are not the same

Thus, industrial quality control demands quality, meaning conformance. But the machinists, assemblers, sheet metal workers and their supervisors upon whom we make the demand think of quality as something different from the common-run-of-things.

It is difficult to estimate the effect of the confusion created within the individual by the conflict between quality defined as conformance, and the deeply inculcated understanding of quality as that something a person or article may have which makes him or it different and unique. This may account for the persistence with which assemblers introduce slight deviations from the monolithic conformity we demand. We call it carelessness, but it may not be. The motivation might be to add that something different which is the mark of excellence.

These comments are not meant to suggest that we should call quality "conformance," but the contradiction with the traditional understanding of quality exists, and we should give it some thought. It might serve as a clue to the behaviour of producers; the products we accept or reject are to a large extent the products of behaviour.   □

---

*A Dictionary of Psychology; James Drever; Penguin Reference Books. Revised 1964.

Quality and conformance

☐ Quality is conformance in the world of industrial mass production. Quality, as understood in the practice of quality control, is conformance ... conformance to a set of engineering drawings, or to a catalog description, or to an advertisement, or to any description of a product authorized as the quality standard by contractual reference.

But quality as traditionally understood, quality as understood by practically everybody except a relatively small group of quality control practitioners (the membership of ASQC is about 20,000), is the very antithesis of conformance.

"Quality" as used in common daily conversation, means that property of an article, or of an individual, or of the performance which distinguishes that someone or something from the mass, from the average. It is what is stated or implied in the many advertisements which claim that "our product has quality." It implies that our cigarettes, or coffee, or steaks, or sweaters, or skirts are better than, or different from, the common run of such things.

To be 'different from' is to be 'better than'

Indeed, to be "different from" is generally understood to mean "better than." It would not occur to many of us to assume that "different from" means "worse than." In this sense, "quality" and "different" are synonymous in the common thought.

In the piece, "What is Quality?", I suggested that the contradiction between quality as conformance (the goal of quality assurance programs), and quality as difference (the ingrained attitude of most managers and operators) was a factor which should be considered in motivation.

I want to add something which is also relevant to attitudes and motivation. The idea of craftsmanship has been revived and we urge production operators to be good craftsmen. But traditional quality, that is quality as difference, was the product of craftsmanship. Do we want craftsmen to produce what craftsmen have traditionally produced? ►

What we want is quality as conformance. But, whereas traditional quality is a product of individual craftsmen, quality as conformance is the product of a system. The system (a quality assurance program) requires that many individuals suppress their culturally indoctrinated tendencies to vary, to differ, in favor of conformance to a common plan.

But will they agree to conform to a common plan?

We all know what a problem it is to get a group of energetic managers to adhere strictly to an agreed plan or system. Not that they will not "agree"; they do, but when an energetic manager says, "I agree," what he means is, "I agree to follow this plan as I see it!"

And he does this because his entire inculturation and education has conditioned him "to think for himself," and to excel in whatever he does. To "think for oneself" is tantamount to questioning the plan or system as given. To excel is to achieve that difference which is the personal hallmark of quality!

Perhaps we should have a new vocabulary. We ask for "quality" when what we want is "conformance." We demand "craftsmanship" when what we want is strict adherence to the procedure, or method, or blueprint as given. But it may be that the powerful drive in such great traditional concepts as "quality" and "craftsmanship" are essential to motivate individuals to conform! But there are hazards, and we see them every day in rework costs, scrap, and in management dissension. ☐

Home on the range

☐ Joe Random was returning from the company picnic with Alpha his wife, Beta his daughter, and his 10 year old son Percy (commonly referred to by Beta as the fraction defective). For the moment, they were in a good mood; there was no sibling bickering; they were behaving like a family should.

It had been a good picnic. Managers, clerks, and machinists had coalesced in a fine democratic melange in which hardly anybody claimed to be more equal than anyone else. Scotch and beer had assisted in the equalizing process, and had promoted spontaneous communication.

Predictably, there had come that moment during the afternoon when the machine shop supervisor wobbled to his feet and, looking directly at Joe, announced, "You can't inspect quality into the product!"

Joe attempted to explain that, while you can't inspect quality into the product, you can inspect the defects out. This, said Joe, could be construed as putting quality into the product. "Conshtrued," said the supervisor, "What's 'conshtrued' got to do with it?" and weaved off in the direction of the beer barrel.

Special agent Six Sigma

Joe had been buttonholed by an administrative assistant who greeted him:

"Look who's here! The man from Q.C. Special agent Six Sigma!"

Joe responded with an amiable grin, and the administrative assistant continued.

"I've got an idea for you. Just the thing for an ambitious quality engineer."

Joe had visions of the Trojan Horse, but he listened.

"Tell me. Why do we have so many defects?"

Joe remained silent, sensing that this was a rhetorical question.

"Because of the inspectors. They spend all day poking around, rejecting this part, and putting that part into review. Isn't that the truth?"

Joe agreed.

"Right then," continued the administrative assistant, "if we had less inspectors, we would have less defects. That would be an improvement.

But just think what would happen if there were no inspectors. No inspectors, no defects!''

The administrative assistant rushed on giving Joe no time to formulate a counter argument.

''All that's needed for Zero Defects is to fire all the inspectors!''

At this moment the administrative assistant was taken in tow by an amorous armature winder (female), and Joe was left pondering the uses of logic.

Joe seemed to be a natural target on such an occasion, almost as though it took something like the company picnic to encourage individuals to confess their innermost thoughts. The assistant sales manager had sidled up to him.

Call off the Indians

''Hi Joe. Just the man I want to see. What are your Indians trying to do—put us out of business?''

''Not this week! But what have they done now?''

''Look at those motors they rejected the other day. $20,000 of my billing shot to Hell on the 28th of the month! What gets into guys who do a thing like that at the end of the month?''

''But Ed, they were out of spec.''

''I know that. But were they too bad to ship?''

''But Ed, a defect's a defect.''

''Yes, and billing is billing. Can't you knock a bit of commonsense into those guys?''

At that moment the chief engineer wandered over. He was moderately smashed, and was being lovingly supported by the receptionist.

''Joe Random, I believe.''

''At your service.''

''Joe, I meant to ask you for a long time. When are you going to tighten up on the production people? When are you going to make a part like the drawing?''

Joe was about to protest that he didn't make the parts, but his escort was already steering the chief engineer off towards the ball game that was starting up between the day-shift and the night-shift. Riot squads were standing by.

And so in the cool of the evening Joe addressed his family: ''What do they all want? Production! Administration! Sales! Engineering! Why can't they agree on what they want?''

Beta his daughter, a smart-alecky kid from MuCLA took his arm affectionately, ''Poor Daddy. Won't you ever learn that one man's mean is another man's poisson.'' □

How did statistics get into quality control?

☐ How did statistics get into quality control? The question was put to me at a recent seminar I had organized for nuclear power plant construction men and quality engineers. I was momentarily nonplused! My immediate impulse was to say that they belong together like man and woman, or like beer and pretzels. But then I realized that a question had been raised which bugs many intelligent men and women: what do ABSTRACTIONS like the MEAN and the STANDARD DEVIATION have to do with good solid HARDWARE?

There's no obvious link . . . unless you are one of the limited number of individuals who automatically apply statistics to large quantities . . . of manufactured parts, or people, or whatever. In which case you're a quality engineer, an operations research analyst, a statistician in some occupation . . .

It all started with the Bell System

Someone, somewhere had to make the first connection between statistics and industrial products. Who? When? And where? That was the question. I responded by relating the remarkable, and historically significant events of the 1920s when Drs. Walter Shewhart, Harold Dodge and Harry Romig, with managerial assistance from George Edwards, labored and brought forth statistical process control and sampling. This seemed to satisfy the participants.

When I got back to Los Angeles, I recalled that I had once written George Edwards about those pioneering days.

I shall paraphrase his reply dated 19 April, 1965, with direct quotes. The Bell Telephone System was just entering the dial switching field in the early 1920s. "In some large central offices the number of inspectors . . . exceeded the number of installers . . . they were falling over each other!"

Bell Lab, a merger of the Engineering Department of Western Electric and the Department of Development and Research of AT&T, did not

▶

exist at this time (it was formed January 1st, 1925). The problem led to discussions between Mr. Edward Craft, the Assistant Chief Engineer for Western Electric and Mr. Clarence Stoll, Works Manager. "It was out of these discussions that the earliest concept came of a new approach to the quality problem . . . I always gave Craft credit for much of the imagination and many of the ideas which went into it. Craft transferred Dr. Reginald Jones from Engineering . . . and put him in charge of all Engineering Inspection work. It was into Jones' branch that I (George Edwards) went in early 1924 . . . I found Dr. Shewhart already there . . . Shewhart's concept of *'quality as a distribution'* and of the *'control'* of that distribution were already in embryo."

George Edwards also found that "Mr. R.B. Miller . . . had already developed the concept of a *'defect tolerance'* and had worked out tables . . . of sample sizes for each lot size of each type of apparatus. . . ."

Jones was made Inspection Engineer, and George Edwards became Assistant, subsequently, succeeding Jones as Director of Quality Assurance.

The two dominant techniques

At this time, writes George Edwards, "it was quite clear that . . . we must work toward a generalized system of sampling inspection." Harold Dodge was persuaded to transfer into the department. So that now the two dominant techniques of industrial quality control: PROCESS CONTROL and SAMPLING were progressing under Shewhart and Dodge. Dr. Arnold Beckman was added to Shewhart's group and Dr. Harry Romig to the Dodge group. Beckman left to form Beckman Instruments. The work continued and Shewhart published in 1931. Shortly thereafter, the Dodge-Romig Sampling plans were being used in departmental handbook form; and were published to the world in 1939.

So statistics got into quality control because, as George Edwards wrote, the situation demanded that something be done and, by a fateful and fortunate coincidence there, waiting on the historic moment, was a union of statisticians and engineers who developed and codified a system of statistical process control and sampling which has since girdled the world and penetrated into every industry. □

Do you know your supplier's capability?

☐ Capability? What do we mean when we speak of a supplier's capability? We are saying that he has the ability to manufacture a quantity of parts, at a given price, and deliver them in a prescribed period of time. Basic is the ability to manufacture parts, of which a large proportion (hopefully 100%), conform to specification. It is basic because the success of the buyer's production schedule depends on the timely arrival of good parts.

The ultimate measure of the supplier's capability is, then, his ability to predict the yield of good parts. This is not quite the same thing as the ability to produce parts, for many can produce, but not all can predict how many will be good.

Which brings us to the use of process capability as measured by the statistical methods of quality control. Do your suppliers know the capability of their processes as statistically determined? Many don't.

Analyzing the problems at Medusa

You are the Quality Manager. You have your receiving inspection records analyzed and summarized weekly. You find that the Medusa Machine Shop heads the list of poor performers this week. They make part # 84842 on which the important dimension is a diameter of 0.4750 in. ±0.0015 in. During the report period they have made two shipments, both rejected, that look to be more than 10 percent defective.

Let us assume that your policy is to use attribute sampling, and to sort rejected lots 100 percent. As a consequence of this policy you know exactly what quality of material is being supplied. You know that the first lot of 1,000 was 15 percent defective.

But let us try an experiment. We've already agreed that lots rejected by sampling shall be sorted 100 percent. Let us tag the second lot. A sample of, say, 50 shall be drawn from the tagged lot. Each of the 50 parts shall be measured and a frequency distribution plotted. Subsequent sorting yields 805 good pieces out of 1,000, or 19.5 percent defective.

Now you study the frequency distribution and much is revealed to you. It is as though you were looking into a crystal ball. Indeed the frequency distribution is the quality engineer's crystal ball.　▶

What do you see?

1. That the natural machine spread, the 6-sigma spread, is 0.006 in.

2. That this is twice the total tolerance allowed by your blueprint so you and the supplier are in bad trouble on that count alone.

3. That the average of the distribution is displaced 0.005 in. from the blueprint nominal dimension of 0.4750. So you're in more trouble because, as this demonstrates, the set-up man missed by 0.005 in.

4. That the yield of good parts would have been 81.9 percent had the distribution been perfectly normal. It was, in fact, 80.5 percent (805 good out of a 1,000) which is pretty close. The standard deviation was computed at 0.001 in. The yield figure was derived from a table of areas under the normal curve you had conveniently in hand.

5. That the supplier's process is varying only from chance causes, as evidenced by the near-perfect distribution.

6. That, if you think back to the previous lot of 1,000, of which 850 were good, you now know on that occasion the set-up man hit the drawing nominal practically right on. Had he been right on the nose, then 86.6 percent of the parts would have been acceptable. You found 85 percent good which, again, is pretty close.

Now you have the answers

Now your Quality Engineer is prepared. You let Purchasing know what you're doing and your man speeds like an arrow to Medusa. The probability is that your engineer already knows more about the process than the supplier. However, he shoots the questions not only at the supplier's inspector, but also at the production supervisor and the production engineer who assigned your part to this machine.

- "Did you inspect these parts before you shipped them?"
- "Did you make any checks during the run?"
- "How come you missed the drawing nominal on the second set-up?"
- "When you heard from our Purchasing that the first lot ran 15 percent defective, why did you make the second run?"
- "If you thought you would get a better yield, why did you think so? How do you predict the yield?"

What will be the upshot in this particular case? The supplier will select a more "capable" machine, in the quality control meaning of the words. Your quality engineer will instruct them in how to make and use a control chart.

See that your supplier knows his capability; it's much to your advantage, and his.　　　　□

The alpha and beta risks

□ At present, I'm on a sampling kick. I hope you don't mind. However, sampling is just too important a part of the industrial scene for any of us to have any doubts. I wouldn't presume to do this if I hadn't learned from experience that those who do know cannot imagine anyone else *not* knowing; while those who don't know, or are in doubt, are reluctant to ask.

Let us imagine we are sampling a lot of 9,000 pieces at 2.5% AQL, inspection level II, normal, single. We're inspecting by attributes and take the plan from MIL-STD-105D. Table I of 105D tells us that the code letter is "L"; Table II-A (single sampling plans for normal inspection) shows that the sample size is 200 with an acceptance number of 10. Let us imagine that the lot is, indeed, exactly 2.5% defective. There will then be 225 defectives in the lot of 9,000 and the lot is, by definition, a "good" lot. This is a mass production situation, and while the buyer would like all good pieces, he is prepared to tolerate 2.5% defectives; this was a factor in setting the price.

The inspector draws at random a sample of 200 pieces. He inspects them and finds, say, 6 defectives. He accepts the lot without further inspection. Good!

But it can be seen that the inspector might find 11 or more defective pieces in the sample of 200, since there are 225 defectives in the lot. If this should happen he would be forced to reject a "good" lot.

What are the odds on bouncing a good lot?

Now, it's expensive enough to manufacture 9,000 parts without having them rejected when they're "good." So we ask, "What is the risk that a good lot may be rejected?" This is the ALPHA RISK, the "Producer's risk," so called by Dodge and Romig in their pioneering work on sampling risks.

The answer is on page 50 of 105D. Looking at the OC curves and extending up from 2.5 on the horizontal axis to the point of interception with the "2.5" curve, the probability of acceptance looks like about 99%.

Hence, the probability of rejection is about 1%. The tabulation below the curves shows that the quality that would have a 99% chance of acceptance, or a 1% chance of rejection, is, more exactly, 2.39% defective.

OK, what are we saying? If and when a lot submitted for inspection happens to be 2.5% defective and, therefore, "good" by definition, there's a risk of about 1% that it may be rejected. ▶

Or on accepting a bad lot?

But what about the BETA RISK or Consumer's risk (again from Dodge-Romig) that a "bad" lot may be accepted?

Let us imagine that the lot is, in fact, 5% defective. In which case there will be 450 defective pieces concealed in the 9,000. But remember, there are still 8,550 good pieces, so it's not impossible for the inspector to find only 10 defectives or less in his sample. In which case he will accept a "bad" lot.

So we ask, "What is the chance that a lot as bad as 5% defective may be accepted?"

Again, the answer is to be found on page 50. Extending up from 5.0 on the horizontal axis to the intercept with curve "2.5," we find there's about a 57% chance of acceptance.

Does this mean that 57% of accepted lots may be 5% defective?

No! Although that's a common misunderstanding. What it means is that IF AND WHEN the submitted lot happens to be 5% defective, then there is a 57% chance it may be accepted. But remember, there's a 43% chance it may be rejected. Of course, the manufacturer may keep his production process under good control so that his quality never drops as low as 5% defective. But if it does, and only if it does, then and only then is there a 57% chance it may be accepted.

Let us look at it another way. Instead of asking "What is the chance that a certain quality may be accepted," we should ask, "What is the quality that may be accepted at a stated risk of acceptance?"

For this purpose, let us consider what may happen at a BETA RISK, or Consumer's risk of 10% (the figure popularized by Dodge-Romig). Again, on page 50, we extend across from 10 on the vertical axis to the intercept with the "2.5" curve; dropping to the horizontal axis we hit about 7.7 which the tabulation below the curves confirms.

Dodge-Romig called this worse-than-the-AQL quality the LTPD (lot tolerance percent defective). 105D calls it the LQ (limiting quality).

But, again, what does it mean? Does it mean, to repeat the common misunderstanding, that 10% of accepted lots may be as bad as 7.7% defective?

No, of course not. It means that IF the quality of a lot submitted for inspection should be as bad as 7.7% defective (REMEMBER IT MAY NEVER HAPPEN, BUT IF IT DOES, AND ONLY IF IT DOES), then there's a 10% chance it may be accepted. But there's a 90% chance of rejection.

In short, if you inspected 100 lots of 9,000 each at 2.5 AQL and if the production process were so out of control that 10 of the 100 lots were as bad as 7.7% defective, only one of those 10 lots might be accepted. □

Closing the gap between the consumer's risk and the supplier's risk

☐ The consumer's risk is the probability that, when using a given sampling plan, a lot of worse quality than the agreed AQL may be accepted. The supplier's risk is the probability that a lot as good as the agreed AQL may be rejected. These aggravating risks cannot be eliminated from the sampling plans; they are part of the scene like death and taxes.

Let us take an example. Customer Ajax is considering ordering a lot of 10,000 parts from Supplier Brown. Ajax estimates that he can tolerate 1 percent of non-conforming parts and so he decides to specify AQL 1 percent. He asks his quality engineer to let him know to what risks he and Supplier Brown will be exposed. The inspection is to be by attributes, so the plan will be selected from MIL-STD-105D. The plan is to be single, normal, inspection Level II.

The quality engineer selects a plan with code letter L, sample size 200, acc. no. 5. He finds that there's no more than 2 percent chance that a lot as good as 1 percent may be rejected (see page 50 of 105D). That's alright for Supplier Brown . . . but what will the plan do to the consumer? The quality engineer finds that the quality which may be accepted at 10 percent risk is as bad as 4.64 percent defective (page 50). This isn't alright for Consumer Ajax, not at all!

Ajax phones Brown and tells him he cannot tolerate the risk he will be exposed to by an AQL 1 percent plan with sample size 200 and acc. no. 5. "Fine," says Brown, "let's find another plan agreeable to both of us." So they agree to find a sampling plan which will assure consumer Ajax that at 10 percent beta risk the worst quality which might be accepted will be 2 percent defective; and which will assure Supplier Brown that the risk of rejecting a lot as good as 1 percent defective will be no more than 5 percent. As you can see, Brown has made a concession, his risk having increased from 2 percent to 5 percent, but things will be better for the consumer, which is what I meant by *closing the gap*.

The quality engineer decides to look for a suitable plan in Cameron's Tables, published in ASQC's *Quality Progress* for September '74. To use Cameron's Table all percentages must be converted to decimal fractions. Thus AQL 1 percent becomes fraction defective $p_1 = 0.01$; 5 percent alpha risk becomes 0.05; AQL 2 percent becomes $p_2 = 0.02$ and 10 percent beta risk becomes 0.10.

To use Cameron's Table, first select the correct column. It is the one headed: ►

$$\alpha = 0.05$$
$$\beta = 0.10$$

Compute the ratio p_2/p_1. It is $0.02/0.01 = 2$.

Find the number in the selected column equal to or next greater than 2. It is 2.029.

Find the acceptance number by checking the number in the "c" column on the same row. It is 17.

Find the sample size by (1) finding the number in the np_1 column on the same row. It is 11.633. (2) divide 11.633 by p_1 (0.01). The sample size is 1163.

Hence the sampling plan is a sample of 1163 with an acc. no. of 17 to be applied to a lot of 10,000. This plan will assure Customer Ajax that there's no more than 10 percent risk that a lot as bad as 2 percent may be accepted. It will assure Supplier Brown that there's no more than 5 percent risk that a lot as good as 1 percent may be rejected. □

(Applicable Portion of Cameron's Table)

Values of p_2/p_1 for:

c	$\alpha = .05$ $\beta = .10$	$\alpha = .05$ $\beta = .05$	$\alpha = .05$ $\beta = .01$	np_1
0	44.890	58.404	89.781	.052
1	10.946	13.349	18.681	.355
2	6.509	7.699	10.280	.818
3	4.890	5.675	7.352	1.366
4	4.057	4.646	5.890	1.970
5	3.549	4.023	5.017	2.613
6	3.206	3.604	4.435	3.286
7	2.957	3.303	4.019	3.981
8	2.768	3.074	3.707	4.695
9	2.618	2.895	3.462	5.426
10	2.497	2.750	3.265	6.169
11	2.397	2.630	3.104	6.924
12	2.312	2.528	2.968	7.690
13	2.240	2.442	2.852	8.464
14	2.177	2.367	2.752	9.246
15	2.122	2.302	2.665	10.035
16	2.073	2.244	2.588	10.831
17	2.029	2.192	2.520	11.633
18	1.990	2.145	2.458	12.442
19	1.954	2.103	2.403	13.254

Rock, beta, rock!

☐ The first time we heard "The Reliability Rock," Jeremiah was on the vibes and Cassandra was belting out the lyric: "Rock, Beta, Rock!"

Most likely, you've heard this combo. Jeremiah is this now prophet with a negative attitude about the future, and Cassandra is the Trojan chick which Apollo desired. She said she would if he gave her the gift of prophecy. He did, but she didn't.

"Okay, baby," said Apollo, "You can keep the gift, but nobody will believe you."

There was enthusiastic applause and Cassandra encored with "You've Got No Confidence in Me." The word "confidence" grabbed us like a vise and held on despite the relentless hammering of the big beat.

Confidence—statistical confidence; not that the mind could assemble the syllables of a word like "sta-tis-ti-cal" in that hurricane of noise, but the idea was there.

Confidence levels stop 'em cold

Reliability experts are familiar with what happens to administrators, engineers, production supervisors and inspectors when failure rates (like one failure in a million hours) are quoted: the slow transformation from eager interest to dazed incredulity. But I think we never rock them so hard as when we get on to the subject of confidence.

Take an example. Assume that a reliability demonstration has been made. Several units were run for a total of 1800 unit-hours. There were three failures, all judged to be random. The MTBF has been estimated at 600 hours. The customer considers the result and says: "If you took another set of units and put them on test, I suppose you'd get the same result?"

"Well, no. You might, although it's not likely. You might get a better result, and then again, it might be worse."

"How much worse?"

"That would depend on the confidence level."

"What d'ya mean, confidence level?" ►

"Well, we're dealing in probabilities. You ask me to make a prediction and I, naturally, want to hedge the bet. So I ask you how much confidence you want to place in the answer. Like 60%, or 80%, or 90%. Sort of how do you feel about it?"

"I see. What's the worst it might be at, say, 80%?"

You do a bit of figuring and reply: "At 80% confidence, the lower confidence limit will be 325 hours MTBF."

"For heaven's sake!" the customer exclaims, "What happened to the 600 hours?"

Maybe you will and maybe you won't

"Like I said, you might get 600 hours or more on a second trial, but then again, you might not."

The customer tries again. "What would it be at 90% confidence?"

You do some more figuring and reply: "Well, at 90% confidence, the MTBF at the lower confidence limit would be 270 hours."

This is likely to rock the poor man good, and the expert must be prepared to restore the customer's confidence in "confidence." This is not easy because the concept of statistical confidence is not as obvious as a traffic light. In general, laymen expect the lower confidence limit to improve at higher confidence levels.

"I thought I'd be better off with more confidence."

"Well you are really. It's just that the more confidence you demand, the more cautious I become. You're better off because now you know the worst."

"Thanks!" says the layman.

Reliability experts must be prepared to indoctrinate their colleagues. Not because the latter are obtuse, but because the subject of probability is a bit obscure. Indeed, it must be, since the future is hidden from us by a veil of uncertainty. The reliability specialist's attempt to pierce the veil must necessarily be characterized by that variability which is the essence of the problem.

Anyway, let us not assume that the mathematics of uncertainty are as clear and forceful as an ad for a new detergent. Let us make sure our colleagues are with us as we plow through the computations.

Then, Cassandra was screaming into the mike, "Lambda, stay 'way from my door!" It was enough. I staggered out into the quiet of the night. □

Sampling: the consequences of the zero acceptance number

☐ It is advisable, when selecting a sampling plan, to keep in mind the consequences of the zero acceptance number. If the inspector shares the fairly widespread belief that finding no defectives in the sample means there can be no defectives in the balance of the lot, he is likely to be badly misled.

Let's work an example. The inspector has to inspect a lot of 100. He wants to assure himself that he has a good lot; that is, a lot in which every piece conforms to the specification. He decides on a sample size of 4 with an acct. no. of zero. Let there be 2 defectives in the lot, although, of course, the inspector doesn't know.

What is the probability that the inspector will draw 4 good pieces and be misled into believing that the balance of the lot is good when it isn't? The probability that the first piece drawn will be good is 98/100; that the second piece drawn will be good as 97/99; the third piece 96/98 and the fourth piece 95/97. The probability that all 4 will be good is, of course, the product of these four fractions.

It works out to 0.923 or 92.3%, say 92%.

Thus, the inspector may be misled, 92 times in 100 tries, into believing that he has put into stock or shipped totally good lots when they are, in fact, 2% defective!

The alternative is 100% inspection

What would the inspector have to do to assure himself that every piece in the lot conforms to all requirements of the specification? Inspect 100%. This creates problems: for example, inspector fatigue. But whatever the problems, they must be overcome if it is required to know that all of the pieces in a lot conform to all requirements of the spec. It's an expensive business to assure that every piece in a lot is 100% good. It's something consumers and producers should keep in mind when negotiating. It's an important determinant of the manufacturing cost and selling price.

What does MIL-STD-105D have to say on the subject? Let us agree that we will follow customary procedure and inspect at Level II, normal, single. We assume the customer has made no recommendation to the contrary. Page 9 of 105D tells us that, for a lot size of 100, the sample size code letter is F. We turn to page 10 where we don't find a plan for zero per cent defective. Indeed, we didn't expect to. However, there is a plan at AQL 0.010, which is fairly close to zero, but still not zero. We locate the intersection of row F and column 0.010, and there's that arrow pushing us

►

all the way down to a sample size of 1250 with an acct. no. of zero!

Even with a healthy lot size of 30,000, for which the code would be M, we would still be pushed down to that same sample size of 1250. It's tough to assure oneself by sampling, that the quality is as good as 0.010% defective, or 0.015, or 0.025. It's impossible if the customer insists that all pieces be free of all defects.

There's another consequence of the zero acct. no. All other things being equal, it increases the probability that a good lot may be rejected. Let us use the same lot size of 100, but this time the customer is willing to tolerate 2% defectives. A "good" lot is now, by definition, one that is 2% defective or better. A sample size of 4 with an acct. no. of zero is agreed upon.

8% probability of rejection

What is the probability that the sample will reject lots exactly 2% defective? This is the same problem we looked at above, except that we're looking at it from a different viewpoint. Since we rounded out the probability of acceptance to 92%, we can round out the probability of rejection to 8%. Thus there is a probability we may reject a "good" lot 8 times in 100 tries. This probability is what Dodge-Romig called the producer's risk. Whether you consider this a high risk or not will depend upon whether you're a producer or consumer. However, the consumer's deliveries are affected if too many "good" lots are rejected.

What happens if the acct. no. is increased to 1 (one)? It can be shown by the following computation:

$$Pd = \frac{n!}{d! \, (n-d)!} \; (p^d) \; (1-p)^{n-d}$$

n = sample size (4)
d = rejection no. (2, since the acct. no. = 1)
p = the fraction defective (0.02)

This works out to 0.0023 or 0.23%, which is quite a reduction. Of course, what Dodge-Romig called the LTPD, that worse-than-the-acceptable quality level which may be accepted at a stated risk, would be worse. But for the moment, it's sufficient to see the large effect on the producer's risk when the acct. no. is increased from zero to one.

It's interesting to note that MIL-STD-105D allows a contractor, with the buyer's consent, to switch from a plan with zero acct. no. to a plan with a larger sample size and an acct. no. of one (see paragraph 9.4 on page 6). The reduction in the producer's risk isn't as spectacular as in our example, but in the two examples I worked, it is appreciable. Anyway, it seems advisable to keep the consequences of the zero acct. no. in mind when choosing a sampling plan. □

MIL-STD-105 or Dodge-Romig?

☐ If you're sampling, when should you go 105, and when should you go Dodge-Romig? If you're the supplier, you select your plan from 105D. If you are the consumer, you will select your plan from Dodge-Romig.

Let us take an example. Let the lot size be 1,000 and let the AQL (acceptable quality level) be 1%. If we are the supplier, we go to 105D and find (on pages 9 and 10) the sampling plan: code J, sample size 80, acceptance number 2. What's the probability that a good lot may be rejected? From the OC curve on page 46, the probability of rejection is 5%.

OK, this is what the 105D plans were designed to do: to provide an alpha risk of about 5% for each designated AQL at the normal (II) inspection level. It doesn't work out every time, but this is one time it does. But what if we are the consumer. What is the probability of accepting a bad lot? We must either nominate some quality level worse than 1% and find from the OC curve the probability of acceptance; or select a low probability of acceptance and find the corresponding quality which might be accepted. Let us select a 10% risk of acceptance (10% beta): we find at the intersection of row 10 and column 1.0 in the tabulation on page 46 that the worst quality that might be accepted is 6.52% defective. We aren't about to tolerate such a probability.

Let's try Dodge-Romig instead

So we go to Dodge-Romig (the 1967 reprint) and on page 182 find a 1% LTPD sampling plan. The LTPD at a stated risk of acceptance is what we, the consumers, are interested in. The plans on page 182 are for a beta risk of 10%. Dodge-Romig give us 6 plans to choose from depending on the process average of earlier lots. Since this is a new part we are buying, we don't know the process average and must take the plan from the right hand end column. The plan is a sample size of 335 with an acct. no. of 1. Compare that with the plan of 80 and 2 for an AQL of 1%. ▶

What about the AQL? Since the LTPD dangles in 105 AQL plans, I suppose we may say that the AQL floats in Dodge-Romig LTPD tables.

Where then, is the AQL floating? Dodge-Romig don't give us the AQL, but do provide the AOQL (average outgoing quality limit). It is 0.17%! This presupposes that we are doing lot-by-lot inspection, and that we are screening rejected lots and discarding defectives. At one time, Dodge-Romig used to require that defectives be replaced, but the 1967 reprint says it's alright to discard them. It makes a negligible difference to the AOQL.

This AOQL of 0.17% raises a question. When we, the consumer, selected a 1% LTPD plan, did we have in mind that an average of 1% over many lots would be acceptable? Almost certainly. Unless, of course, we were selecting a plan for a single lot. In which case we, the consumer, would stick with the LTPD and let the AQL float. But in lot-by-lot inspection the consumer can go for an AOQL plan. In which case, we go to page 200 in the Dodge-Romig for a 1% AOQL plan. It is a sample size of 120 with an acct. no. of 2.

Mil-Std-105D has no nice round numbers

Dodge-Romig tables are strictly consumer-oriented. They protect the consumer whether in the case of the inspection of a single lot (LTPD plans) or lot-by-lot inspection (AOQL plans). However, we can do it all with MIL-STD-105D, except we can't get the nice round numbers (1.0%, 4.0%, etc.) provided by Dodge-Romig for LTPDs and AOQLs.

In the case of our example of lot size 1,000 and AQL 1%, had we wished to find a plan for a single lot with an LTPD of approximately 1% at 10% beta risk of acceptance, we would have found it on page 50 of 105D. This is a sample size of 200 with an acceptance number of zero, (see the intersection of row 10.0 and column 0.065). The LTPD quality is 1.15% defective. If we care to look up at the "floating" AQL, that's it at the head of the column: 0.065% defective.

If, as the consumer, we intended to do lot-by-lot inspection of many similar lots, then we could find a plan by selecting the AQL 1% and going "tightened." The code letter is still J and, according to page 11, the sample size is 80 with an acct. no. of 1. From page 23 we learn that the AOQL factor is 1.1 (row J and column 1.0). This must be multiplied by $(1-n/N)$. The bracket equals 0.92; the AOQL equals 1.1 times 0.92, which is near enough to 1.0%. □

The LTPD, or who's on first?

☐ Four bases confine the baseball diamond and four parameters (the AQL, Alpha Risk, LTPD, and Beta Risk) enclose a sampling plan. I suppose there is some analogy although I must admit it's stretching it. What gave me the idea was a humorous dialogue in which the straight man of a comedy team is constantly demanding, "Who's on First?" As I recall, there's a lot of confusion and the straight man never does find out. Anyway there's a lot of confusion about the LTPD and many sampling plans are in use that have no fix on it.

Why should you want a fix on the LTPD? Let us assume that you are sampling at, say, 2.5% AQL. One may reasonably expect the quality of an accepted lot would be about 2.5% defective, however, it may be better—or worse.

The LTPD, remember, is the lot tolerance percent defective, a term originated by Dodge-Romig to designate a level of quality worse than the AQL. The LTPD or worse than AQL quality must be tied to a probability of acceptance called the Consumer's Risk or Beta Risk.

The problem for many consumers is that they've never heard of the LTPD, let alone the Beta Risk. Indeed, it's frequently the case that they aren't aware of the Alpha Risk either. As a consequence, many sampling plans in use are identified only by the AQL. Alpha Risk, LTPD, and Beta remain unknown and unsuspected.

But let us assume that our consumer knows. Let us further assume that he knows that the LTPD is particularly relevant when he's buying and preparing to consume a single lot. He knows that in lot-by-lot inspection, where the risk of accepting a lot worse than the AQL is present in the inspection of every individual lot, it is a fact that some lots will be rejected and must be inspected 100%. Theoretically, all defectives will then be replaced making such lots zero % defective. They offset, therefore, those lots worse than the AQL which may be accepted.

Let the consumer be buying one lot of 9,000 at 2.5% AQL (the same example we used in an earlier piece on Alpha and Beta Risks). He wants to put a fix on the LTPD. But first, being an orderly man, he asks, "What is the LTPD at 50%, 10%, and 5% Beta Risk?"

We turn to page 50 in the MIL-STD-105D and read off from the tabulation below the curves:

Beta Risk		LTPD
50%	=	5.33% defective
10%	=	7.70% defective
5%	=	8.48% defective

▶

This information shatters the consumer and he then asks what can be done to protect his single lot from such a fearful probability. We explain that we can use MIL-STD-105D to find an "AQL" plan which will protect his desired quality of 2.5% at a stated Beta Risk. We explain that since we must use the sampling plans listed in 105 and cannot interpolate, we may not hit it right on 2.5% but we'll get fairly close.

We turn to page 50 in 105 and use the tabulation. Entering the table at 50.0 (extreme left column) we move across the row to a number close to 2.5. We find this to be 2.84 in the column headed 1.0.

This is the first plan we offer the consumer. It requires us to specify AQL 1.0% which will assure us that if the lot quality should be equal to or worse than 2.84% defective, there's a 50% chance it will be rejected.

"Try again," he says. We enter the table at 10.0 in the extreme left column and move across the row looking for a number close to 2.5. We find it at 2.66 in the column headed 0.40.

Again entering the table at 5.0, in the left column and moving across for a number close to 2.5, we find it at 2.37 in the column headed 0.25.

Thus we offer the consumer three sampling plans which will fix the LTPD at approximately 2.5% defective at three different values of the Beta Risk.

LOT SIZE 9,000. SINGLE, NORMAL, LEVEL II (REF. MIL-STD-105D)

AQL	LTPD	Beta Risk
1.0	2.84	50%
0.40	2.66	10%
0.25	2.37	5%

The sample size remains constant at 200; the acct. no. changes as follows:

AQL 1.0%	acct. no. 5
AQL 0.40%	acct. no. 2
AQL 0.25%	acct. no. 1

Which plan would the consumer select? That's up to him. The main thing is that, while 105 plans are indexed for the AQL, it's easy to construct a plan that will hold a specified LTPD (worst quality of a single lot) at a stated risk of acceptance.

I went through this drill using the OC curve tabulations to emphasize that all such information derives from the OC curves. However, we could have found the plans for 10% Beta Risk and 5% Beta Risk from Table VI-A and Table VII-A on pages 24 and 26 of 105.

It can be anticipated that there will be an increasing use of plans tied to the LTPD and Beta Risk as companies tighten procedures in response to consumer complaints. □

Selecting the AOQL

□ The AOQL, the average outgoing quality limit, "limit," not level, is the worst the accumulating inventory from lot-by-lot inspection will be—but only if certain procedures are followed conscientiously, no fudging!

Let's first select a sampling plan which will provide a specified AOQL; and then have a look at the inspection procedure which must be followed, not fudged.

Assume the part to be inspected is one which has been classified "major," and it is convenient for production to group parts into lots of 800.

Inspection by attributes

Inspection is to be by attributes, so we shall use MIL-STD-105D.

1) Turn to page 9 for the crucial code letter. The lot size of 800 is grouped in with lots 501 to 1,200. We will inspect at Level II, so that the code letter is J.

2) Turn to page 10 for the sample size; it is 80. We shall need it to compute the AOQL.

3) Turn to page 22 for the AOQL. We find the number 1.7 at the intersection of row J and column 1.0. This is a factor which must be multiplied by $(1-n/N)$ to get the AOQL. Since n = 80, and N = 800, then the bracket equals 0.9 and the AOQL equals $(1.7 \times 0.9) = 1.53\%$. It won't do!

Let's try again

4) Turn to page 23 to see what the AOQL sample will be if we sample at AQL 1% tighten instead of normal. The factor is 1.1 which, when multiplied by 0.9 (sample size and lot size are the same), gives an AOQL of 0.99, which is close enough. ▶

5) Turn to page 11 (because we're going to tightened) to find the acceptance number; it is 1. The single sampling plan is, then, a sample size of 80 with an acc. no. of 1.

6) The all important procedure: As each lot is submitted for inspection, the inspector will draw at random a sample of 80 and inspect each part. If he finds one or zero defects in the sample, he accepts the lot without further inspection. If there is one defect in the sample, he discards it. If 2 or more defects are found in the sample, the balance of the lot must be screened 100%. All the defects must be discarded.

By following this procedure we are assured that the average outgoing quality will not be worse than 1% defective. It may be better, but it won't be worse.

Use the "tightened" version

In general, the "tightened" version of a normal AQL plan will provide an AOQL equal to or better than the AQL. Try it again: Let N equal 3,000 and let the desired AOQL be 2.5%.

Page 9 provides code letter K; page 10 says the sample size shall be 125; page 23 (tightened) provides a factor of 2.5 in column 2.5 and on row K; the bracket $(1-n/N)$ equals 0.9584 and the AOQL equals 2.4%. Don't forget the acct. no. According to page 11, it is 5. The plan is: $n = 125$; $c = 5$.

And again: Let an AOQL of 4.0% be required for lots of 200. Page 9 provides code F; page 10, a sample size of 20; page 23 (tightened) provides the factor 4.2 which, when multiplied by $(1-n/N)$ equals 3.8%. The acct. no. is 1 (from page 11) and the plan is $n = 20$; $c = 1$.

Note: Dodge-Romig, who developed the AOQL procedure, used to require that defects be replaced. But in the 1967 reprint of the Dodge-Romig Sampling Tables (John Wiley & Sons), it says it makes very little difference and it's OK to discard defects without replacement. □

A funny story—or is it?

☐ The other day I was in the office of the Purchasing Manager of a new client. We were talking about supplies and suppliers.

"D'you specify AQL's on purchase orders?"

"No. Well, I haven't so far. What do you have in mind?"

"Don't you buy a number of non-critical items?"

"Yes, we do."

"Well, if you specified AQL's on those items, that would mean less inspection for the supplier. So you ought to get a price break."

The Purchasing Manager looked skeptical, perhaps because he felt he already had the prices down to rock bottom.

"Why not try it?", I asked. "Let's try it on the phone."

So he picked out a hardware item which he buys in fairly large quantities.

"What AQL?", he asked, and I suggested AQL 4%.

How does 4% AQL grab you?

He phoned the supplier and, after exchanging the usual amenities, he said, "On the next order for part number so-and-so I'm thinking of specifying 4% AQL. How's that grab you?"

The Purchasing Manager listened attentively to what, judging from his pained expression, must have been a heart-rending dissertation. Then he asked, "How much?"—paused for the reply and concluded, "OK, I'll let you know the next time I place an order."

"What did he say?"

"Double!"

"Double what?"

"The price. He says he'll have to DOUBLE the price!!"   ▶

"No!"

"Yes," said the Purchasing Manager, laughing. "Yes, that's what he said. And that's a concession to me because I give him so much business!"

We were fractured! We agreed that he and QC, with some assistance from me, should launch a program to educate the suppliers.

And so we did, and it's getting along fine.

But this is the kind of "happening" that can really shake the professional. It reveals the gap that exists between the few who have a firm grip on statistical sampling and the many who don't.

The supplier is no fool

Let's get one thing clear. It's not my intention to suggest that the supplier was a fool. Far from it! It's an almost certain bet he drives a Cadillac, or a Ford Lotus if he's the sporting type. He's prosperous enough not to have to wear a tie; he's been in business 10 years or more and he employs 85.

I asked the Purchasing Manager, "Did he want to know what 4% AQL meant?"

"No. In fact, from the moment I put the question, he sounded like an infuriated bull."

"Did he offer any explanation for upping the price?"

"Oh, yes. He said if I was going to stick him with government type quality control, I would have to pay for it!"

The poor government! They try so hard to be fair and "objective" and look what it gets them. It is more ironic when one considers that the sampling plans indexed for AQL, and published by DoD as MIL-STD-105, were specifically developed to minimize the probability of the rejection of good lots. "Good," meaning as good as the AQL or better.

Indeed, MIL-STD-105 might reasonably be called the "producers sampling tables" in contrast to, say, the LTPD and AOQL indexed Dodge-Romig Tables, which might be thought of as favoring the consumer. Anyway, I thought it might amuse you. □

Range conflict

☐ I've been searching for a phrase that would symbolize the constant danger in mass production of conflict between process capability and engineering tolerance limits. I think "range conflict" does it. Range conflict is at its worst when the process range exceeds the tolerance range. Nothing can then prevent a large fraction of the parts produced from being out-of-spec.

I must admit that the phrase also brings to mind the great days of the Golden West, when conflicts on the range were so frequent that one wonders whether a cowboy ever found time to light up a cigarette.

Scrap is scrap, period!

However, conflict between the tolerance range and the process range is every bit as deadly as any shoot-out in the sage. Indeed, more so, because the cowboys who die so valiantly in today's movie revive to shoot again. But in the machine shop, scrap is scrap, period!

Why, at this late date, should so much scrap be made because of range conflict? Why are jobs loaded onto production processes when the drawing tolerance range is less than the process range? Can it be that Production personnel are not aware of the phenomenon of inherent variability? Can it be that they, or many of them, are not aware of statistical quality control techniques for the measurement and control of variability?

It cannot be. Dr. Shewhart's "Control of Quality of Manufactured Products" has been out since 1931. Many other books are in publication. Many seminars have been conducted by competent instructors.

I think the reason may be that many are informed but few believe. "Belief!" you say, "What has belief to do with the science of statistics?"

►

Well, plenty. Bear in mind what happened to Galileo as recently as 1632. He asserted what every schoolboy now believes: that the Earth moves 'round the sun. But people weren't ready to accept the idea that their beloved Earth was not the center of the Universe. Furthermore, the Inquisition threatened dire action and Galileo kept his head on his shoulders only by withdrawing his ridiculous assertion.

Now, many people are as opposed to the idea of variability in man-made mass production processes as our ancestors once were to Galileo's shocking proposal. They can accept it as a part of nature because they see it all around them. They see it in people, 3 billion of whom readily accept the idea that each and every one of them is unique and different from all the others. They recognize the tendency to variability in dogs, horses, and many other species mass-produced by nature. But they cannot accept that it also occurs in machine tools and plating vats and heat-treating ovens.

What is the inherent amount of variation?

Personnel responsible for loading jobs on to production processes have to arrive at the point where they believe that on any given process there is an inherent amount of variation, like .0002 in., or .002 in., or whatever, which cannot be reduced either by perspiration or by prayer.

How are they to be brought to a proper state of mind? It's not simple, or it would have happened long ago. It's not the statistical techniques; the statisticians have made them simple enough to use. I think it may be that we haven't recognized the necessity to propagate the idea of variability as a necessary precondition to the acceptance and use of statistical techniques. Like all practitioners in possession of a body of esoteric knowledge, we have assumed that what's self-evident to us is equally self-evident to everyone else. But it isn't! Not by a long chalk!

Range conflict is a fact of industrial life that must cost millions of dollars in scrap every day. Statistical quality control is the only technique that can make a radical reduction in this appalling loss. But the broadest possible application will not be made unless and until we recognize the necessity to induce, in production executives, a belief in the universality of variability. When they accept that, they will appreciate the disastrous effects of range conflict. Only then will they request the quality engineers to measure all process ranges, and instruct the industrial engineers that no job be loaded onto a process unless the tolerance range exceeds the process range. □

Who was Vilfredo Pareto?

☐ I thought you might enjoy a change from being lectured on how to persuade your employers to allow you to improve product quality at no extra cost! Pareto seems like a good subject. Here's a man whose name we have appropriated to a most elegant system of analysis; simple courtesy dictates that we should desire to know a little about the man behind the system.

Vilfredo Pareto was begotten of a French mother by Raffaele Pareto, a Genoese nobleman, in Paris in the year 1848. Poppa had fled to France because he had been involved in the struggle for the unification of Italy he felt he had a better chance of keeping his head on his shoulders in some other country. He was a hot-tempered man and so was his son—as we shall see.

Can you imagine Italy without Rome?

Incidentally, Italy *was* united in 1861; but, united Italy did not include Rome! Can one imagine the U.S. without Washington, D.C.? Or England without London? Or France without Paris? No! That's how the Italians felt about Rome, and so they "annexed" it in 1870.

The family returned to Italy in 1858. Vilfredo began a course of studies which culminated in a Doctorate in Engineering in 1869. He embarked upon the profession of engineering and became general manager of the Italian Iron Works.

Direct experience in industry turned his mind to economics which, in turn, led him to sociology. By the early 1890's, he was well-known as an economist. His stature in that field is demonstrated by his inclusion in Joseph A. Schumpeter's *"Ten Great Economists."*

But he was also known as a malcontent. As hot-headed as his father, he was now inveighing against the members of the democratic government who ruled the united Italy his father had so ardently desired. Schumpeter writes: "He saw nothing but incompetence and corruption. He fought with impartial ferocity the governments which succeeded one another." In fact, he became known as an "ultra liberal" which in those times meant an uncompromising advocate of *laissez-faire* instead of, as the word is now used, an opponent of what is left of laissez-faire.

Realizing that his denunciations had made him unpopular with the authorities, he was considering a move to Switzerland ... when he was offered the Chair in Economics at the University of Lausanne!

In 1893, he moved to Lausanne and there lived happily, lecturing, writing and fulminating against government until 1906. In 1906, he resigned and moved to Geneva where he continued to write and fulminate until 1923. In that year, he joined other great controversialists in the Beyond.

Arriving at the Pareto Analysis

What was it he did which enabled us to arrive at what we now call the Pareto Principle of Analysis? He observed that as society splits up into classes, there are in each class a few, an elite, who can be relied upon to work their way to the top. As one government succeeds another in the periodic convulsions of parliamentary democracy, it must be kept in mind that it is the few, the elite, within the winning party which will rule. Therefore, it behooves the wary citizen and the watchful observer to know who the few are, and what they might do. Always, he said, we are ruled by the few, by a minority, regardless of the party in power. Note that "minority" was then used in the proper dictionary sense, not in the present sense whereby one "minority" alone, the women, outnumbers all other "minorities" added together, as well as the majority!

Many things have changed since Pareto's time, including the political vocabulary. But the principle still remains: where many items or individuals in a closed system (a factory, a country) may vary, a few will vary the most—and those few must be identified and corrected. Correction in the case of hardware is possible and is facilitated by Pareto analysis. In the case of politics we do the best we can at each election.   □

A system for all seasons

☐ The phrase, "A something or someone for all seasons," has become a bit hackneyed since it was applied to poor Sir Thomas More. More was all things to Henry VIII except submissive, and so he lost his head. But I think we can put it to good use once again for that inestimable, all-purpose, analytical system: the Pareto.

Pareto (1848-1923) was an Italian economist and sociologist. He was interested in the cyclical rise and fall of ruling elites and observed that, while populations are large, only a few individuals exert themselves to claw their way into the governing elite, or to knock others out of it. Sound familiar?

Many are called, but few are chosen

As a proposition, it may be said that while many may act, only a disproportionate few act the most (for better or for worse). It's important therefore to identify the most active few and to investigate why they act the way they do. As adapted to quality control (by Dr. Juran), we look for the defects which occur the most frequently and feed back this information to Production as an indication of where corrective action can do the most good most quickly.

The most familiar application of the Pareto is to assembly lines for fairly complex products; an electronic assembly is a good example. To recapitulate the steps: 1) code the defects; 2) design a report sheet with boxes in which defects can be tallied; 3) periodically compute the frequency of occurrence of each kind of defect; 4) tabulate kinds of defect in rank order with the most frequently occurring defect at the head of the list; 5) expect to find that about 10 percent of the kinds of defect account for about 90 percent of all recorded defects. (This frequently quoted ratio is by no means rigid; it could be 20/80, even 30/70. It is almost certain that at the beginning of a program there will be a startling disproportion);

▶

6) feed back to Production; 7) don't do any of the above until you have established the pre-existing quality level. Who will believe that it was you and Pareto who effected that spectacular quality improvement unless you have the "before" and "after" figures?

Hardware quality isn't all that the Pareto can do. Consider *purchased supplies* which arrive late so often that you would think it was the law of the land. It's a problem all over, but especially in electronics where purchased supplies may be 50 percent or more of the sales dollar.

Design a report sheet to record the day of arrival of each lot. Score 0 (zero) for each lot arriving on the scheduled day; score plus one, ten or whatever for days late; score minus one, ten or whatever for days early. Analyze monthly, computing the algebraic sum of days late and early for each supplier. Compose a Pareto display with suppliers in rank order, the worst offender at the head of the list. Feed back to Procurement. Keep an eye on the *range* for each supplier. You might get a perfect score of zero on two deliveries, one 20 days late and one 20 days early! Such a case would be worth investigating in its own right.

Costs also may be studied

Costs can be subjected to Pareto discrimination: on which parts or at which cost centers do deviations from standards occur the most frequently?

Absenteeism and *tardiness* are great disrupters of schedule and cost. The Pareto will identify the individuals absent or late the most frequently and on which days. The latter will almost certainly be Mondays and Fridays, but the Pareto will give you confirmation of it. You may know who the worst offenders are, but the Pareto may still shock you with its demonstration of the magnitude of the disproportion.

The Pareto can shed light on any situation where many things may vary but where a disproportionate few may vary the most. And it does it so simply! Well, more or less. It seems incredible that such an essentially simple system can reveal so much . . . but there it is. □

Pareto probes physician's practices

☐ Is it true that too many malpractice suits are brought against doctors?

Is it true that juries make excessive malpractice awards?

Is it true that competent doctors are as likely to be sued as incompetent doctors?

All three allegations are a matter of common belief among doctors. Many members of the public believe them too because of the great publicity that is given to the large awards. When malpractice insurance premiums shot up sky-high two or three years ago, there was a lot of sympathy for the doctors. There was a feeling that while patients who suffered from malpractice should certainly be compensated, the compensation in many cases was excessive. This was attributed to the tendency of juries to favor the suffering patient, possibly because each member of the jury could imagine himself or herself in a similar situation.

All three beliefs are untrue!

Who says so?

Such were the findings of a study made by the Rand Corporation and reported in the September 1978 issue of *Psychology Today*. The study was made by Dr. William Schwartz of the Tufts University School of Medicine, Boston, Massachusetts, and Professor Neil Komesar of the University of Wisconsin Law School, Madison, Wisconsin.

One of the channels of inquiry was a study of the malpractice records of 8000 doctors in the Los Angeles area, all covered by one insurance plan. The records covered a period of four years. That's 32,000 doctor-years, which is a pretty good sample.

The investigators found that 10 percent of the claims were entered against only 46 of the doctors! That is, less than one percent of the doctors accounted for 10 percent of the claims! ▶

A Pareto disproportion

This is a Pareto disproportion of the first rank. It would be impossible to find a more convincing example of the value of the method of analysis based on the Pareto principle. The Pareto principle states that where many individuals or articles may vary (for better or for worse), it is likely that a disproportionate few will vary the most.

The disproportion was even more severe in the matter of claims paid. Every suit is not successful; payments are made against only a fraction of the claims entered. The 46 accounted for 30 percent of the claims paid!

It is interesting to consider what would have happened if the investigators had stopped at the average performance for the 8000 doctors. The average number of claims entered against each of the 46 for the four-year period was five. Hence the total of claims against the 46 was 230. Since this was 10 percent of all claims, the grand total against 8000 doctors for four years would have been 2300 claims. The average would then compute out at less than 0.1 percent of a claim per doctor per year; the actual figure is 0.07!

1/10 claim per doctor per year

Now, although it is regrettable that even one patient should suffer from malpractice, an average of less than one-tenth of a claim per doctor per year doesn't sound very terrible. The investigators might have stopped there, leaving the impression that things weren't all that bad.

But fortunately, and whether prompted by Pareto or not, they broke down the original, amorphous mass of data in pursuit of the individual performance of each doctor ... and discovered the spectacular disproportion.

Once more Pareto performs its indispensable task of identifying the "vital few." □

Dig Sigma!

☐ Saint Sigma, the patron saint of quality assurance, decided to test a recent recruit to the ranks of his followers. He appeared, therefore, in a dream to Joe Random, a quality engineer.

"Get-up"—commanded St. Sigma—"and answer a few questions. You don't mind being catechized do you?" Joe really had no alternative, but he agreed politely.

St S: D'you do any sampling?

JR: Oh yes. Plenty.

St S: What plan are you using at present? Just name any one.

JR: Well, we're using a 1% AQL from 105.* Single sampling. General inspection level II.

St S: What's the average lot size?

JR: They run about 400.

St S: So you're using a sample of 50, with an acceptance number of 1 and a rejection number of 2?

JR: Yes—yes sir.

St S: Is this acceptance inspection? Is it written into the contract with your customer?

JR: Yes, we sample—and if it's OK, we ship.

St S: Does your customer sample after you?

JR: Oh, yes. In fact, his rep comes right in and samples in final inspection.

St S: Does he ever find a bad sample? You know, like 2 or more defectives in a sample of 50; we'll assume the lot size is 400.

JR: (With bitter emphasis): He sure does! Just today he sampled a lot of 400 right after us. My inspector found no defects in a sample of 50 and bought the lot. This character from Metalunar draws a sample of 50 (my fellow had thrown his back in the lot), and what d'you know, he finds 3 defectives!

St S: What happened?

JR: What happened! He ranted and raved for 10 minutes and wrote a Defect Report that says we're blind, or incompetent, or both!

St S: D'you think he was justified?

JR: What's there to think about? I saw them with my own eyes: three big fat rejects! Right after we said there were none.

St S: But that's the point. When your inspector drew a sample of 50 from 400 and found no defectives, what did that tell you about the quality level of the lot? That it was exactly 1% defective? Or better than 1%? Or worse than 1%? Or you don't know? ►

JR: 1% or better.

St S: No.

JR: NO?

St S: No. You don't learn too much by sampling about the quality of a single lot. Let us assume that the lot was exactly 1% defective. In 400 there would then be 4 defectives. Right?

JR: Right.

St S: Your inspector could have selected 50 at random and missed all of the defectives; as he did. The customer's rep could draw 50 and find 1, 2, 3, or 4 defectives; he found 3.

JR: So?

St S: Take a further example. Assume there are only 2 defectives in a lot of 400. In that case, the lot is twice as good as it need be according to the contract. It would still be possible for your inspector to find no defectives in a sample of 50 and accept; while the customer's rep might find the only 2 defectives and reject! Again, the lot might be as bad as 5% defective in which case there would be 20 defectives in 400. You could draw 50 and find one defective, and accept the lot. The customer's rep could do the same, and accept the lot too! If you look on page 44 of 105 — No! Don't put the light on now — you'll see there's about a 27% chance that that could happen.

JR: Wow!

St S: Yes, indeed. So you see that a buyer is not justified in automatically condemning the seller for incompetence when he finds a "bad" sample. Assuming, of course, that acceptance sampling at some agreed level was written into the contract.

JR: D'you mean I can challenge the Defect Report?

St S: Certainly. However, make sure you have it all worked out in your mind before you do so; make sure you dig it good; you'll have to explain it convincingly to the customer's rep.

JR: I see. So that customer's rep had no right to reject that lot. I can't wait to get at him!

St S: Take it easy, Joe. He had every right to reject it and to require you to screen it. But he should not have hit you with a harsh Defect Report. He should know, as you should know, that what happened, could legitimately happen. You and he should keep a record of all such inspections and compute the process average periodically. As long as the process average remains fairly near to 1% you're all right. That's the key, the process average; not what happens in the inspection of a single lot.

JR: Gee, thanks!

St S: You're welcome. Goodbye Joe — and Joe — dig me! □

*MIL-STD-105D, Sampling Procedures and Tables for Inspection by Attributes.

Statistics, life and labels

☐ Life and statistics do not agree. Life is lived by individuals, but statistics happen to masses of anonymous consumers.

Objectively, every individual is surrounded by a host of potential dangers, each crouching on its statistical probability just waiting to spring! But we are blissfully unaware of them. Even when the statistics of injury are quoted we tend to disregard them. We live subjectively; each of us unique, subject perhaps to a personal fate, but not to the blind groping of random chance. Certainly not!

This indifference to statistical threat makes it possible to leave the house in the morning, to blast onto the freeway, to use elevators which may fail, and so on. But this mind-saving indifference also discourages us from reading warning labels, or from acting on them if we happen to glance at them, or from paying attention to broadcast warnings.

To take an example: every holiday weekend hundreds are slaughtered on the highways. Broadcast warnings fill the air: "Drive safely; the life you save may be your own!"

Why doesn't anybody listen?

Does anyone listen? No! Well ... hardly anybody. Why not! Because individual drivers do not feel that the warnings are addressed to them. Nor do they feel that *their* lives are in danger; they would freeze at the wheel if they thought so. And so the first accidents are announced, and the next, and the next. The holiday winds on to its appointed end. The statistical forecast of fatalities is fulfilled.

How was the trend reversed? Not by warnings, not by dread statistical threats. The trend was reversed incidentally as an unplanned consequence of another series of events. War broke out between Israel, Egypt and Syria; the Arabs cut the flow of oil to the U.S.; an energy crisis was declared; the national speed limit was reduced to 55 MPH; and ... the death rate dropped by one third! ►

Many individuals were exasperated by the reduction of the speed limit. Some declared that it made driving more dangerous because drivers kept their eyes on the speedometer instead of the road. Nevertheless the anonymous mass responded to the change in the objective condition with an almost automatic precision!

To take a second example: I was listening to another speaker at a Wisconsin University Safety Seminar. He was talking about farm equipment. He mentioned a yearly figure of 700 tractor roll-overs. I was appalled! The few tractors I had ever seen at work seemed to be as incapable of turning over as a Hindu juggernaut. Yet here was a statistic which implied that tractors moved as precariously as an acrobat on a high wire.

The operators are the problem, not the equipment

I spoke to him later and asked what was wrong with the equipment. Was the center of gravity too high? "It isn't the equipment," he said, "it's the drivers. They try to make turns too near to ditches. They try to pull loads too heavy for the tractor (in which case the tractor may rear up and fall over backwards). They work on steep slopes. If you got the center of gravity down to the ground, they'd try going up a vertical wall!"

"Even so . . . they must really work at it to run up a total of 700. The countryside must be littered with them."

"Oh no . . . that's not the total. That's the roll-over death rate. Roll-overs run into the tens of thousands."

"Why don't you warn them?"

"Warn them? We plaster the tractors with warning labels. We provide safety manuals. But it goes on. You'd think they couldn't read."

The problem is not that they can't read . . . but that they don't. Or if they do, they feel these "ridiculous" warnings are meant for less skillful drivers. The moral of the story is that we should not expect to reduce the injury rate by "educating" the potential victims. We shall have to concentrate on foolproof design and meticulous quality assurance, and we can exercise our imaginations in the hope of composing warning labels which will convince the reader they mean *him* . . . and not *them*; not the anonymous but statistically sensitive mass of which no individual can feel he's a part. □

Cost reduction and sampling

☐ Why do we talk so much about cost reduction and do so little double and multiple sampling?

The customary answer is that it's too difficult to train the inspectors. There's some truth in this explanation since it's obvious that there's more complexity in the procedure for double and multiple sampling than in the simple procedure of drawing one sample. However, what would it do for us if we should go double or multiple?

On successive lots of 10,000 at 1 percent AQL, the single sample size for each lot would be 200. If we should go double, and if the quality of successive lots is about equal to the AQL, the average lot size would be 140. A reduction of 30 percent. Multiple sampling would reduce the average sample size to 120, a reduction of 40 percent from the single sample of 200.

Where do you get the numbers?

How do we arrive at the average sample sizes of 140 and 120? It's on page 29 of MIL-STD-105D. But first we should complete the details of the sampling plan. We are inspecting at inspection Level II, normal. This information directed us to page 9 where we picked up the code letter L. Page 10 provided the sample size of 200 and acceptance number (c) 5. With this information we identify the diagram we require as the fourth over on the top row, where $c = 5$. The proportion defective is the incoming quality; we are assuming that this is the same as the AQL of 1 percent, so that $p = 0.01$, and $np = 2$.

At this point on the horizontal axis the authors of 105D have obligingly drawn an arrow. Following it up to the points of intersection with the "double" and "multiple" curves and extending to the left, we strike the vertical axis at approximately 70 percent and 60 percent. The vertical axis is 100 percent of the equivalent single sample size. The average sample sizes for double and multiple sampling are, therefore, 140 and 120.

▶

What happens if we are using a "tightened" sampling plan? First, we must check the single plan information again. The sample size is still 200 (see page 11); "c," the acct. no. has changed to 3; "p" is still 0.01 and np is still = 2. This information puts us into the third diagram over on the top row of page 29. Following the same procedure, up from 2 on the horizontal axis to the points of intersection and across to the vertical axis, we find that the average sample size for doubling sampling will be 80 percent of the equivalent single sample of 200 (160); for multiple sampling the average sample size will be 75 percent of the single sample, or 150.

What if you're inspecting "reduced?" Page 29 is silent.

I phoned the statistician at Los Angeles DCAS. He suggested that a reasonably reliable estimate of the average sample sizes for "reduced" double and multiple plans could be obtained by reducing the single sample sizes for double and multiple plans in the ratio of the single sample size for reduced to the single sample size for normal. Thus, in our example, the single sample size for the reduced plan is 80 (page 12), while the single sample size for the normal plan is 200 (page 10); the ratio 80/200 = 0.4 or 40 percent; 40 percent of 140 (see above) is 56, which will be the average sample size for "reduced" inspection of lots of 10,000 at 1 percent AQL. Forty percent of 120 = 48, which would be the average sample size for multiple sampling, "reduced."

Everybody likes a second chance

Apart from the economic benefit, there is a psychological appeal in double sampling. Everybody likes a second chance. One would think that everybody would then like seven chances (as in multiple sampling) better. But no! Double sampling is seen as a lifesaving second chance. But multiple sampling is too much! It is perceived only as so much trouble and confusion.

There's a temptation, when double sampling, to fudge on the second sample if the first sample does not accept the lot. The fudge is to take only enough further pieces from the lot to make up the single sample size and to use the single plan acct. no. In our example, the two double samples would be 125 each (page 14). If we failed to accept on the first sample of 125 (and if we did not exceed the single acceptance number of 5), the fudge would be to take a second sample of only 75. Don't do it. It increases the probability of acceptance for any value of lot quality and, therefore, for values of lot quality worse than the AQL. Thus, it's not only honest to play it straight, it's beneficial to the quality, too. □

Reliability: camp or reality?

☐ "Camp" was a popular word in 1966; perhaps you saw it in the slick periodicals. It has been used to describe the discotheque—a contemporary institution which consists of a small dimly-lighted cave, a thunderous beat, and a horde of stunned, quivering adults protesting that they have never felt younger. Or, the cult of affecting to believe that the mono-syllabic moanings of immature minstrels have more to say about the allurements of love than, say, Henry Miller.

Is there any similarity between dazed discothequers and designers, producers and procurement personnel solemnly discussing the merits of electronic components with failure rates of, say, 0.1% per 1000 hours or 0.001% per 1000 hours?

As every schoolboy knows (to quote Macaulay), the mean-time-between-failures is the reciprocal of the failure rate. The MTBF for a component with a failure rate of 0.001% per 1000 hours is 100,000,000 hours, whereas the MTBF for a failure rate of 0.1% per 1000 hours is only 1,000,000 hours. Not that this greatly increases the credibility. If we assume 10,000 hours to the year (it's actually 8760), then in the one case we are confronted by a mean-time-between-failures of 10,000 years, and in the second case by an MTBF of 100 years.

Two questions arise: Why do we demand such MTBFs? and: How do we convince ourselves that the components have them?

An MTBF of 10,000,000 hours?

Let us take a fairly typical case. A major subsystem of a complex device is required to have a reliability of, say, 0.999 for an operating period of one hour. The statisticians tell us that the device must have an MTBF of 1000 hours! That's a fairly fabulous jump, from one hour to 1000 hours! But that isn't all. Assume that the subsystem has 10,000 components each essential to satisfactory performance and, for the sake of argument, each having an equal effect. Then, the statisticians tell us, each component must have an MTBF of 10,000,000 hours! Well ... we have some misgivings, but we don't like to challenge the statisticians, so we look around for components.

The question arises whether, for example, in the case of a component with the relatively modest MTBF of 100 years, it would be permissible to put 100 components on test for one year or 200 for six months? If 200

▶

survived for six months without failure, can we conclude that each component has an MTBF of 100 years?

Once again, the statisticians provide the answer. Yes, they say, but only if every component has been completely debugged before going on test, so that every assignable cause for failure had been detected and removed, and only chance causes for failure remain. Would the same statement hold in the case of components required to have an MTBF of 100,000,000 hours, or 10,000 years? Could you put 10,000 on test for a year and demonstrate the MTBF? Yes, they say, provided that the components have always been completely debugged.

Now, why don't lay personnel challenge these statements more frequently? No amount of "common sense" can convince the intelligent layman that a system must have a mean-time-between-failures of 1000 hours to assure performance without failure for one hour. Common sense cannot make such a big leap. Yes, says common sense, if you want to be sure of it for an hour, I can see that it ought to be able to go for more than an hour. Like two hours, for example, or even five hours; but 1000 hours! I just don't dig it! It's even crazier when a further leap is made from the systems MTBF of 1000 hours to component MTBFs of 10,000,000 hours! And the testing program for components; that's far out beyond common sense!

Just a big private joke

And yet, as we said, there are few challenges to this logic considering the thousands of people directly involved with it. This is where the "camp" may come in: administrators, purchasing men, contracts personnel, practically everybody except the reliability elite and some indoctrinated designers, suspect it's a big private joke. But they're reluctant to ask because we throw these numbers about with such straight faces. So they play along. This is the danger, and a constant hazard to the successful execution of reliability programs. It should be remembered that a reliability program is not just a series of computations by the reliability specialists, but a program involving the entire organization.

Everyone must be motivated by knowledge and a conviction of necessity. There can be little motivation in those who wonder whether reliability figures are real, or whether somebody is kidding. To find out who thinks what, the question must be debated with non-technical personnel.

Indeed, the best way to give an immediate and powerful boost to any reliability program is to convince non-technical personnel by indoctrination and instruction that, while reliability numbers are not immediately obvious to common sense, they are valid.   □

The high cost of confidence

☐ How much statistical confidence is a lot of confidence, and what does one have to pay for it?

A confidence level that is much quoted is 90%. Let's see what it means. Assume we have to inspect a lot of 3,000 parts. Let it be agreed that the part is not critical. It has been judged that if 2.5% of parts are beyond the tolerance limits, they will not be detrimental to the performance and safety of the end product. Thus the AQL (acceptable quality level) is 2.5%.

This judgment is usually made by quality engineers. It ought to be made with the consent of the designers, since the proposal that some of the parts may be out of specification is, in effect, a modification of the design. Furthermore, management should be involved too. Anyway, let's assume that the selection of 2.5% AQL was made with the consent of the engineers and the approval of management.

Lay it on the table

We will use MIL-STD-105D because these "military" sampling tables are equally applicable to commercial and military production. From page 9 of 105D we select the code letter K, because we elect to work at inspection Level II. We turn to page 10 because we also elect to go single sampling normal. Row K tells us the sample size is 125 and the acceptance no. is 7 (for 2.5% AQL).

We would reasonably expect that any accepted lot would be in the vicinity of 2.5% defective; and so it will be if the process is properly controlled. However, the process may go out of control, making a higher percentage of defective parts. So we ask, "At 90% confidence, how bad a lot may be accepted?"

We go to page 48 of 105D for the answer. At the intersection of row 10 and column 2.5, we find the quality, 9.42% defective! The complement of the 10% risk of acceptance we selected, is a confidence of 90%. We are now in a position to say that we are 90% confident that no accepted lot will be worse than 9.42% defective. A reasonable response would be to ask, "What do we have to do to be able to say we are 90% confident that no accepted lot will be worse than 2.5%?"

Check row "10" again. Follow it along until we arrive at a quality equal

▶

to, or near to 2.5%. Well, there are 1.84 and 3.11. Let us choose 1.84. The column heading is 0.10 (AQL). Back to page 10 where we find the acct. no. has dropped to zero. The sampling plan is now: n = 125; acct. no. = 0.

With this plan we can now say we are 90% confident that the quality of any accepted lot will not be worse than 1.84% defective. It's better than we required, but ... however. What is the cost of the confidence we have acquired? Well, if the quality of a submitted lot happens to be 1.84%, there is a 90% chance it may be rejected! There's only a 10% chance that it may be accepted. If the submitted quality happened to be 2.5% (which is what we were willing to accept), the chance of acceptance would drop to about 4% (check the O.C. curve on page 48). The complement of a 4% chance of acceptance is 96% confidence.

We could have used 0.40 AQL. It would have increased the acct. no. from zero to 1 for the same sample size of 125. This plan would assure us that no accepted lot would be worse than 3.11% at 90% confidence. If, by chance, the quality of a submitted lot were 2.5%, there would be a 15% chance of acceptance. The complementary confidence is 85%.

But what does it all mean?

To summarize: if we use a plan of sample size 125, acct. no. 0, there will be a probability of 4% of accepting a lot of 2.5% quality; with a complementary confidence of 96% that no accepted lot will be worse than 2.5% defective. If we use the plan, 125 and 1, there will be a 15% chance that a lot of 2.5% quality will be accepted; the complementary confidence being 85% that no accepted lot will be worse than 2.5%. What happens if we use the original plan of 125 and 7? The O.C. curve on page 48 assures us that the probability of acceptance of a lot 2.5% defective is almost 99%. The complement is the confidence that no accepted lot will be worse than 2.5% defective!

It sounds terrible, doesn't it ... but it's not so bad in practice. These figures mean what they say all right ... but the assumption behind demands for confidence levels of 90% or 95% is that production processes may go out of control with consequent rapid deterioration of the quality. And so they can ... but they shouldn't be allowed to. That's what statistical process control is for ... and there's not nearly enough of it. But if the process is kept under control then lot after lot submitted for sampling will be in the vicinity of 2.5% quality with a probability of acceptance of 98 to 99%. Make sure, therefore, that when someone in your organization, or a customer, demands 90 or 95% confidence that a given sampling plan will not accept any quality worse than a specified level, that all understand what it will mean in execution, and what it will cost by way of frequent rejections of lots having the specified level of quality. □

The eye of a needle

☐ Intending to write about switching in sampling, I was going to use some prosaic title like, "How to Switch," until it suddenly struck me that it's easier for a camel to pass through the eye of a needle than to switch from normal to reduced!

Let me give you an example, but first I would like to point out a common misconception in the use of MIL-STD-105D. Page 9 tabulates sample size code letters for various lot sizes and inspection levels. General Inspection Level I is not "reduced" in relation to "normal" Level II; and Level III is not "tightened."

Now, for the example. We are inspecting lots of 1,000 at 1% AQL, Level II, single, normal. The all-important code letter is J (page 9); the sample size is 80 and the acceptance number is 2 (page 10).

The first lot arrives (either from a supplier or from one of our own fabrication areas). The inspector draws the sample and finds 2 defectives. He discards the defectives, accepts the lot and passes it into stock or to the shipping area. He records the results. For the purpose of switching, record only the results of original inspections (resubmitted lots don't count in switching).

They bounce 2 out of 5 lots

Let us assume that we are unfortunate and that 2 out of the first 5 lots are rejected. We must go to tightened inspection (paragraph 8.3.1 on page 5). What does this do to us? According to page 11 of MIL-STD-105D, the sample size remains at 80, but the acct. no. drops from 2 to 1. To get back to normal inspection with an acct. no. of 2, we have to have 5 acceptable lots in a row (paragraph 8.3.2 on page 5). Since we pushed for corrective action when 2 lots out of 5 were rejected, we will assume that the action taken was effective, so that we soon get back to normal inspection level.

Now that the process is in control, we can hope to progress from normal to reduced inspection. What must happen? 10 consecutive lots must be found acceptable (paragraph 8.3.3 on page 5). But, that's not all. The total

▶

number of defectives found in the 10 samples must not exceed the number shown in Table VIII on page 28. We find (at the intersection of row 800-1249 and column 1.0) the number 4. Which is quite a shock! Because we could have accepted each of the previous 10 lots by finding 2 defectives in each sample of 80. We could have accumulated a total of 20 defectives while still accepting all 10 lots; but that won't get us into reduced. Not only must the total of defectives not exceed 4, but production must be at a steady rate and the government inspector must still consider the switch desirable (paragraph 8.3.3 on page 5).

But let us imagine that we manage to qualify; what does it get us? Page 12 of 105 tells us that the sample size drops to 32 with an acct. no. of 1 (row J and column 1.0). So if we ever make it, it's going to be worthwhile.

Now, if it is difficult to get into reduced, it's terribly easy to fall out. All we have to do is to have one lot rejected; or production becomes irregular or delayed; or "other conditions make it desirable to revert to normal" (paragraph 8.3.4). Subparagraph "b" is a reference to double and multiple sampling; we are concerned with single.

Your horoscope says . . .

A word about the stars on page 28. Let us say that we are still working with lots of 1,000 but at 0.15% AQL. The sample size would still be 80, but the acct. no. would drop to 0 (page 10). Assume that we find 10 lots in a row all acceptable. The total number of inspected pieces in the 10 samples is 800. Bear in mind that we did not find one defective among those 800. We go to page 28 and look for the number at the intersection of row 800-1249 and 0.15. We find a star. No go! We move down column 0.15 to the first number; it is 0 in row 1250-1999. Which means that, to qualify for reduced, the sum of the previous consecutively accepted samples must be equal to 1250 or more! The nearest we can get to 1250 is 1280 (16 times 80). Thus, working with lots of 1,000 at 0.15% AQL, we would have to find 16 consecutive original lots acceptable to quality for reduced.

We ought to take note of paragraph 8.4 on page 5. It states that if tightened inspection remains in effect for 10 consecutive original lots, sampling should be discontinued pending action to improve the process. Which seems reasonable whether one is producing for the government or the commercial market. □

Sampling, the super cost reducer

☐ In the March '75 issue of ASQC's *Quality Progress,* there is an excellent article on sampling by L.W. Miller of Kaiser Aluminum and Chemical Co. The title is "How many should you check?" Mr. Miller demonstrates that with certain conditions and by making certain assumptions, it is possible to make a substantial reduction in the size of the sample.

Fine! The reduction in the size of the sample reduces the cost of inspection. But what about the immense reduction in the cost of inspection brought about by statistical sampling as opposed to 100 percent inspection? I'm not looking at Mr. Miller when I raise this question, but at all of us in quality assurance. We are constantly called upon to justify what we do, and the cost of it, but I cannot recall any recent reference to the savings effected by the basic switch in manufacturing technology from 100 percent inspection to statistical sampling. But when one is confronted by it, it is staggering!

Sampling will allow some defectives

It was brought to my attention by a recent event. The assembly supervisors at a plant manufacturing a complex electro-mechanical device complained that they were finding defectives in parts and components drawn from stock. The defects were sometimes obvious and the assemblers put them aside; but occasionally the defective part was built into an assembly and was not discovered until the assembly failed on test. The assembly people then had to tear down such assemblies and rework them.

The quality manager and consultant explained to the assembly supervisors and the plant manager that the probability of some defectives in accepted lots was an unavoidable result of sampling; that the willingness to accept some defectives in accepted lots was a necessary precondition for the use of sampling. (You may think that everybody knows this; but they don't, or they don't seem to.) ▶

Then give us 100% inspection!

"In that case," said the production people, "let us have 100 percent inspection on incoming material."

"If it costs less than the cost of rework, then we'll be glad to. But let us see what it would cost. There are 20 inspectors sampling supplies. The average lot size is 1000, the average sample size is 80. If we go to 100 percent inspection we shall require an increase in the number of inspectors in the ratio of 1,000 to 80. Which is 250."

The production managers were appalled! The qc people hastened to point out that if they went to 100 percent inspection, they would require less than 250 inspectors because they were already doing some 100 percent inspection. But there was no way the 250 could be brought down to an acceptable figure. It was agreed to continue sampling.

Why don't we bring this massive cost reduction to the attention of employers and clients? Mainly, because over the years we have "sold" sampling as being more reliable than 100 percent inspection. But this argument, as I pointed out previously in "To sample or not to sample," also casts doubt on sampling when the sample is moderately large.

We'll do it if you pay for it

If 100 percent inspection had to be done (as every engineering drawing implies), we could make it reliable. We, who put men on the moon, surely could accomplish such a relatively simple task. It would just be horribly expensive. Occasionally designers are willing to classify characteristics, but more often they are notoriously reluctant to do so. They usually leave it to the quality manager to take responsibility for this task and for the acceptance of a proportion of non-conforming parts.

When the designers decline to participate, and if the quality manager has not obtained top management sanction for sampling, he alone is responsible for the presence of non-conforming parts in end products. This fact will be brought out with dire effects for quality managers and their employers when plaintiffs' lawyers rest the case for their injured clients on the defendant's practice of sampling and its consequences.

Employers, clients and consumers all benefit costwise from sampling; they should be made aware of the magnitude of the benefit, and should share responsibility for the concommitant probability of defects. □

CPSC improvements act of 1976:
No Sampling!

☐ The Consumer Product Safety Act was passed into law in October 1972. It took some time to get the Commission together, to hire a staff and get to work. The "work," bear in mind, was to write and promulgate safety standards for common consumer products.

The manufacture of vast quantities of consumer products at competitive prices is made possible only by mass production methods, which include inspection by sampling. But the first step in sampling is to select the AQL (Acceptable Quality Level). The AQL sounds good, but it is, in fact, the permissible or tolerable percentage of non-conforming parts in sample-accepted lots; it can be quite low but it cannot be zero. This concept runs smack into the intent of the Act, which is not to have safety standards which protect 99% of consumers, or even 99.9%, but all of them!

To sample, or not to sample

By 1974 a hot debate was in progress: to sample, or not to sample. The CPSC held hearings at which some harsh comments were made regarding the inclusion of sampling in safety standards. Typical was that by James Brodsky, attorney for Consumers' Union, who said that the use of sampling plans "would gut the Act's effectiveness."

At that time, the Commission was tentative about the use of sampling and published a "Proposed Statement of Policy on the Use of Sampling Plans" in the Federal Register for August 23, 1974. It raised the very practical point that 100% inspection would increase costs which must be "balanced against the increments in safety flowing from the increments in cost." In general, there appeared to be a willingness to include sampling plans in safety standards. Interested persons were invited to submit comments to the Commission. ▶

In the meantime, no safety standards with sampling plans were issued. Sampling plans are, of course, included in safety standards for flammable fabrics, but they are issued under another Act: the Flammable Fabrics Act. Now the matter has been settled and the answer is . . . NO SAMPLING!

On May 11, 1976, the "Consumer Products Safety Commission Improvements Act" passed into law. It is Public Law 94-284 of the 94th Congress, S.644. Among a number of amendments to the original Act of 1972, it requires that the following new paragraph be inserted in paragraph 7:

> "No consumer product safety standard promulgated under this section shall require, incorporate, or reference any sampling plan. The preceding sentence shall not apply with respect to any consumer product safety standard or other agency action of the Commission under this Act (A) applicable to a fabric, related material or product which is subject to a flammability standard or for which a flammability standard or other regulation may be promulgated under the Flammable Fabrics Act, or (B) which is, or may be applicable to glass containers."

So there it is. I suppose we should have expected such a conclusion. But where does it leave the producers . . . and the safety standards?

Must every item be tested?

Since the latter will not specify sampling, but will specify safety-assuring characteristics which must be measurable, does it imply that every item must be tested? What will happen if a producer elects to sample, since the standard will neither say that he can or that he can't? If he should find himself the defendant in a product liability suit, will he then be subject to punitive action over and above the claim for compensation of injury?

Let us assume that the first suit is brought against the producer; that there is no history of negligence on the part of the manufacturer; and let it be assumed that proper consideration had been given to the nature of the product in the selection of the sampling plan; and that the records showed that the plan had been meticulously adhered to. Would the court still take punitive action on the grounds that 100% inspection is implied in the absence of a specified sampling plan? It remains to be seen. □

The forgotten sampling plan

☐ The forgotten sampling plan: defects per hundred units. Well, not forgotten exactly, but rarely used. The title, defects per hundred units, tends to discourage would-be users. It's sort of confusing to have to think about constructing a sampling plan based on permissible defects per hundred units when you have only, say, 35 units. But, in fact, it's easy.

Let us suppose that each of 35 units has 10 quality characteristics; each characteristic falls into the same classification. Let's see what happens if we go the percent defective route. We select an AQL of 1% defective, inspection Level II, single, normal. Page 9 of MIL-STD-105 provides us with the sample size code letter D. Page 10 provides sample size 8 . . . but moving along row D in search of the acceptance and rejection numbers, we run into an arrow which pushes us down to code letter E, sample size 13, and an acceptance number of zero.

We're sampling 130, not 13

We must now draw a sample of 13 and inspect each of 10 characteristics on each unit. We may accept the lot if we find no defect in any one of the 13 units. But look! It's implicit in percent defective sampling plans that each unit in the sample has one chance of being found acceptable or defective. But each unit of our sample had 10 chances of being knocked out! In effect, we were judging the lot by the inspection of a sample of 130 instead of 13.

We do this every day because of the apparent ease of finding a percent defective plan. It's sometimes said that we prefer such plans because of the difficulty of explaining defects per hundred units to the inspector. This may be true on occasion, but it's worth the effort.

Now, let's go defects/100 units. Each of our 35 units has 10 characteristics (potential defects). There are, therefore, 1000 characteristics in 100 units. What percentage may be defects? Let's say 1%. One percent of 1000 is 10. The plan is, then, 10 defects/100 units.

▶

Inspect 10 characteristics on 8 units, instead of 13

The lot size is still 35 and the plan is still to be inspection Level II, single, normal. The code letter is still D (see page 9), the sample size is still 8, but now we have to move along row D to the column headed 10. There we find acceptance and rejection numbers of 2 and 3. So, we draw 8 units and inspect each of 10 characteristics on each unit; if we find only 2 defects or less, the lot is accepted.

Ten characteristics per unit does not make the unit complex. Let us imagine that each unit has 40 quality characteristics. Thus, there are 4000 in 100 units. What percentage of defects can we tolerate? Say 1%; then the plan is 40 defects/100 units. The code letter is still D and the sample size 8. On page 10 of 105 under the column headed 40 we find the acceptance number 7. Draw the sample of 8; inspect each of 40 characteristics on each of 8 units; accept the lot if there are 7 defects or less.

Let the classification be such that we can tolerate an AQL of 4% of defects in 100 units. What I wanted to point out to those who may not have recognized it is that the number of quality characteristics in each unit is automatically 1% of the characteristics in 100 units, which is what makes it easy to use such plans. Since we can tolerate 4% of defects in 100 units, the required plan has an AQL of 160 (40 X 4) defects/100 units.

There is no AQL of 160 on page 10, so we use the one to the left: i.e., 150. The sample size is still 8, and as we can see the acceptance number is 21. Inspect each of 40 characteristics on each of 8 units; accept the lot if there are 21 defects or less.

Why don't you give them a try. They might save some product that would otherwise be penalized by percent defective sampling when there are multiple quality features per unit. □

The marketing manager and quality statistics

☐ It's about 10:30 on Monday morning. The situation's cool; everyone's recovering from the weekend. No accusation of sabotage has yet been made against an inspector. You're just settling down to a nice cup of coffee when the marketing manager storms into the office.

"Hi," you say hopefully and offer him a cup of coffee. But he's in no mood for the amenities, he's obviously all wound up.

"When are we going to stop shipping junk?"

"Who says we're shipping junk?"

"This guy at Endsville. I was at this conference on marketing. I was the luncheon speaker. I said that our product was the best, better than Mom's homemade apple pie. Afterwards this guy comes up to me and tells me a tale of woe as long as your arm about the trouble he's had with one of our products."

When did it happen?

"Did you ask him when it happened?"

"Why should I ask him that? I mean, if it happened, it happened."

"Yes," you say, "But it matters whether it happened last week or three years ago."

"Why? A defect's a defect whenever it happens."

"That's true, but it matters whether the defect has a low probability of occurrence, or a high probability. You have to know the statistics of quality, especially you in marketing."

The marketing manager rests his head on one hand in a posture of resignation and asks, "Can't you guys in quality assurance ever get away from statistics?"

"If we do, we're lost, and so are you."

"OK," he says, simulating utter boredom. "Let me have it. Tell me about the statistics of quality."

"Right. Complaints from the consumers now average 0.5 percent. They've been stable at that figure for the last nine months. A couple of years ago that figure was about five percent." ▶

He interrupts, "Isn't that when you joined the company, about two years ago?"

You admit it, but, you add with becoming modesty, what has been done since then couldn't have been done without the cooperation of management, engineering and production.

Nero fiddled while Rome . . .

He affects to play a fiddle to accompany this worthy sentiment. You both laugh; the ice is breaking.

"All right, so what am I going to tell the next customer who approaches me with a tale of horror? If it happened two years ago should I have told him that he was one of the unfortunate five percent, but not to worry because this year the probability of being unfortunate is only 0.5 percent? His chance of getting a defective product has diminished ten times?"

"Very funny! But that is, indeed, the situation. As far as you and the other managers of the company are concerned you have no certainty as to the quality situation except in statistics."

"All right. What am I going to do at the next promotional conference? Am I going to tell them that no more than one in two hundred is likely to get a lemon?"

"No, but it's a pity you can't, because that's the real world. But *you* know it. It will keep you steady when the odd consumer grabs you by the lapel and pours his troubles into your unwilling ears. It will help you to keep the faith."

"That's fine, but what do I *tell* the guy who's hanging onto my lapels?"

"You break his grip. Politely of course. Then you commiserate with him . . . and hand him a replacement."

"Just like that?"

"Well," you say, backing off a little, "It should be a matter of company policy, of course. But since the price of our products varies from about $5 to $10, and since we know production is in control at an average quality level of 0.5 percent, we can agree on a replacement policy and incorporate the cost of it in the selling price. That way you don't hassle the occasional consumer who gets a lemon. And you should be the man to recommend such a policy."

The marketing manager pauses. "Aren't we ever going to get that 0.5 percent down to zero?"

"I doubt it. Not with mass production. And not at competitive consumer prices."

The marketing manager fires his parting shot, "Why didn't I know all this before?"

"Because you don't read my memos." Touche.   □

Quality as a distribution

☐ I read with great interest the article by Nat Wood in the September 1979 issue of *Quality* about the marriage of Memorex and quality control. Not that they had been strangers in the past, but this was the full treatment from A to Z—no compromise.

Thinking about what it takes to put together a full scale quality program—empathizing with Ed LaChance, Jack Payne, Ed Theis and John Heldt—it occurred to me that it would have been no more than an elegant academic exercise had it not received the approval and support of Chairman Robert C. Wilson. Which started me speculating on the question of what should be in the minds of men at the top to predispose them to favorable consideration of quality control—since this is, as we all know, the prime requirement.

What does your boss think about quality?

Speaking in general of top men, how would we wish them to perceive quality control? As something cheaper to do right the first time? Or even as something which is free? Both of these are excellent and to be highly desired, but they emphasize economic benefits without implying knowledge or perception of quality control as such.

Should they think of it as a body of procedures which must be adopted as the price to be paid for a military contract? Or as protection against possible personal injury suits? These are weighty factors but, again, they too may be given consideration without a perception of the nature and necessity of quality control itself.

Postulating only that the organization shall be in mass production, and in the market to make a profit (as distinct, for example, from corporations engaged in government sponsored space research), quality control would be assured of an informed hearing if the man at the apex were familiar with the concept of quality as a distribution. ▶

This brilliant encapsulation of the vast corpus of quality control theory and practice was propounded by Dr. Walter A. Shewhart in the mid-twenties. It was a revelation then, when the vast quantities of material poured out by mass production had swamped conventional methods of inspection. It is a revelation now.

Process variation is fact, not theory

Quality as a distribution places the emphasis on the phenomenon of variability as it manifests itself in repetitive production processes. It directs attention to the range of variation as an incompressible, nonnegotiable parametric characteristic of a given process (assuming the process to be in good repair). Which leads directly to practical recognition of the fact that the range of variation of a given process may exceed the engineering tolerance on the part assigned to the process. This would assure, beyond any doubt, the production of a proportion of out-of-specification parts.

And so on, by logical extension, to the recognition of the necessity for statistical techniques:

- to measure process variability
- to make predictions as to yield on long runs
- to control processes during the run to assure that predictions will be fulfilled, etc.

It does not require that top men should know the variety of statistical techniques as quality professionals know them. It requires only that they recognize the necessity for statistics where quantities are large and that they be familiar with the concept of quality as a distribution.

Let us congratulate all concerned at Memorex and take satisfaction in the knowledge that one more corporation is on the right course with a good pilot at the helm. ☐

Victims & victors of variability

☐ We are all victims of variability, none more so than the manufacturers of industrial products. Variability is there to confuse and dismay them, generating scrap and rework, causing havoc with their best laid plans from the moment the factory opens Monday morning to closing time on Friday.

The victors are quality engineers trained in statistics. They are specialists in variability, adept in the measurement and control of variability as it manifests itself in the mass production of many products: mechanical, electronic, hydraulic, pharmaceutical, etc.

It would appear that there should be a natural symbiosis between victims and victors of variability. And so there should be; U.S. industry will never operate at peak efficiency until such a symbiosis occurs. Out-of-spec products and parts of products will continue to pour off production processes in shockingly high proportions, causing scrap or rework and the attendant disruption of schedules and delivery promises.

Variability is inherent within any process

The problem is that the victims are, in general, not aware that the enemy is variability. Production executives know that they get far too high a percentage of scrap and rework, and they know the added cost and delays they cause. But they don't think "variability" when they read the depressing reports.

We may assume that most industrial executives learned at school about population statistics and the normal curve. But it does not occur to them that the characteristic distribution of human variables would also occur in metal and plastic parts. Why would it occur to anyone unfamiliar with the work of Walter Shewhart and his successors that mass-produced human beings and metal gadgets would be equally susceptible to the same phenomenon of variability? So management beats on the production foremen, who beat on the set-up men and operators, and the demon of variability lurking within the process grins fiendishly and produces just as many defective pieces the next time! ▶

Why don't the producers turn to quality control for help in reducing scrap and rework? Well, they do of course, but they tend to think of quality control as a program of inspection and monitoring. Quality control may be doing some variability measurement and control with good results; but unless top management has been made aware of the nature and prevalence of variability the effort will not receive the proper budgetary and moral support.

When top managers think of variability as an all-pervasive threat, then they will turn to specialists in variability, priests of variability if you like, to exorcise the demons of variability from their processes! If you're thinking of the movie, "The Exorcist," don't be alarmed. On that occasion the departing demon took the exorcist with him. There are far too few qualified variability specialists to lose even one of them. What quality control exorcists do is to put the demon on a short leash. The process is analyzed statistically, the demon is located, measured and tied up!

Keep drawing tolerances within process limits

To continue with the metaphor, we have to make sure that members of management understand that the way to keep scrap and rework at a minimum is to keep the drawing tolerance limits beyond the reach of the chained demon! For which purpose we have developed a relatively simple device: the control chart.

We have to get to top policy-making managers; we have to meet them in their offices and at top level conferences. An immediate task is to train more quality engineers and managers in the art of preparing and presenting a convincing demonstration of the nature, behaviour and universal incidence of variability. It's not the statistics, although these are indispensable tools, it's the idea of variability which has to be "sold."

It's not only industrial executives who have to be indoctrinated with the idea of the primacy of variability; it's quality engineers and managers, too. When they are functioning as variability specialists they are performing what could be called the profession-specific activity of the quality control specialist. The quality engineer performs the customary tasks we are familiar with: inspection, monitoring, etc., but as a specialist in variability he performs the unique function which identifies and distinguishes him. □

Lady Chatterly's statistician

☐ Let us imagine that Lady Chatterly has sent for us; with sampling tables in hand and modest demeanor we enter the august presence. Lady Chatterly, picking at the remains of a couple of kippers, looks up.

"Good morning, Mellors."

"Good morning, m'lady."

"Mellors, we're almost out of horseshoe nails. We have to buy more and I thought we might get a price break if we specify an AQL."

"Yes, m'lady. What AQL did you have in mind?"

"Well, something like 4%."

"I see, and what did you want to know?"

"Am I right in assuming that what this means is that when the bag of nails arrives it won't be worse than 4% defective?"

"Well, not quite m'lady. It might be 4% defective exactly, or better, or worse."

"Oh, come on Mellors. You'll have to be more definite than that!"

"I wish I could. However, let us say that we order a bag of 250 nails to be inspected by sampling at 4% AQL, inspection level II. The sample size would be—let me see—32, and the acceptance number would be 3."

"What's that you're squinting at Mellors?"

"A book of sampling procedures and tables m'lady. It's called MIL-STD-105."

"Where does it come from?"

"From America m'lady. You know, the ex-colony."

"Of course. The one across the Atlantic. Well, what else does it say?"

"There are certain risks in sampling m'lady. There's the risk that the bag of nails may be rejected by the sampling plan even if it's good. That is, if it's 4% defective or better."

"Ridiculous!"

"Maybe m'lady, but such risks cannot be eliminated from sampling."

"Oh, alright. In that case, what are the odds against a good bag being rejected?"

"About 20 to 1."

"Hm, a bit of an outsider. What else?"

"There's the risk that a bad bag may be accepted. That is a bag of nails worse than 4% defective."

"How much worse?"

"To reply to that m'lady, I have to know what odds in favor of acceptance you have in mind." ►

"Let's say one in ten."

"Right. The quality that has a one in ten chance of acceptance is 20% defective."

"What? On a 4% plan. You can't be serious!"

"Indeed I am. Look, it says so here."

"You mean that bunch of bananas?"

"It's a family of operating characteristic curves m'lady."

"What a family! Try again Mellors. I'm not willing to take a chance the bag may be 20% defective."

"What worse quality would you consider with a 10% chance of acceptance?"

"I hadn't thought about it. I just had an idea that sampling seemed like a good way to save on the cost of inspection. I didn't know all this stuff about the risks of rejecting a good bag or of accepting a bad bag."

"I suspect you're not alone in your ignorance."

"Mellors!"

"Beg your pardon m'lady. No offense meant."

"Granted. Well, what should I say? Certainly not any worse than 8% defective. That's twice as bad as the 4% I had in mind."

Mellors studies 105 while Lady Chatterly peers over his shoulder.

Mellors mutters as he putters through the OC curves, "8% defective at 10% chance of acceptance—let me see—we shall have to switch to a 1% AQL plan, inspection level III."

"D'you know Mellors, we could have saved a lot of trouble by naming the worst quality and the acceptance odds at the beginning."

"Yes, indeed. Of course, it's true that the AQL numbers are meant for lot-by-lot sampling. In that context, and if one follows prescribed procedures, the quality level of the accumulating inventory approximates the AQL in time. Whereas the worst quality, or the lot tolerance percent defective, or the limiting quality as it is called is a single lot concept."

"Now Mellors, what does all that mean?"

"I'm just confirming your conclusion m'lady. If all you want is one bag of nails, the things to do is to decide on the worst quality you're willing to accept and the beta risk."

"The beta risk?"

"The odds in favor of acceptance m'lady."

"Oh—y'know Mellors, it might have been simpler to ask the horse."

"Yes, except he might be a statistics major."

"Heaven forbid! Well, that's enough statistics for today. Let's go into the woods."

"With pleasure m'lady." □

CREDITS

Cover design and typographical format by *Jean Kempf.*

Text type used in this book is London Roman II with Toledo Bold II heads. Type was set by *Annette Mola* on Hitchcock Publishing Company's high-speed, electronic typesetting equipment.

Production and paste-up by *Joyce McNeely.* *Margaret Moffett* proofread and corrected final copy.

Thanks to all.

Cover stock is 160 pound rust red Curtis linen. This fine cover paper is famous for its smooth, elegantly embossed linen finish.

Body stock is 60 pound regular finish Mountie Matte. This high-quality blade coated matte finish paper features extraordinary ink holding capabilities and an ultra-smooth, white surface.

Printed by W. M. Carqueville Co. in Elk Grove, IL.